D1106009

GENUINE INDIVIDUALS

AND GENUINE COMMUNITIES

Other recently published titles in the series include

Rorty and Pragmatism: The Philosopher Responds to His Critics
edited by Herman J. Saatkamp, Jr.

The Relevance of Philosophy to Life
John Lachs

The Philosophy of Loyalty
new paperback edition
Josiah Royce

The Thought and Character of William James
new paperback edition
Ralph Barton Perry

GENUINE INDIVIDUALS AND GENUINE COMMUNITIES

A ROYCEAN PUBLIC PHILOSOPHY

▲

Jacquelyn Ann K. Kegley

Vanderbilt University Press • *Nashville and London*

First edition 1997
97 98 99 00   4 3 2 1

This publication is made from recycled paper and meets the minimum requirements of American National Standard for Information Sciences—Permanence of Paper for Printed Library Materials ∞

Library of Congress Cataloging-in-Publication Data

Kegley, Jacquelyn Ann K.
    Genuine individuals and genuine communities : a Roycean public
philosophy / Jacquelyn Ann K. Kegley. — 1st ed.
        p. cm.
    Includes bibliographical references and index.
    ISBN 0-8265-1286-0 (alk. paper)
    1. Royce, Josiah, 1855-1916—Political and social views.
2. Political science—Philosophy. 3. Individuation (Philosophy)
4. Community. I. Title.
B945.R64K44 1996
320'.092—dc20   96-35640
                                                                          CIP

Manufactured in the United States of America

This book is dedicated
to the memory of my soulmate and late husband,
CHARLES WILLIAM KEGLEY.
My deepest love and gratefulness
for support go to my family:
Jackie and her soulmate, Ted;
Stephen, Charles II, and John
and his soulmate, Mary.

CONTENTS

PREFACE

THIS BOOK is about individual persons, who they are and what they can be, and about their necessary existence in communities. It is also about how we humans might create more genuine communities that foster and support more genuine individuals who, in turn, create more supportive and fulfilling communities and sets of human relationships. It is my conviction that the individual-community issue is one of the most significant and yet most troublesome problems confronting us as human beings. This issue, in fact, resides at the center of a swirling host of other, often interrelated, issues: for instance, the conflict between our rights as individuals and our obligations, an issue that, in turn, is at the center of vexing issues like abortion and the right to die, as well as many others.

In my judgment, the thought, teaching, and writing of the American philosopher Josiah Royce represent one of the best attempts to create a philosophical scheme that successfully deals with the individual vis-à-vis community dilemma. Further, Royce provides us with an understanding of persons and communities that, I believe, is especially relevant to issues we are confronting today. Thus, in the first chapters of this book I set out an understanding of individual 'person', of human personal development, of human obligation, of genuine community building, and of human loyalty to community and to the widening of community, all based on the thought of Josiah Royce.

In the remaining chapters, that view is tested in application to contemporary issues in the areas of family, education, and medicine. These "public issues" are of great concern to most people today. Unfortunately, most discussions of the problems of family, of the educational system, and of health care are not informed by any clear and adequate concept of human personhood or by the ways in which each individual might be supported to reach fuller human development. It is my hope that this book will begin to provide such a foundation.

This book also represents the coming together of a number of personal interests and aspects of my own life. My interaction with the thought of Josiah Royce has been a career-long endeavor, and it has now coalesced with a life-long interest in applying philosophy to problems of everyday concern. Professionally, I have struggled with ethical and other philosophical issues in medicine and in education, and as a wife and mother I have personally struggled with the concept of family and how that institution might be structured as a context for the fullest self-development of each of its members. This book has provided a fruitful way toward the resolving of those issues.

My personal appreciation goes to John McDermott for suggesting the topic of Royce and public philosophy, as well as to John Lachs and the other members of the Society for the Advancement of American philosophy. It was they who stimulated my original interest in American Philosophy and who have carried forth this venerable tradition so very well. I express the fondest memories for Justus Buchler, who was my Ph.D. mentor and who led me to Royce. I also wish to honor the superb work of Frank Oppenheim, a true Royce scholar. My final and deepest appreciation goes to my family, especially to Jackie and Stephen who sustained me through the most difficult of times.

GENUINE INDIVIDUALS
AND GENUINE COMMUNITIES

1

Introduction
Is a Roycean Public Philosophy
Viable or Possible?

"Human affairs are neither to be wept over nor to be
laughed at, but to be understood."
—*Josiah Royce*

"Every transformation of man has rested on a new
picture of the cosmos and the nature of man."
—*Lewis Mumford*

Is There a Public or a Public Philosophy?

ANY PROJECT worth its salt should provide its audience with both a
rationale for its undertaking and a foretaste or forecast of its outline
and content. We turn first to the rationale. Why, then, a book on public philosophy and especially one focused on the thought of Josiah Royce, American philosopher and Harvard professor, who lived and wrote in the period
1855–1916?

The first answer to this question "why" is that there is an expressed need,
almost a public cry for something akin to "public philosophy." For a number of years there have been voices announcing both the death of any sense
of "the public" and of anything resembling a "public philosophy." These
voices claim that there is no "public" in the United States. The prominent
social commentator, Walter Lippman, for example, in his book *The Phantom Public*, criticized the United States and its democracy for having an ex-

1

aggerated and undisciplined notion of "the public." Lippman says that the public is a creature, if it exists at all, which is certainly "volatile, elusive, ignorant and shy."[1] In 1974, Richard Sennett, historian-sociologist, presented the provocative thesis that the private psychic scene in America had so upstaged and overpowered any sense of a public world stage that there had been a "fall of public man."[2] Christopher Lasch's *The Culture of Narcissism* argued that the new consciousness in America was indeed one of "intense subjectivism."[3] There has been seeming agreement among many that the United States, reacting to the horror of the Holocaust and Hiroshima and led by a politics of affluence and Cold War posture, turned to Freud, horror films, science fiction, the suburbs, gardens, and a very "privatized view of life."[4] The "public" seemed a clear fiction.

Equally clear to many also has been the non-existence of any public philosophy. Not only have the people retreated "inward," but so have the culture's intellectuals. Russell Jacoby, in 1987, summarized this retreat in a book with the provocative title *The Last Intellectuals*. In this study he speaks of the "new high-tech intellectuals"—the consultants, the professors, the "anonymous souls" who do not "enrich the public culture" and of younger intellectuals "whose lives unfolded almost entirely on campuses and who are "inaccessible and unknown."[5] There are, claims Jacoby, no "public intellectuals," that is, "writers and thinkers who address a general and educated audience."[6] As a result, argues Jacoby, the public sphere is "less a free market of ideas than a market; what is publicly visible registers nothing but market forces."[7] In 1988, Charles Sykes echoed Jacoby's condemnation of intellectuals in an academic culture. Today in academia, he argued, we have the "erudite professors belaboring tiny slivers of knowledge, utterly without social value" producing scholarship cloaked in "stupefying, inscrutable jargon."[8]

Of all the classes of intellectuals, Jacoby is particularly scathing toward philosophers: "The philosophical self-scrutiny . . . may be the weakest because American philosophy has promoted technical expertise that repels critical thinking . . . [I]ts fetish of logic and language has barred all but a few who might rethink philosophy. Philosophy seems the most routinized of the humanities, the least accessible to change."[9] Jacoby's criticism of philosophy was stated earlier by John E. Smith who notes: "The wholesale victory of British analytic philosophy has reduced philosophy to "an internal dialogue among professionals. . . . Philosophy has become completely an academic affair."[10]

There is then in the United States certainly a vacuum—no sense of public and no "public philosophy." But is there really a *need* for a formation both of a "public" and "a public philosophy"? Lippman, Dewey, and others give us a partial answer to this question. In his *Phantom Public*, Lippman's central picture was of a weak, ineffectual, even dangerous "public" that was really a conglomerate of many publics, with many competing self-interests and who as "a public" fell easy prey to the spurious member who would act "to bend the rule in their favor while pretending or imagining that they are moved only by the common public need."[11] Lippman was concerned that there were no members of the public, "no ordinary bystander" who could help the public "purge itself of the self-interested groups who would become confused with it."[12] Lippman often spoke of the need for an "omni-competent citizen," that is, one who possesses in common with other citizens a universal moral code, a keen and impartial public spirit and a command of all the facts necessary to make public policy decisions.[13] John Dewey, in his *The Public and Its Problem*, states the issue in a slightly different way. However, like Lippman, he focuses on a crisis within democracy itself, a failure in the accepted theory of popular government, namely, that it rests on the belief that "the public" directs the course of events. For Dewey, "the essential problem of government thus reduces itself to this. What arrangements will prevent rulers from advancing their own interests at the expense of the ruled?"[14]

In this regard, the issue of "the public" becomes clearer. A number of recent events, in fact, verify this problem: Watergate, the Iran-Contra affair, the Post Office scandal, and various ethics trials for public officials. Further, there are the familiar facts of voter frustration and the control of politics by strong interest groups. Dewey, in 1927, could easily have been writing today when he penned these words: "Skepticism regarding the efficacy of voting is openly expressed . . . What difference does it make whether I vote or not? Things go the same anyway. . . . And of them [those who vote] it is a common remark that a large number vote against someone or somebody rather than for anything or anybody."[15] A number of economic theorists, for example, have recently noted citizens' unwillingness to support government, either by taxes or voting.[16]

Looking more broadly at the issue today, human society seems utterly fragmented, at home and abroad, by ethnic, racial, and religious conflicts—each little group demanding its own territory, identity, and rights. America today is known not only as a "self-absorbed culture" but as a "litigious" one, where the courts become battlegrounds for persons pitted against each other—husbands against wives, parents against parents, children against parents. Perhaps only in the United States can a child divorce his parents. In our cities, violence erupts everywhere, guns or brute physical force resolves dilemmas resulting in death and/or various forms of abuse—of spouses, of the aged, of children. Yet in all of this despair there is hope. Out of the hell and fire of the 1992 Los Angeles riots, a strange voice in the wilderness sounded a desperate need for a "public." It said, "We must learn to live together." There is, in other words, a true need in the United States for some sense of a "public" or at least of some link in common. William Sullivan, in his book *Reconstructing a Public Philosophy*, envisions the development of a "public life," a condition "when a society realizes that reciprocity and mutual aid are worthy of cultivation both as a good in themselves and as providing the basis of the individual self."[17]

Further, Sullivan argues that a crucial element in the development of a "public" and a "public life" is a public philosophy. We emphatically agree. A public philosophy would address the issue at the center of the democratic crisis identified by Lippman and Dewey; namely, it would interpret and delineate "what political association is all about and what it deems to achieve."[18] A public philosophy would help address the need for a test and criticism of the partisan clothed in the suit of public interest and good, and it would address the need for a sense of living together. A public philosophy, writes Sullivan, provides "a continual tradition of understanding about what it means to be not just a responsible member of this or that community, but a participant in forms of life that are the common concern of many diverse communities."[19] Further, there are issues today of tremendous private and public import that must be addressed critically and sensitively, and with a broader vision of what counts. Among these issues are the many raised by science and technology—life and death support, definitions of heritage and parenthood; aging and health; and responsibilities to self, others, and nature, whether as organ or gene donors or as caretakers. There are also those issues of ethnic, racial, and cultural identity, of cultural literacy and multiculturalism. There are issues of a continual "racial divide," as raised, for instance, by the O. J. Simpson trial, and of deep religious controversy, exemplified in the abortion issue. Here again we see a need for a "public philosophy" which is, argues Sullivan, "both a cause and an effect of awakened discussion of those things most important and at issue in the life of the nation. What is ultimately at issue is the radical question of what is a worthwhile life?."[20]

Finally, the need for public philosophy is not only a general one but one internal to philosophy itself. For too long philosophy has turned inward, focused on esoteric, narrow concerns of the discipline without social, personal, or even intellectual significance. For too long many philosophers have fit the mold of "the professor" described by H. L. Menchen, namely "an obscurantist . . . he has a special untouchable talent for dullness; his central aim is not to expose the truth clearly but to exhibit his profundity."[21] To engage again in the construction of a public philosophy would signal a return to philosophical roots, to a concern for "civic community" and to the belief that "the unexamined life is not worth living." There is, argued Dewey, no better way to realize what philosophy is all about than to engage in issues of "public import," for this would bring to light the "things that are morally and intellectually fundamental in the direction of human affairs."[22]

There is then not only a need for a "public" and a "public philosophy," but indeed it is evident that it goes beyond need: it is a moral imperative. Human affairs demand to be reflected upon, to be dealt with and perhaps to be understood. William Ernest Hocking in 1958 wrote eloquently of the world's "cultural psychosis," of the "loss of man's native rapport with the whole, the loss of significance and meaning in experience itself."[23] Paul Tillich argued, in *The Courage to Be,* that to separate an "interpreting consciousness" in a radical way from the world of experience generates "the anxiety of emptiness and meaninglessness, when the self feels its connectedness to others and to the whole of existence severed or reduced to a minimum."[24] There is a deep sense of alienation today and a hunger for meaning.

Josiah Royce: No Public Philosopher?

To endeavor the exploration of pubic philosophy, then, seems both relevant and badly needed. But why base such an exploration on the work of a late nineteenth century philosopher, Josiah Royce? Indeed to focus on Royce to some observers of American philosophy is almost ludicrous. Thus Bruce Kuklick, in his study of American philosophy at Harvard in the period 1860–1930, and with reference particularly to the thought of William James and Royce, provides the following scathing evaluation: "The quality of Harvard's political and social philosophy was poor; the structure of the university and of the discipline well-nigh guaranteed that first-rate work would not be done; and the work that was done ignored critical texts and has been subsequently ignored by significant communities of scholars."[25] Although

Kulick is not entirely blind to Royce's value—he recognizes in Royce a belief conducive to public philosophy and identifies Royce's lifelong desire for a social order that would reconcile isolated, lonely selves, acknowledging Royce's belief that there was a desperate need for a "harmony-creating policy"[26]—his summary view is, nevertheless, a dim one. It should be obvious in my undertaking of this book that I disagree with Kuklick's overall evaluation, at least for Royce. I shall let others argue on behalf of William James. It is my hope that the arguments of this book will overturn Kuklick's judgment. However, at this juncture I would like to suggest what has led Kuklick and others to their poor opinion of Royce.

Kuklick's error arises, I believe, from his ill-chosen criteria for evaluating Royce's contributions to social and political philosophy. These criteria are Royce's ignorance of the critical texts and a lack of reference to Royce's work by other social and political theorists. Without expanding on the issues I would suggest that these criteria betray Kuklick's own concordance with the isolated, academic world so criticized by Jacoby and others. The index of worth in a closed academic world where conformity, patronage, provincialism, enclavism abounds is the "footnote." "Many citations to an individual's work indicates he or she is important; conversely few or no references implies someone is unknown and irrelevant."[27] Connected with this type of academic philosophy is a narrow, authoritative view of what counts as "true," "quality" philosophical work in a particular area. In political philosophy, such work would be in the tradition of Locke, Mill, and Kant, or Rawls and Nozick, that is, of liberalism with its emphasis on the market and the minimal state, rights, justice, contract theory, and a universally justified neutral procedure for choosing rightly among alternative courses of social action and polity.[28] In social philosophy, the "real" view of social life would be utilitarianism, where social action is guided by interests, with the greatest good for the greatest number equaling the sum of individual interests. In psychology the accompanying doctrine is of an egoistic, instinctual psyche pitted against organized society but needing its civilizing influence. The point is that Royce provides a critical and alternative view to this kind of social and political philosophy as well as to the accompanying views of the psyche. Thus, he would not easily fit the notion of "social political philosophy" that underlies Kuklick's evaluation.

Ignoring those who are outside of and counter to one's own view has, of course, condemned a number of creative and presumably excellent philosophers to the margins of academic concern, including many philosophers in classical American philosophy. Even Dewey, acknowledged by many outsiders as the last of the great "public philosophers," has been thus marginalized. Royce is faulted by Kuklick for not reading Marx or Weber. Dewey also admitted an ignorance of Marx. Although both Royce and Dewey were nonreaders of Marx, they were certainly astute critics of capitalism. And, in my judgment, Royce's analysis of the effects of rampant capitalism rival, if not surpass, those of Marx. Likewise, though not Weberian, Royce's analysis of the nature of religious thought is astute and deeper than Weber's explication of the "Protestant ethic."

Further, the liberal social-political philosophy so fundamental to "academic" philosophy, and presumably informing Kuklick's evaluation, is now under strong attack from within philosophy and without and is itself in retreat. William Sullivan summarizes some of the elements of the assault on philosophical liberalism, which he labels, properly I believe, as "deeply antipublic." This liberalism, he argues, sees humans as exclusively and unchangeably self-regarding and human association as a necessary evil. The role of the polity is to accommodate civilly the clashes of individual and group interests. This philosophical liberalism, Sullivan contends, "exalts the supremacy of self-interest and the development of institutional means for pursuing these interests. . . . Yet no nation could remain a self-governing, communicating whole if it were only a precarious assemblage of mutually suspicious segments."[29]

Later in this text I shall summarize the attacks on philosophical liberalism and show how Royce's analysis of "community" and of "fruitful provincialism" provide a significant alternative view of what public life could and should be about. It should also be noted that Dewey criticized many aspects of this classical philosophical liberalism and sought to provide a more adequate revisionist liberalism consonant with a creative democracy.[30] However, in the text I shall argue that Royce offers a more significant base for an alternative social-political philosophy than Dewey because he breaks more completely out of the individualistic mold of liberalism, while Dewey does not completely do so.

We have suggested that Kuklick's evaluation of Royce's social-political thought might be suspect. But there is more to be said. In addition to his citation criterion, Kuklick provides "three philosophical reasons to "help explain the death of social theory" at Harvard. These are: (1) that the Harvard pragmatists had a hierarchical view of the branches of philosophy, stressing logic, epistemology, and metaphysics; (2) that logic and the physical and natural science were the model for philosophizing at Harvard; and (3) that the outlook of Royce and James derived from Kant's *Critique of Pure Reason* and the problems it generated. All of this led, says Kuklick, to an emphasis on the technical rather than on the social-political. These philosophers, contends Kuklick, joined their philosophic ideas to their personal and moral experience and thus if they did apply social and political theory it tended to be anti-institutional and concerned "largely with the amelioration of personal troubles."[31] Several comments are in order about the adequacy of Kuklick's characterization, especially as it fits the work of Royce.

First, and undeniably, Royce's interest in metaphysics, epistemology, and logic were lifelong. His doctoral dissertation (1878) was on epistemology; his first published book was a *Primer of Logical Analysis for the Use of Composition Students* (1881); and two of his greatest works were on metaphysics, *The World and the Individual* and *The Problem of Christianity*.[32] However, he was equally concerned throughout his life and career with social and political issues. His first published essay at Lincoln School in San Francisco in June 1869, was entitled, "Is the Assassination of Tyrants Ever Justifiable?" His very last philosophical effort concerned the great war and Germany's betrayal of human society. His last statement and vision, *The Hope of the Great Community* (1915) was decidedly about social, political, and moral issues.[33] Royce's philosophy is, in fact, of one integrated artistic piece; his metaphysics and epistemology are ground in and interweave with his ethics and his social and political philosophy. Indeed, Royce's philosophy of self and his metaphysical understanding of the nature of the individual and the relationship of individuals to each other and to the community are what give substance and fecundity to his social and political philosophy, making Royce's work peculiarly relevant and useful to today's needs. Much of the vacuum in public philosophy today is due to a social, political, and economic philosophy that operates with a hidden and unexamined metaphysics and epistemology—a reductionistic betrayal of human selves, their relationships, and the reality they encounter.

The dominant American social and political thought is a "detached individualism," which is based, in turn, on an "ontological individualism" that claims that reality is composed ultimately of individuals only. All communities, then, are seen as mere collections of individuals with no essential reality of their own other than the sum of individual thoughts and actions. Royce, in his later philosophical work, attacked and exposed the weaknesses of this belief system, which he called "nominalism." In contrast to such a metaphysical view, Royce sees reality as essentially social and affirms the reality of *both* individuals and communities.[34] Likewise in epistemology, Royce asserts the essential social nature of all knowledge-seeking and, with Charles S. Peirce, argues for a third type of knowledge, interpretation, which is triadic: social, community building, and the essence of knowledge of mind (and self), whether one's own or that of another.[35]

Although we cannot, in a book on public philosophy, give any substantial space to a discussion of Royce's metaphysics, it must be clear that metaphysics, ethics, epistemology, and, thus, social and political philosophy are vitally interconnected in Royce's philosophy and that his metaphysics of community makes his thought fruitfully relevant to contemporary public issues and public philosophy. For an enlightened discussion of Royce's metaphysics, especially as it relates to public philosophy, I recommend that of Frank M. Oppenheim in his book, *Royce's Mature Ethics.*[36]

This brings us also to Kuklick's criticism that Royce's outlook derives from Kant's *Critique of Pure Reason* and therefore leads to an emphasis on technical rather than on social and political philosophy. Royce did study and work with Kantian philosophy. However, in *The World and the Individual,* in his third mode of Being, he criticizes as inadequate the understanding of reality presented in the *Critique of Pure Reason.* He continues this criticism into his later work, even in his last course on metaphysics taught in 1915. Further, although *The Philosophy of Loyalty* is often cited as evidence of Royce's affinity with Kant's *Groundwork of the Metaphysics of Morals,* Royce's mature ethics also is critical and transcendent of the Kantian universalist ethic of duty.[37] Indeed, as Oppenheim has shown, Royce's mature ethics integrates freedom, goodness, and duty and highlights the personal, interpersonal, and communal dimensions of ethical life. This makes Royce's work particularly relevant to contemporary issues, especially to the universalism—particularism debate in recent ethical thought, that is, to the question of obligation to the universal principle and duty versus one's obligation to personal and particular others— to one's child or spouse, for instance. Royce's work clearly goes beyond Kantian ethics and beyond mere technical philosophy.

As for logic, Royce did not earnestly turn to it until late in his life, using it primarily to work out a significant philosophy of community, of communication, and of community life in *The Problem of Christianity.*[38] Stanley Scott, in discussing the work Royce and Peirce did on a theory of interpretation, based on a triadic logic, sees this work not as 'technical' or 'personal,' but as of significant import for a social philosophy. He writes: "Both Royce and Pierce attempted to articulate the process of coming into the presence of the inner influence of others in a community."[39] Kuklick's characterization of "a technical philosophy grounded in Kant," in fact, more aptly fits philosophical liberalism than it does the work of Royce.

Kulick's reference to logic and the physical and natural sciences as a model for philosophizing at Harvard also applies to most of "academic philosophy" after Royce. This view of science saw it as neutral truth seeking, as rationality par excellence, as the realm opposed to the social, moral, and personal.

Contrary to this view, Royce held forth science as a model for intelligent inquiry and communal experience. Science, as a human endeavor, was, for Royce, a social endeavor, involved in the social construction of reality. For Royce, our knowledge of the external is fundamentally bound up with our being-with-others. In his *The World and the Individual*, Royce writes:

> Our belief in the reality of Nature, when Nature is taken
> to mean the realm of physical phenomenon known to com-
> mon sense and science, is *inseparably bound up with our be-
> lief in the existence of our fellow men*. . . . Whatever the
> deeper reality behind Nature may turn out to be, our Na-
> ture, the realm of matter and of laws which our science and
> our popular opinion have to do, is a realm which we con-
> ceive as *known or knowable to various men,* in precisely the
> general sense in which we regard it as known or knowable
> to our private selves.[40]

Further, Royce constantly cites the scientific community as an example of true community, that is, one endlessly committed to newer and broader truth, to continuous seeking for common agreement.[41] With such a view of science Royce does not easily fall prey to the errors of either the critics of science and technology or the liberals, both of whom identify science with a particular time or view. The critics thus blame science for all the present social ills while ignoring humans' task to render science and technology as servants of humankind and society and the common good. The liberals, on the other hand, conflate the accomplishments of science and technology with laissez-faire capitalism. In understanding science as a social mode of inquiry and technology as a human mode of productive activity, Royce, is able to see technology as "social" and "political," open to critical questions of ends pursued. He is also able to provide a basis for seeing various forms of technology as building "common bonds" or as "isolating individuals." Thus, historian Robert V. Hine, in reviewing Royce's history of California, argues that, in the tradition of the modern French Annales school of historians, "Royce foresaw the critical interaction of technology, society, and culture by underlining the social effects of mining techniques." "The shovel and pan allowed pure individualism, while the miner's cradle brought social change and the sluice became the basis for the social life of a civilized community."[42]

Kuklick's criticisms of Royce's social political philosophy, then, are more cogent for Harvard academic philosophy and philosophy in general as it developed after Royce. This is also true of a final criticism posited by Kuklick, namely, that Royce and James were "successful big time American academics, ultimately self-satisfied and uncritical of the social order."[43] As John Clendenning's definitive biography of Royce makes abundantly clear, Royce was neither self-satisfied nor ever satisfied with the state of the human order. Indeed, he saw his own self and life not as a finished product ever, but as a "history, a drama, a life quest."[44] As for philosophy and a human order, they too are quests, ever seeking a "better view of things, never resting content with a final answer." Royce's own words on the philosopher's work speak eloquently to this point.

> The philosopher's work is not lost when, in one sense, his system seems to have been refuted by death and when time seems to have scattered to scorn the words of his dust-filled mouth. His immediate end may have been attained; but thousands of years may not be long enough to develop for humanity the full significance of his reflective thought.[45]

In condemning Royce as part of the Harvard milieu of the late nineteenth century, Kuklick also fails to appreciate that Royce was born in California in a mining town, grew up in San Francisco, and was the graduate of the first public university in California. These California roots were deeply ingrained in Royce's total person, as R. V. Hines's book on Royce makes so clear. In fact, he wrote two extensive studies of California, one a history and the other a novel, both concerned with the struggle for order and community in a setting of racial hatreds and rugged individualism that placed wealth above responsibility. The history particularly contains insights about race relations and about social and political order that spring from Royce's California experience and that could not have been aspects of the experience of someone born into the Bostonian milieu, which was highly commercial, stabilized, and imbued with European culture.[46] Royce, in fact, lived a life of marginality and in poverty in California, as Clendenning's biography so well describes. Further, he always remained to some extent a "stranger" at Harvard. He was much disliked by Mrs. James and was worried how people would endure his slipshod Western manners. His figure was squat and stout, his face was round and freckled, he had astonishingly red hair, and his clothes defied all standards of fashion. An undergraduate described him as "a miniature figure, well compacted, with an enormous red head which had a gigantic aspect . . . and also an infantile look like that of an ugly baby."[47] Royce left the impression with many of "the John L. Sullivan's of philosophy."

Albert William Levi, in his book *Philosophy as Social Expression*, reminds us that emphasis upon the philosophizing individual can help us see a philosophy as expressing a *cognitive lifestyle*, a form of life. I will suggest that Royce's cognitive life style was that of a lonely Californian who developed a philosophy of adequate communal life. Robert V. Hines, in his *Josiah Royce: From Grass Valley to Harvard*, explores Royce's California intellectual heritage in excellent and expert detail. Hines claims rightfully that Royce was both a "product of and reaction to the West."[48] He was, for example, unlike many Westerners, and unlike many today, not an admirer of the "Western loner." He found the brutal freedom of the pioneer vile.[49] Indeed, Royce's observations and diagnosis of this "radical individualism" is highly relevant today. Hines writes: ". . . Royce was one of the first to diagnose alienation, the American neurotic illness, the 'inward revolt' of people who increasingly find it difficult to attach themselves to the community."[50] Royce's California experience also provided him with evidence of the deep longing for community so prevalent in the United States today. He was able to observe directly the birth pangs and struggles of a "young, immature community." Indeed in 1915 at the very fine Philadelphia tribute to him, he fondly recalled his Grass Valley and San Francisco childhood. He said he had come to see that "my deepest motives and problems have centered around the Idea of Community" and by what "I nowadays try to express by teaching that we are all saved through the community."[51]

Royce's California heritage, I believe, added a richness of experience to his philosophy and especially to the relevance of his work to public philosophy and public issues today. He was personally acquainted with divisiveness of various kinds—racial, class, religious, political; he had lived in poverty and as a social misfit, he knew, intimately, the manifestations of greed and restless economic pursuit; he experienced the struggles for family and commercial unity, for civility in the midst of hostility; he was well acquainted with lack of commitment and rebellion against commitment; he saw nature's beauty as well as mankind's drive for brutal conquest of nature. Hines describes Royce as "a philosopher who was by destiny forever a frontiersman."[52] As a frontiersman, he believed in the unique value and worth of the individual as well as the community, and he set out to develop a philosophical point of view that focused and expanded both concepts, providing us today, I believe, with a superb foundation for a vital and relevant public philosophy.

A final telling point against Kuklick's negative evaluation of Royce as a social and political philosopher, is the fact that Royce had a background of literary and public writings before he began his philosophical career. As a student at UC Berkeley, he was a prolific writer for the *Berkeleyan*. His published articles have a distinctive public flavor. Two in 1874, for instance, were on "Class Feeling" and another was on "The Modern Novel as Conveying Instruction and Accomplishing Reform."[53] He wrote extensively in literary criticism, and he never abandoned his interest in literature as a medium for "exploring the potentials of consciousness for growth out of its present limitations."[54] Royce considered himself a public philosopher. Even Kuklick acknowledges that James and Royce thought the "philosopher had a public duty to speculate on real-life problems."[55] Royce did write and speak on public and cultural issues. Like Dewey, he was much concerned with education, and he wrote on educational issues and often addressed educators. Among his articles in 1891, for example, we find one entitled "Present Ideals of American University Life," and another asking, "Is There a Science of Education."[56] Chapter six in this book will deal with the implications of Royce's thought for public educational issues today, such as the canon, cultural literacy, multiculturalism, pedagogy, and the role of the teacher/scholar.

Given all that has been said in answer to Kuklick's negative view of Royce's contribution to social and political philosophy, we can confidently assert that Royce does *not* fit the negative characterization provided and indeed, rather, that he has important things to contribute to public issues today. Royce's work may be particularly relevant to our present task of creating a sense of "the public" and of "public philosophy." A few comments on the present scene will make this clear.

Three Major Issues

There is today, in fact, a great deal of ferment in the area of social and political philosophy. As indicated above, philosophical liberalism is under attack and seemingly is retreating or moving toward a revisionist position. The specifics of the issues in this debate will be undertaken in a later chapter. Among the central issues are three seeming dualisms or stark contrasting pairs, namely, Individualism versus Collectivism (or Society), Impartialism versus Particularism, and Universalism versus Communitarianism. Royce, in his philosophical work dealt with and attempted, I believe with relative success, to overcome all three pairs.

As indicated above in Sullivan's remarks, philosophical liberalism is highly individualistic in that the rights and values of the individual are seen as opposed to organized social action. The individual has priority over the state in time because the origin of the state, its legitimation, is based on a contract between self-interested individuals. The individual also has primacy over the state in moral authority because reason, on which the morality of the good will is based, is an inherent endowment of individuals. Further, the primary value to be protected by the liberal state is liberty or freedom, which is interpreted in the negative sense as non-interference in the individual pursuit of life, property, and happiness. Even the civil liberties of freedom of speech and assembly are individually based rather than seen as guarantors of cooperative communal decision making that allows views to be aired and tolerated. Such an individualism, especially one that has been transformed into the self-interested pursuit of success and wealth, leads to atomism and loneliness, and an attitude of everyone for self. Tocqueville, in his early observations of American society, described this outcome succinctly when he writes: "They [individuals] form the habit of thinking of themselves in isolation and imagine that their whole destiny is in their own hands. Each man is forever thrown back on himself alone and there is a danger that he may be shut up in the solitude of his own heart. . . . Each one of them, withdrawn into himself, is almost unaware of the fate of the rest."[57]

Further, John Dewey, in his various analyses of liberalism, often spoke of the split in philosophy in the United States between (1) the notion that free market competition would lead to human interdependence, harmony of interests, and automatic care for individuals and (2) the notion that government must regularly intervene to help equalize conditions between the wealthy and powerful and those less fortunate. This split, which reflects a conflict between the ideals of liberty and equality, is one with which John Rawls, in his *Theory of Justice*, attempts to deal. Thus, we have his notion of the "veil of ignorance" (which equalizes individual conditions) and the principles of justice, one of which attempts to account for inequalities in a just society.

Again, the details of dealing with the conflict between individual and social interest, between freedom and equality will be addressed in chapter 2, but here we can indicate that for Royce individuality and community, individual and social interests, are inextricably bound together; each is uniquely valuable, and each arises out of their mutual interaction in a creative, ongoing infinite process. For Royce, individuals are inescapably rooted in the social context, and true individuality and freedom are forged out of that context. Individuals are both self-made and a social product. As we shall see, Royce enables us to deal with freedom not just in its negative aspect as noninterference but also in its positive aspects as circumstantial—providing conditions for individual development and exercise of choice. Royce can also see the civil liberties as providing enabling conditions both for individual and community. Individuals are not in conflict with communities; rather, they, as free, self-conscious, self-committed individuals, who are also essentially social beings, build communities whose obligation, in turn, is to foster *both* communal action and harmony and the development of true individuals. Individuals need communities for self-extension, to develop morality, and to overcome error. But, equally, individuals keep communities from stagnating into inveterate habit or degenerating into mob madness.

Another aspect of the individual-society conflict is the question of patriotism and loyalty to a community. Are patriotism and loyalty goods, or are they dangerous traits and more akin to racism or sexism? Is a preference for the well-being of one's country or group subject to blind allegiance without giving any moral weight to the interests of others? Can there even be loyalty or patriotism in a context of many conflicting self-interests? Is Alasdair MacIntyre correct when he declares, "Patriotism turns out to be a permanent source of moral danger"?[58] George P. Fletcher in his book, *Loyalty: An Essay on the Morality of Relationships*, raises a number of important issues surrounding the concept of loyalty, including the problem of patriotism—expressed in patriotic ritual, the pledge of allegiance, and responses to the the flag—in building a sense of political community in the United States today.[59] These issues will be addressed in chapter 4, but it can be said that Royce's work on loyalty, on provincialism, and on "religious community" contains many valuable insights for dealing with a number of contemporary issues, including those involving loyalty and racial, ethnic, and sexual identity, and those of religious practice and belief in a pluralistic democracy.

Turning to the impartialism—particularism debate, which also is related to questions of loyalty, again Royce's work in ethics and on the psycho-social development of the self will provide us with an excellent foundation to deal with pressing contemporary issues, including a theory of moral development adequate to deal with today's pressing crises of psyche and of family. The impartialism-particularism debate, as it manifests itself in contemporary controversies in social, political, and ethical philosophy, has been succinctly stated by John Cottingham. He characterizes the two positions in the following way:

> Impartialism maintains that morality requires us to allocate our time and resources without according special preference to our own goals and interests and without displaying favoritism or partiality to those to whom we happen to be in some way specially related.
>
> Particularism is the thesis that it is (*not merely psychologically understandable) but morally correct to favour one's own.*[60]

Related to issues of loyalty and moral duties referred to above, various forms of "partialism" or "particularism" are familism, kinshipism, clanism, patriotism, racism, sexism, planetism.[61] Again, Royce's extensive work on loyalty, duty, and provincialism offers valuable insights to issues related to these partialisms and their value or lack of value. In addition, his writings on nature and evolution also will allow us to tackle such contemporary debates as animal rights and the charge of specieism.

Another aspect of the impartiality-particularism debate, however, to which Royce can also speak focuses on the nature of the moral task. Here the moral philosophy of Iris Murdoch comes to the fore. Lawrence Blum, writing on Murdoch, puts the issue as follows:

> Iris Murdoch suggests that the central task of the moral agent involves a true and loving perception of another individual who is seen as a particular reality external to the agent. . . .
>
> For Murdoch the moral task is not a matter of finding universalizable reasons or principles of action, but of getting oneself to attend to the reality of individual other persons.[62]

This dimension of moral theory, claims Blum, has been theorized away in contemporary ethics. Contemporary ethicists have claimed that it is good to act with the mere intention to benefit, independent of any genuine grasp of the need or good of others. This claim has caused much difficulty in attempting to deal with ethical issues in complex medical or biomedical situations where conflict among the principles of autonomy, beneficence, and justice and the conflict of the interests of many concrete individuals are often present. Royce's work again provides excellent grounds for dealing with this aspect of the impartialism-particularism debate. At one point in her book *The Sovereignty of the Good*, Iris Murdoch defines love as "knowledge of the individual."[63] Knowledge, she argues, is "refined and honest perception of what is really the case, a patient and just discernment and exploration of what confronts one."[64] Royce, like James, wrote extensively on the role of "selective attention" in perception, knowledge, and action; in his *The World and the Individual*, Royce defines individuality in terms of an act of love. "The individual is primarily the object and expression of an exclusive interest, of a determinate selection."[65] His emphasis is upon love as a form of exclusive interest that we devote to a being or an object. This love leads us to declare it as unique, irreplaceable and without any possible equivalent. At the root of love is a spontaneous affirmation, namely, "There shall be no other."

Royce would also find inadequate the claim that it is good to act with the mere intention to benefit independent of any understanding of the need or good of the other. In his *The Problem of Christianity*, Royce dealt with the meaning of the Christian notion of love or *agape*. The real issue, argues Royce, is that although we know we are to love God and our neighbor, we cannot easily answer the question *how?* How can I be practically useful in meeting my neighbor's needs? The intention to benefit, claims Royce, is not enough. He writes, "What constitutes, in this present world, the pathos, the tragedy of love is that, because our neighbor is so mysterious a being to our imperfect vision, we do not know how to make him [our neighbor] happy, to relieve his deepest distresses, to do him the highest good. . . ."[66] In chapter 3, where I deal with the issue of particularism in ethics, I will discuss many affinities between Royce's views and those of Murdoch, as well as crucial differences. However, it should be clear at this point that Royce's thought contains hidden riches for dealing with this contemporary issue in ethics, which, in turn, has practical implications for issues in medical dilemmas where the fulfillment of obligations to self and family are so difficult, as well as implications generally for the roles of parents and children and their mutual obligations.

Another set of pressing contemporary issues arising out of the impartialism-particularism debate concerns the question of moral development and the adequacy of theories of moral development and of self-development. These issues come out clearly in the implications of the theories of moral development of Lawrence Kohlberg and Carol Gilligan. Kohlberg's theory assumes that final mature morality is to be found in an impartialist view with an emphasis on impartiality, formal rationality, and the principle of justice. Gilligan, in contrast, emphasizes a morality of care and responsiveness within personal relationships and a concern for maintaining the web of relationship. There is here also the issue of possible gender differences in moral concern and judgment, for Kohlberg's research is based on a male population, whereas Gilligan's reveals that females respond to ethical dilemmas primarily on the base of care and concern for relationships. Further, this debate involves the question of moral feelings; in the case of Kohlberg, guilt and shame; in the case of Gilligan, compassion, love, and sorrow. And then there are those who claim that feelings and emotions have or should not have any role at all in moral judgment and action.

We are brought back to matters already discussed, namely, the claim that moral action involves an irreducible particularity, a particularity of agent, other, and situation. There are also political issues, those of equality and power, for instance, and of sexual difference. Thus, Carol Gilligan writes:

> If recurrent childhood experiences of inequality are less mitigated by experiences of attachment in boys' develop-ment and then compounded by social inequality in adoles-cence and a high cultural valuation of male dominance, feelings of powerlessness may become heightened and the potential for violence may correspondingly increase.[67]

The problems of violence today cry out for both some explanation and some remedy. Practical solutions may be extremely difficult, but on a theo-retical level, which is a beginning in giving guidance to educational and clin-ical practice as well as to social policy, Gilligan urges that we become convinced that a perspective on relationships—their development, their ad-equacies and inadequacies—is crucial to understanding mature, moral de-velopment and judgment. Lawrence Blum has urged that we explicate a "mature morality," which involves the complex interaction and dialogue be-tween concerns of impartiality and those of personal relationship and care.[68]

The specifics of these very difficult dichotomies and questions will be discussed extensively in the remainder of this book. However, as I have ar-gued elsewhere,[69] Royce has a theory of self and self-development that pro-vides us with many insights useful for examining the Gilligan-Kohlberg debate as well as problems of attachment and rebellion. Above all, he has a view of self and of person as relational, developmental, contextual. As a cru-cial part of this theory of self, Royce sees the self as eminently social in na-ture, developing in consciousness through significant relations with others and, in turn, through our own estimation of ourselves. This development af-fects our understanding and need for both a sense of difference and of sim-ilarity and belonging. For Royce, also, there is an essential ethical dimension to self-involving choice, rights, responsibilities, and feelings of guilt, shame, love, and loyalty. Royce adds to these aspects of self a religious dimension, which would be welcomed by Murdoch, but scorned by others. This allows him to deal, more adequately than Kohlberg or Freud, with guilt and self-division and their overcoming in community relationship and atonement. Kohlberg and Freud see mature morality and self-development as autonomy in the negative sense of standing outside and against society and conventional rules. Royce would argue that such a view fails to deal with the depth of "original sin," namely, that deeply rooted egoism by which man "orients everything to himself instead of opening himself . . . to others." Likewise, Freud and Kohlberg do not see how this egoism is fostered by the social situation itself. Guilt is rooted by Freud and Kohlberg in the sense of disobeying social rules and is related to fear of punishment and public exposure. For Royce, guilt is self-loss because true self is rooted within autonomy within relationship. Sin, likewise, is "absolutizing of self, a withdrawal into a world of self-sufficiency." The overcoming of such is in reconciliation of self with self and with community. Again, these aspects of Royce's thought will be developed more fully in what follows. However, it would appear that Royce's thought will provide a fruitful new perspective on the debates surrounding moral and self-development.

A final relevant controversy within contemporary moral, social, and political theory is that of universalism-communitarianism. This debate has definitely gone "public." There is a "communitarian" agenda, a "communitarian" network," and a journal, *The Responsive Community*. The communitarian agenda is spelled out by Amitai Etzioni, a social scientist, in *The Spirit of Community: Rights, Responsibilities and the Communitarian Agenda*.[70] The communitarian movement, writes Etzioni, is "an environmental movement dedicated to the betterment of our moral, social and political environment."[71] Communitarians claim John Dewey as their mentor with his emphasis on participatory democracy. The key, says one communitarian, is "building grass roots communities, where people make their own decisions.[72] Josiah Royce with his "wholesome provincialism," a process of community building at grass-roots level, would certainly agree with this aspect of communitarianism. However, Royce would have had serious reservations about the charge that communitarianism, in its criticism of individualism, has "scapegoated individual rights by pitting them against community needs."[73] As indicated above, individuals and communities need each other. Individuals without community are without substance, whereas communities without individuals are blind. Stable unique selves develop out of a genuine communal context, and genuine communities are constituted by and require individuals capable of self-expansion and thus of communal loyalty.

Further, rights would be important, from Royce's point of view, but in the context of both individual protection and development and community building. He would not, as some communitarians do, pit rights against "public virtue." In chapter 2 I will discuss Royce's affinities with and differences from public communitarianism, with respect to such public issues as moral voice, the communitarian family, the communitarian school, rebuilding and starting communities, beyond the melting pot, public health and safety, and special interests versus public interests.[74]

What then about the more theoretical debate between universalism and communitarianism? This will lead us into a discussion of the work of Habermas and Alastair MacIntyre and a critical comparison with Royce's work. Thus Royce's theory of interpretation and the development of community and communal consensus will be set in critical interaction with Habermas's communicative theory of justification for norms based on the notion of rational consensus. This will allow an extensive discussion of Royce's view on how interpretation can be used to build consensus while respecting diversity and also to resolve conflict between dyadic "dangerous pairs." Dealing with MacIntyre's views will allow us to see how Royce's philosophy might interpret and deal with important concepts developed by MacIntyre, namely, "virtue," "narrative quest," "tradition," and "practice." As these concepts are discussed, we will seek to deal with a serious question for education and for other areas as well, namely, the nature of professional and vocational training. Dewey, in his article "The Challenge of Democracy to Education," writes, "there is very little understanding of the place of these . . . professions in the social life of the present and of what these vocations and professions may do to keep democracy a living growing thing."[75] Discussion of this issue will develop a Roycean understanding of profession as both communal tradition and practice, and of fiduciary responsibility based on trust, mutuality, and community.

The juxtaposition of Royce and MacIntyre's views will also allow me to argue why I believe a Roycean public philosophy is more adequate than the attempt by Sullivan to reconstruct such a philosophy on a base very similar to that of MacIntyre. It fails, as does MacIntyre, because of its Aristotelian teleological base.

Finally, the communitarian-universalist debate, particularly in its public form of the communitarian agenda will allow the argument that Royce's thought provides a better base for public philosophy than does that of John

Dewey. Dewey's public philosophy is related to contemporary communitarianism especially in its emphasis on participatory democracy and political action. Dewey, however, does not fall, as do the communitarians, into the trap of pitting individual and individual rights against community needs. Communitarism overemphasizes community; yet Dewey fails in underestimating the communal. He is too much an individualist at heart, even in the application of the scientific method of inquiry. If one juxtaposes Dewey's *Liberalism and Social Action* with Josiah Royce's *The Problem of Christianity*, the difference, in my mind, becomes clear. Dewey asks whether it is possible for a person to continue honestly and intelligently to be a liberal.[76] Royce's question is: "In what sense, if in any, can the modern man consistently be, in creed, a Christian?"[77] Dewey's question, spelled out, is how can an individual committed to free and open inquiry build a creative, radical democracy, one which questions the economically based society, thus transforming it into a true participatory democracy based on both liberty and equality? Royce's question is, How can essentially sinful, egocentric, individuals and communities build a genuine community in which genuine conversation and communication is possible, where there is "unity within variety" and where each person cares for the other? John Winthrop provides us a version of such a community in his essay, "A Model of Christian Charity":

> We must delight in each other, make each other's condition
> our own, rejoice together, mourn together, always having
> before our eyes our communion and community in the
> work, our community as members of the same body.[78]

Unlike Dewey, Royce has a developed doctrine of evil and of sin that allows not only for the notion of sin on the level of the individual but for communal sin and failure as well. He also deals with ways to overcome both. Thus, I believe he has partial answers at least to John McDermott's criticisms of Dewey's thought, namely, (1) that "he underestimated the capacity of the corporate world to operate, hydraheaded, in areas that Dewey took to be the vanguard of liberalism: education and labor-unions" and (2) that he had "an undeveloped doctrine of evil, the demonic, the capacity of human beings *en masse* to commit heinous crimes against other human beings."[79] Royce, I believe, would see labor unions as essentially "difficult" organizations too involved in a dangerous dyadic relationship and thus too fragile as communities and too open to the sin of capitalistic egoism. As for the schools, Royce, I believe, would argue that Dewey overly individualized science as a method of inquiry and failed to see it also as a community with a communal (moral) spirit, that is, the will to interpret. For open inquiry to accomplish genuine individual moral development, it must be operative in a genuine communal context. I shall develop these theses more in chapter 2 in the section on Dewey and Royce as public philosophers.

In seeking to justify a Roycean public philosophy, I have at the same time obviously given a substantial foretaste of what will follow in the succeeding chapters. It must be clear, however, that this will be no mere explication of Roycean thought, but rather an attempt to create a "great conversation" between Roycean ideas and contemporary issues and problems in social, political, and moral philosophy proper and in the public arena as well. It will be an attempt to begin to construct a public philosophy for today in the sense of discerning and articulating a common project for both concerned citizens and philosophers. The project is this: to struggle courageously with how we might build a sense of a "public," both as shared meanings and ideals and as a shared sense of community, while also earnestly addressing specific imperative issues with profound individual and communal impact. As I undertake this adventure, I do so with a deep sense of humility and limitation. With Sullivan, I look with awe upon the achievement of the Americans who created our democracy out of a context of deep and abiding conflicts. I also wholeheartedly concur with Sullivan's judgment that recent historiography shows us "how historically rare and difficult an achievement a genuine public philosophy really was."[80]

The Quest for Genuine Community

"The community is a fictitious body composed of the individual persons who are considered as constituting as it were its members. The interest of the community then is what?—The sum of the interests of the several members who compose it."
—Jeremy Bentham

"In order to be thus lovable to the critical and naturally rebellious soul, the Beloved Community must be quite unlike a natural social group, whose life consists of laws and quarrels, of a collective will and of individual rebellion. The community must be a union of members who first love it. The unity of love must pervade it, before the individual member can find it lovable."
—Josiah Royce

"Rebellion to Tyrants is Obedience to God"
—Thomas Jefferson

"Surely the individual, the person in the singular number, is the most fundamental phenomenon."
—William James

THAT INDIVIDUALISM has been at the heart of American thought and life from the beginning is hardly an issue for contention. In the fight to develop the new land called America, freedom of various kinds was the watchword—freedom from political tyranny and the control of government, freedom of mind, soul, and lifestyle, freedom of opportunity and freedom of the pocketbook. In the land of opportunity and abundance, and freed from the past and traditions, self-reliant individuals were to pursue their own interests. However, this is not the whole story. A new nation also had to be forged, and the question of social order and integration could not be ignored. Calvinist John Winthrop, aware that new land and the challenging of order would make social integration difficult, urged his band of immigrants bound for New England on the Arbella to pursue community. We must try, he said, "to be knit together in this work as one man." Thomas Jefferson, the ardent spokesman for individual freedom and rights, also believed community and concern for others a necessary ingredient of any new life forged in America. In his letter of June 13, 1814, to Thomas Law, he writes:

> Nature has implanted in our breasts a love of others, a sense of duty to them, a moral instinct, in short, which promotes us to heal and succor their distress. . . . The Creator would have indeed been a bungling artist had he intended man for a social animal without planting in him the social dispositions.

In the next two sections I shall explore briefly this American pursuit of individualism that nevertheless embraces the longing for community. As we shall see, individualism seems to have done much better in the American milieu. However, I will argue that the quest for genuine community and concern for others is not only very human but very American. Consequently, the work of Josiah Royce should touch a responsive chord in Americans currently interested in building and maintaining community.

Individualism Runs Rampant—Individuals Alone and in Conflict

Indeed, it may be accurate to say that in America our ideological stance has been that of individualism, but our philosophical quest has been for community.[1]

How, then, should the individual be related to society, community, the public interest, and/or the common good? This question has been a perennial and significant one for American thought and life. It is no surprise, then, that the issue of the individual vis-à-vis the community has again come to the foreground of public consciousness in the United States today. This question, this tension manifests itself in many ways. For example, two issues of *Time* magazine (August 16 and 20, 1993), one on guns and teenagers and another on the Brady bill and other Law and Order reforms, highlight the conflict between the individual's right to bear arms and public safety, especially the safety of public places such as medical facilities, libraries, and restaurants. Safety is indeed an issue in the United States. Violence of all kinds fills the news in the United States—carjacking, child, spousal and elderly abuse, the killing of parents by children. There is also news of increasing ethnic and racial conflict. Neo-Nazism and the Ku Klux Klan are today resurging. Gays and Lesbians often fear for their lives, and skinheads are even attacking skinheads; hate speech has become a public issue. Further, terrorism has now struck the United States with the remarkable tenure of the Unabomber, the bombings of New York's World Trade Center, and the Oklahoma City disaster. In many ways our society seems a warlike one with individuals and groups pitted against individuals, groups, and institutions.

Furthermore, U.S. society is a very adversarial society. In our court system, an adversarial attitude runs rampant. Lawyers defend clients against the encroachment of others; rights are set against rights, parent against parent, husband against wife, child against parent. William May has argued that the "adversarial game," in law and in accounting, encourages a kind of "antinomianism," that is, functioning as collaborator in unrighteousness by "letting the client know what he can maximally get away with." Even the press, says May, largely defines itself in adversarial terms. "It behaves as though it has not done well until it draws blood from those interviewed."[2] Another example of the adversarial nature of present American society is the polarization that has occurred around the issue of abortion. Pro-life opposes pro-choice, and violence has resulted, including the murder of two doctors.

Not only does contemporary society appear adversarial and warlike, it also appears greedy, self-interested, shallow and cynical. Rampant greed displayed itself in the savings-and-loan debacle, in the B.C.C.I. scandal, and in the junk-bonds scandals on Wall Street. Hypocrisy reins and there are ethical scandals in politics and in religion. Thus, we have endured Watergate, the Contra affair, sexual harassment charges against politicians, and sexual immorality and fraud charges against religious figures such as Jimmy Swaggart and Jim Bakker. Psychoanalyst Jules Henry has argued that "Psychosis is the final outcome of all that is wrong with a culture."[3] It is not surprising then that psychiatrists have discovered that the main psychosis of our time is that of "the narcissistic, liberated personality"—a person with charm and a drive to win, who also avoids intimacy but needs the admiration or fear of others, who has little or no spirit of play, who cannot mourn, and who dreads old age and death.[4] Further, narcissistic persons are definitely antisocial.

This personality is everywhere but is particularly found in the corporate world. Michael Maccoby, in a survey of 250 corporate managers, discovered a personality he describes as the "gamesman." This person likes running teams, being a winner, and never being a loser. This "gamesman" has little capacity for social intimacy or social commitment and indeed "avoids intimacy as a drag."[5] Ours is an era of mobility in the "executive success game;" loyalty means little, "style" and "panache" count. Success is performance and "arriving on time."[6]

On the more personal side, and fostering narcissism, is a 'therapeutic ideology' that encourages endless self-scrutiny. One must have continual physical and psychic checkups and pursue a normative schedule of psychosocial development—progress through stages at the right time and place. One must be intensely concerned about self and about personal growth. However, in addition to feeding narcissism, this ideology may be no more than one of self-preservation and psychic survival.[7] At bottom, this ideology of personal growth, though superficially optimistic, says Lasch, radiates a profound despair and resignation. It is the faith of those without faith.[8] Not only is today's society labeled warlike, adversarial, and narcissistic, but it is also named an age of deep cynicism. The cult of personal relations, manifested in endless seeking of vicarious warmth with others, conceals, we are told, a thoroughgoing disenchantment with personal relations. This reflects the conviction that "envy and exploitation dominate even the most intimate relations."[9] Jeffrey Goldfarb finds cynicism at the heart of our society when he writes:

> For the yuppie anything goes. Wealth is accumulated, but so is anomie—a commitment to nothing at all. Yuppie cynicism is power without culture. For the underclass, the absoluteness of poverty testifies to the absence of value in the way things are. Their cynicism constitutes a culture of powerlessness. . . . The struggle of power versus the powerless is crucially fought among the middle class. Cynicism of the middle is where democratic capacity may be lost.[10]

The cult of the bottom line, argues Goldfarb, steers and dominates all aspects of American life. People do not necessarily believe it is so, but they act as if it is so.[11]

Today, then, individualism, that is, the pursuit of self-interest, even against others, seems not only prevalent but permeating and ubiquitous. This individualism has a definite economic cast, namely, the pursuit of wealth and success. It is interesting, in this regard, to note that both Alexander Hamilton and John Adams foresaw that "affluence" was more to be feared in this new country of America than the tyranny of an aristocracy. In a letter to Thomas Jefferson, Adams raised the following questions: "How can we prevent riches from producing luxury and luxury from producing effeminacy, intoxication, extravagance, vice and folly?"[12] A half-century later Henry David Thoreau wrote of wealth as an illusion, arguing that with the triumph of *homo economicus*, the spiritual man dies. He saw the pursuit of wealth as morally stunting, leading to exploitation, alienation, and a life of "frantic meanness and quiet desperation." Possessive individualism, Thoreau believed, feeds upon and destroys itself, because when all people desire to possess the same thing and consume the same objects, the result is not competition and freedom but conformity, standardization, and compulsion.[13]

Alexis de Tocqueville, always on astute observer of America and American democracy, saw individualism as a key to democracy but also as its problematic. Democracy, observed Tocqueville, provides for the positive norm of individual autonomy. The individual, for his or her own life, becomes the authoritative judge and jury; but, at the same time, since the constraints of cultural norms, religion, family, and locality all reach beyond the individual, these are undermined. Social cohesion becomes highly problematic. Individualism, he predicted, could lead to a new tyranny. He characterized this tyranny as

> an innumerable multitude of men, all equal and alike, incessantly endeavoring to secure the petty and paltry pleasures with which they glut their lives. Each of them, living apart, is as a stranger to the fate of all the rest; his children and his private friends constitute to him the whole of mankind. As for the rest of his fellow citizens, he is close to them, but does not see them; he exists only in himself and for himself alone.[14]

Tocqueville refers to a subtle power which will render free action less and less frequent. That power is mass society and the tyranny of the majority. This subtle power is that described by Thoreau that produces a life without principle or conscious purpose, a mundane existence full of compulsive possessiveness, and a drive to produce without concern for the value of the product.[15] At the center of such a mass society is despair and cynicism. The cynic today, argues Goldfarb in his book *The Cynical Society*, is not the constructive, skeptical cynic like Diogenes—who renounced excessive expectations, who sought for an 'honest man,' and who was concerned for social change. Rather, says Goldfarb, the archetypal cynic of this contemporary time is the mocking cynic who knows that life is a sham but sees such knowledge as universal, that is, "they all do it," all engage in sham! Everything is elaborate rationalization! All are engaged in self-interested pursuit. As a matter of fact, Goldfarb believes that perpetual cynicism is the necessary result of the individual vis-à-vis community tension at the heart of American life and thought. He writes:

> Perpetual cynicism is produced and reproduced in democracies because the necessary balancing act between individual interests and the common good provokes suspicions and differences in judgment. People suspect that actions in the name of the public good actually serve individual private interests.[16]

Tocqueville, however, was not a cynic in this regard. He carefully distinguished egoism (mere selfishness) from individualism and he talked about "enlightened individualism" or "individualism properly understood." This individualism is one where the individual takes account of his or her place in a larger society. He saw a commitment, in America, to what he called "public freedom," and he believed that the public's participation in democracy and the voluntary associations of enlightened individuals would be the key to warding off the tyranny of mass society.

Goldfarb also refuses to give in to a full-blown cynicism about cynicism in American society. He sees great value in open, pluralist, cultural, literary work—such as that of present-day African American women like Toni Morrison and Alice Walker, which speaks critically, clearly, openly, and imaginatively—because it urges and teaches citizens to think for themselves about their society, so that they can act democratically.[17] In what follows we will show that Josiah Royce, struggling with individualism vis-à-vis community and society, was able to discover ways to revitalize community and democracy without violating individual rights or freedom. He argued that individuality and community were not necessarily in conflict, but that, in fact, individuality and community are inextricably bound together, arising out of their mutual interaction in a creative, ongoing, infinite process. Before turning to Royce's work on this issue, however, we need to deal with that other aspect of American life and culture, parallel to its individualistic ideology, namely, the quest for community. Again, I will be concerned to show that this quest is, like individualism, very human and very American.

America's Quest for Community and Concern for Others

There has been a tendency, in viewing the history of America, to focus on the political ideas of the founders, and on the roots of their ideas in classical Lockean liberalism. Such a focus tends to ignore other influences on American life and thought, particularly the influence of religion. Tocqueville, again, proved to be an accurate observer when he wrote:

> Upon my arrival in the Untied States, the religious aspect
> of the country was the first thing that struck my attention,
> and the longer I stayed there, the more did I perceive the
> great political consequences resulting from this state of af-
> fairs, to which I was unaccustomed.[18]

Tocqueville observed that America does not have the union of church and state that has resulted in intolerance and tyranny in Europe. There is, however, a lasting influence of religion. This is the case, thought Tocqueville, because religion's circle of influence is limited to certain principles under its own domain. Tocqueville does not spell out those principles, but they are central to the controversy of individualism vis-à-vis community. They concern humanity's sinful nature, his tendency toward prideful self-assertion, and, thus, his need for community and social dispositions.

George Santayana, also an observer of American life and culture, argued that liberalism and Protestantism dominated the American mind. "Liberalism," he wrote, "gave the American male the natural right to be free, become rich, and escape his marital vows, while Calvinism taught that one could do none of this without experiencing guilt."[19] John Patrick Diggins, in his history of American political thought, argues that historians have slighted the religious convictions that have undergirded American political ideas, "especially the Calvinist convictions that Locke held: resistance to tyranny, original sin and the corruptibility of man, labor and 'calling' as a means to salvation and the problem of man's infinite and insatiable desires, which compel him to be 'in constant pursuit of happiness.'"[20] Diggins argues that John Adams in his *Defense of the Constitution of the United States of America*, synthesized religion and politics in the manner observed by Tocqueville, namely, his theory of government derived from classical liberal ideology, while his psychology of political behavior derived from Calvinist theology.[21] Thus Adams, in this document on government, reflected on the weakness of individuals and their need for community, expressed his ambivalence about America's claim to 'social providence,' and expressed his troubling doubts about human nature and its depravity.[22]

It has been argued, in fact, that recognizing the tendency of human nature to pursue self-interest, Hamilton and Madison developed their theory of "equipoise" for government, that is, the balancing of powers. Their view, often called "liberal pluralism," deals with limitations on the power of the state by dispersing power as widely as possible. A fundamental thesis is that power can only be tamed, civilized, and controlled when there are multiple centers of power and competing of interests, no one of which is in a position to dominate the other. However, dispersal of power, in America, also had its drawbacks. In a land of vast space, it led to fragmentation of sovereignty and loss of interest in government and democratic participation. Alexander Hamilton, in *The Federalist Papers*, recognized this danger when he commented:

> Man is very much a creature of habit. A thing that rarely strikes his senses will generally have but a transient influence upon his mind. A government continually at a distance and out of sight can hardly be expected to interest the sensations of the people.[23]

Distance can dilute patriotism in the self-interested individual, an issue to be addressed in the next chapter, and encourage the cynicism and influence of mass society eluded to earlier. Later in this chapter, we will see how the notion of revitalizing small and local communities addresses the dangers of cynicism and mass-society influence. The issue immediately before us, however, is the influence of religion on American thought and life.

America's religious heritage has emphasized not only humanity's sinful nature and his guilt but also his need for community. The idea of community was central to a Puritan notion of a "holy commonwealth." Puritanism, as we recall, was the dominant religious influence in New England in early colonial days. Earlier, we spoke of John Winthrop's call "to be knit together in this work as one man." In his essay, "A Model of Christian Charity," Winthrop goes on to defend a Christian organism: " We must delight in each other, make each other's condition our own, rejoice together, mourn together, always having before our eyes . . . our community as members of the same body."[24] This is the vision of the Puritan "Holy Commonwealth." The great Calvinist, Jonathan Edwards, believed community to be "beautiful;" it was so, he said, because it realizes both a common design and, through this common design, the fulfillment of each member.[25] Community, it was believed, would temper and control individuals in their acquisitiveness, competition, and cupidity.

However, the concept of community faded in a land of great opportunity, abundance, and space. It was assumed that there was enough for everyone and no need to exploit and oppress others. Further, in conquering the land, virtue easily equated with fortitude and the stance of rugged individualism.

Throughout American history, however, the sense of sin and guilt and the call for community and social dispositions have been continually reasserted. Facing the tragic breakdown of community and the threat to political union, Abraham Lincoln was to unite liberalism and Christianity, proclaiming slavery as a transgression of God's law and pushing forward the principle of human equality as the foundation for all true liberty. Lincoln also recognized that economic pursuit was not the prime purpose of life, and he argued that "man must come before the dollar." Thus he advocated a role for the conflict between the principle of equality and that of freedom, another manifestation of the tension of individual vis-à-vis community. The equality-freedom tension is one that has troubled contemporary political theory and is the focus of John Rawl's liberalism. This Rawlsian liberalism is now under attack today, and we shall deal with this controversy near the end of this chapter. Lincoln also recognized that individuals were not necessarily self-sufficient; he thus advocated a role for government in carrying out the spirit of benevolence. He wrote: "The legitimate object of government is to do for a community what they need to have done but cannot do at all, or cannot do so well for themselves, in their separate and individual capacities."[26]

During this same period, novelists Herman Melville and Nathaniel Hawthorne were writing about America's sins of pride—political, religious, and technological. It is perhaps reflective of our situation today that the recent Hollywood production of Hawthorne's *Scarlet Letter* has removed the sense of sin and guilt from the story. Lincoln, however, often spoke of guilt, particularly the guilt of the nation because of the war. He felt the war reflected a "double" curse. He believed "labor" was an original curse for the human race in its transgression against God and that placing this burden of labor exclusively on a part of humanity in slavery doubled that curse. Lincoln also spoke of "lusting after labor," asserting that religion was not "a convenient fiction, but a painful truth."

Again and again in American history there have been voices for restoration of a "moral sense" and for "moral education." In the nineteenth century, John Witherspoon, president of Princeton, spoke of education as the moral custodian of the nation's character and conscience. Horace Mann saw education as laying the foundation for character development, social harmony, and civic responsibility. Catherine Beecher called for a submission of self to the general good and for social activity as a form of piety.[27] This was also a time when the family was identified as providing a "moral haven" against the aggressive pursuits of the public arena. However, the public-private split was an unfortunate reality and is related to the individualism vis-à-vis community tension. The contest between public and private is an issue that will be discussed later in this chapter and elsewhere, particularly in chapter 5.

The quest for community, for a social and moral sense, as well as a sense of sin and of guilt, seems to be part and parcel of American life and thought as does the strong individualistic drive. It is no surprise then that there are calls today for a return to moral education, as well as for a commitment of self to the common good. George Bush campaigned under a rubric of "a kinder and gentler America" and called for "a thousand points of light." Conservative Republicans call for a restatement of "family values." Bill Clinton, recalling the spirits of Lincoln and Kennedy, has urged Americans to engage in self-sacrifice for the common good. In this spirit of the quest for community, we have also the sociological works of Robert Bellah, et al., namely, *The Habits of the Heart, Individualism and Commitment in American Life* (1985) and *The Good Society* (1992).[28] The title for the first book comes from Tocqueville in *Democracy in America*, where he writes of "habits of the heart" of the American people, that is, those mores that form the American character. Among those aspects of the American character is, of course, "individualism." As indicated above, Tocqueville feared this characteristic might eventually isolate Americans one from another and thereby undermine the conditions of freedom. Bellah's *Habits* has the same concern as Tocqueville—that individualism "may have grown cancerous" and, thus, may be threatening the survival of freedom itself. These researchers studied individualism in America through interviews and other means. They also studied cultural traditions and practices "that, without destroying individualism, serve to limit and restrain the destructive side of individualism and provide alternative models for how Americans might live."[29]

Habits is concerned to explore ways to restore a sense of "the public," of the "common good" for America today. In a companion book, *Individualism and Commitment in American Life: Readings on the Themes of the Habits of the Heart* (1987), Bellah and his coauthors issue a call "to see ourselves as part of a political whole, part of a commonwealth." They also point out that "there are [in America today] echoes of moral traditions that could be used by committed leadership to anchor [lifestyle] enclaves in the life of national community."[30] The moral traditions that Bellah wishes to recall are "biblical religion" and "civic republicanism."

We have discussed briefly "biblical religion" as a strand in American thought and life, and we will see how Royce draws on this to spell out the essential elements of community and communal life. However, Royce's views contrast sharply with "civic republicanism," especially as exemplified in the contemporary work of Alasdair MacIntyre. I will argue that Royce's view overcomes a number of weaknesses in MacIntyre's position and, indeed, I agree with the assessment of Diggins that "civic republicanism" never took hold in American thought and life. It is not the direction America should pursue in building community.

The third work in the Bellah trilogy, *The Good Society*, published in 1992, addresses, among other things, these twin concerns: the way certain institutions profoundly impact our lives, and how we can change these impacts to "community enhancers" rather than having them function to frustrate the quest for the common good.[31] The book is concerned to deal with a number of troubling questions, namely, What constitutes a family, a home, a job, a community? We will explore these same questions but from a Roycean point of view.

In concert with these books has risen a political, activist group called the communitarians. The agenda for this group appears in *The Spirit of Community* by Amitai Etzioni.[32] Communitarianism, writes Etzioni, is "an environmental movement dedicated to the betterment of our moral, social, and political environment."[33] Community is a clear concern of this movement: "We suggest that *free individuals require a community*, which backs them up against the encroachment by the state and sustains morality by drawing on the gentle prodding of kin, friends, neighbors, and other community members, rather than building on government controls or fears of authorities."[34] As we shall see, one of the important roles of "others," for Royce, is criticism of our views, as well as expansion of our vision. The emphasis of communitarianism is clearly on the moral role of community. Etzioni tells us: "*Communities speak to us in moral voices . . . The best way to minimize the role of the state, especially its policing role, is to enhance the community and its moral voice.*"[35]

In what follows we shall contrast Royce's search for community with the communitarian agenda. Royce seeks proper balance between individualism and community while communitarianism tends to see community opposed to individual and individualism. Communitarianism also remains too much in the adversarial, negative mode of traditional liberalism. The emphasis is on freedom *against* the state. Not enough attention is given to positive freedoms and the conditions for building freedom. Further, there is little attention given to what constitutes a "genuine" community and how one deals with dangerous social groups. Do we wish to heed the moral voice of all communities? Further, what prevents the tyranny of these communal moral voices?

We need a concept of "genuine" community, for as Scott Peck tells us, "It is virtually impossible to describe community meaningfully to someone who has never experienced it . . . and most of us have never had an experience of true community."[36] Peck rightly asserts that we falsely apply the word "community" to any collection of individuals. We should reserve this word for groups of individuals who have learned to "communicate honestly with each other and who have a significant commitment to rejoice and mourn together, to delight in each other's condition."[37] Royce describes such a community and the conditions for building and maintaining it. In setting out Royce's views, we will find that they conjoin in many areas with Peck's views on community. Since Peck is engaged in creating in fact many such "genuine" communities, this allows us to believe that Royce's vision of community and of the proper relationship of the individual to such a community is not only timely, but also the realistic, alternative model of American living that Bellah seeks. It is to that model we now turn.

Today's Moral Imperative:
Building Enlightened, Genuine Individualism

Josiah Royce provides a realistic and alternative model for American life today because he values and honors the individual, as did William James, as a "most fundamental phenomenon," while also addressing community and the problem of competing forms of human community.[38] As indicated earlier, his metaphysics recognizes the full-fledged reality of both individuals and community. In the practical social and political realm, Royce also had the courage to tackle the dual issues of "enlightened/genuine individualism" and "true/genuine community." He recognized that the task of building authentic individuality and that of encouraging the growth of fulfilling, moral communities are inextricably bound together—worthwhile individuality and community arising out of their mutual interaction in a creative, ongoing, infinite process. Thus Royce was to develop the following claims: (1) Individuals are inescapably rooted in the social context and true individuality is forged out of that context. An individual is *both* self-made and a social product and the worthiness of the end result, the individual self, is the responsibility of *both* the individual and the community, and a worthwhile self is *both* individual and communal; (2) community is a social product, but true community is created by the hard work of free, self-conscious, self-committed, self-creative, moral individuals; (3) the task of the individual is both to fashion a "beautiful" life and to build a "beautiful" community, while the obligation of community is to build a harmony of wills while also fostering the development of true individuals; (4) individuals are finite, sinful, and fallible and need to extend self to develop morality and overcome error. Further, individuals crave harmony. On the other hand, individuals keep communities alive, moral, and sane by keeping them from stagnating into inveterate habit, moving toward exclusivity and intolerance, or degenerating into mob madness. In other words, stress must be equally on the individual and on the community. For Royce, *individuals without community are without substance; while communities without individuals are blind.*

The notion that the individual is inescapably rooted in a social context is pivotal for Roycean thought, as for contemporary communitarians. Royce argues that our very self-consciousness arises out of a social contrast between the self and not-self, between what is mine and not mine. Royce writes:

> I affirm that our empirical self-consciousness, from moment to moment depends upon a series of contrast effects, whose psychological origin lies in our literal social life. . . . Nobody amongst us men comes to self-consciousness, so far as I know, except under the persistent influences of his social fellows. . . .[39]

In other words, the distinctive human trait, self-consciousness, is a result of a dialogue between self and others. I need others to develop a sense of my own independent, individual self. However, like a number of contemporary psychoanalysts. Royce saw this interactive process to be a very delicate one, and he freely recognized that it could lead to both healthy and unhealthy individual development. Not all social interactive processes or social relationships are healthy ones, productive of the ability to be both individual and communal. Royce saw the developmental process as involving contact and separateness, similarity and contrast, imitation and creativity, accommodation, and nonaccommodation, assertion and mutual recognition. The interactive process of self and other is a delicate one, and if the balance of these various tensions shifts too heavily or too much to one side of the pair, difficulties for building a truly individual self will result.

In Royce's view, the difficulties were of two essential kinds. First, the process of the formation of self out of a social context can develop individuals who are too individualistic, too private, too unsocialized, too rebellious, too unsoftened by social sympathy. Secondly, the formative power of social situations can be too strong, producing too much accommodation to others, too much of a "me-self" that becomes lost in the mass "they" that terrified the existentialists and became a reality in Hitler's Germany. In other words, rampant individualism or stifling collectivism are the two dangers to be avoided and that can result from the breakdown in the delicate balancing process of self-development. This is why there must be a dual emphasis on the creative role of the individual *and* the obligation of the community of others to foster true individuals.

In the relationship between self and other, the other provides me with a sense of intersubjective *reality* both as "external world" and "social world." For Royce, our knowledge of the external is fundamentally bound up with our being-with-others. Royce points out that community experience distinguishes inner from outer, the outer world being the world whose presence can be indicated by definable communicable experience.[40] He further notes that spatial definiteness is important to externality because only the definitely localizable in space can be independently viewed and agreed upon by a number of socially communicable beings.[41] Finally, the data of sight and sound are more reliable because they are most open to social confirmation. We can grasp and see a pole together or lift a weight, but we cannot literally share smells and tastes.[42] If the delicate process of self-building in relation to others goes wrong, an individual's sense of reality and distinction between inner and outer can go astray. These Roycean insights are truly contemporary, as we shall see in the chapter 3's discussion of personhood and self-development. Psychoanalyst D. W. Winnicott, in his book, *Playing and Reality*, discusses how vital proper understanding and use of objects are to a self's sense of reality and ability to engage in play. Further, he argues, on another occasion, that one of the most important elements in feeling authentic as a self is "the recognition of an outside reality that is not one's own projection and an experience of contact with other minds."[43] Recall that the narcissistic personality is unable to engage in the spirit of play and that this type of person sees others and events as "the mirror of himself." Royce, on the contrary, believes others provide us with needed contrasts and criticisms so that self-developmental occurs.

Thus, not only does the relationship and interaction of self and other provide a sense of the "external world," but it also gives a sense of the "social world." The 'other' provides me with roles and models that I can act out and imitate, by which I can create an external me-self, "a social self." The 'other' allows me to internalize the objectivated world of culture, to become socialized. In this regard, several points are important to stress. The first is the need to permit creativity and exploration for the self in this process. The interactive process of self and other must be one which allows me to have a distinct sense of my own self and action, in which I begin to distinguish my thoughts, feelings, and behavior from those of others. I must carve out my distinctive biography and develop my individuality while also sensing my being-with-others. Psychoanalyst Jessica Benjamin gives extensive consideration to the *differentiation* process in human development, that is, the ability to be aware of distinctness from others. What is involved, she argues, is *mutual recognition* in which each self recognizes the other as an independent agent.[44] This is simultaneous mutuality, as, for example, in sophisticated facial interlay where mother and baby adapt "each facial and gestural response to the other's mutual influence."[45] This is a delicate, easily conflictual process, but it also provides for creativity and exploration as well as a sense of 'being with.' This can be seen, says Benjamin, when a baby who is crawling about checks back to see if mom is feeling her sense of adventure. There is for the self in this situation a sense of the "pleasure of being attuned."[46]

Benjamin believes it is human to desire to "remain attuned." Royce speaks of humanity's desire to be "in harmony." However, both recognize the pull and danger of accommodation. The desire to remain attuned, says Benjamin, can be "converted into submission to the other's will." If a self fails to exercise creativity or if social conditions do not permit such exercise, accommodation to the "mass," to others will occur. This failure of the developmental process is also evident today in the increase in various forms of fanaticism, whether Christian or Islamic fundamentalism, or Neo-Nazism and Klanism. Another aspect of the breakdown of the delicate and necessary tension between self-assertion and mutual recognition, says Benjamin, is domination, which is also a form of submission and dependency. We shall discuss these issues more thoroughly in chapter 3.

Individuals, then develop in a social context, but free, self-created, self-conscious individuals need the proper social milieu; communities have an obligation to foster the development of true individuals. We shall discuss the essential characteristics of these authentic communities shortly, but first we need to stress the role that social context places in developing knowledge of external reality of self and of others. The individual self is finite, fallible, and incomplete, and community is needed to overcome this finitude and error, as well as our sin and treason. For Royce, one guilty of treason attempts to destroy "the community in whose brotherhood, in whose life, in whose spirit he has found his guide and his ideal."[47] Participation with others diminishes the actual amount of error and ignorance for individual and group. Knowledge of the external world, as already indicated, is dependent on others. Royce writes:

> Our belief in the reality of Nature, when nature is taken to mean the realm of physical phenomenon known to common sense *is inseparably bound up with our belief in the existence of our fellow men.* . . . Nature is a realm which we conceive as known or knowable to various men in precisely the general sense in which we regard it as known or knowable to our private selves.[48]

Further, for Royce, community is a fundamental condition for scientific knowledge and progress and science as a communal enterprise serves, for Royce as we shall see, as a model for community. Individuals, without community, remain in ignorance about reality as well as about self. We have already seen how a breakdown in early self-other interaction leads to inability to distinguish inner and outer and to have an authentic view of self. As I see others as conscious actors, I can become a conscious actor myself. Further, others "stretch" me by criticizing or stimulating me to develop my self in new directions. Royce writes:

> Our fellows are known to be real and have their own inner life, because they are for each of us, the endless treasury of *more ideas.* They answer our questions, they tell us news, they make comments, they pass judgments, they express novel combinations of feelings, they relate to us stories, they argue with us, and take counsel with us. . . . *Our fellows furnish us the constantly needed supplement to our own fragmentary meanings.*[49]

My knowledge of my self and my neighbor is, for Royce, essentially a social and communal process, a third type of knowledge, knowledge as interpretation which we shall discuss shortly.

Community, then, helps us extend ourselves, helps us overcome ignorance, and allows the possibility of understanding and tolerance of the mutual recognition and appreciation of others. Individuals as true individuals truly need each. Scott Peck expresses the issues very well. Individuals without community in its genuine sense are lonely, fearful, shallow, driven to pretend. Rugged individualism, he says, recognizes that we are called to "individuation, power and wholes," but it denies the other part of the human story, namely, "that we can never fully get there and that we are of necessity in our uniqueness, weak and imperfect creatures who need each other."[50]

The denial of this other half of our human story has tragic results, seen in the narcissistic psychosis and other psychic ills. Peck writes:

> This denial can be sustained only by pretense. Because we cannot ever be totally adequate and self-sufficient, independent beings, the ideal of rugged individualism encourages us to fake it. It encourage us to hide our weakness and failures. It teaches us to be utterly ashamed of our limitations. It drives us to attempt to be superwomen and supermen not only in the eyes of others but also in our own. It pushes us day in and day out to look as if we 'have it altogether' as if we were without need and in total control of ourselves. It relentlessly demands that we keep up appearances. It also relentlessly isolates us from each other.[51]

According to Peck, this denial of the other half of the human story of need and limitation makes genuine community impossible. He calls, as does Tocqueville, as does Royce, for a more "genuine" individualism that will help make community possible. Peck labels this form of individualism "soft individualism," which teaches

> that we cannot be truly ourselves until we are able to share freely the things we most have in common: our weakness, our incompleteness, our imperfection, our inadequacy, our sins, our lack of wholeness and self-sufficiency. . . . It is the kind of individualism that acknowledges our interdependence not merely in the intellectual catchwords of the day but in the very depths of our hearts.[52]

This kind of individualism, says Peck, makes real community possible. Royce also believed that a new kind of individual was necessary for the building of genuine communities. We will discuss extensively in another chapter his understanding of genuine personhood. It can be briefly noted here that

Royce's first condition for building community is the power of individuals to "extend themselves in time." This had a number of meanings for Royce which we will discuss later, but at least one aspect of this "time extension ability" relates well to Peck's "soft individualism." Peck writes: "It is a kind of softness that allows those necessary barriers, or outlines, of our individual selves to be like permeable membranes, permitting ourselves to seep out and the selves of others to seep in."[53]

Today's Moral Imperative: Building Genuine Community

We have said much, then, about individualism and the need of the individual for community. Genuine individualism needs genuine community to foster and maintain it. What, then, are the characteristics of genuine community, and how are such communities built? Royce addressed these questions in his work *The Problem of Christianity*, and it is to this discussion we now turn.

The first condition of community, as we indicated, is "the power of an individual to extend his life, in an ideal fashion, so as to regard it as including past and future events which lie far away in time, and which he does not now personally remember."[54] These aspects of self will be discussed, as indicated, in another chapter. However, a brief remark can be made at this time. The self's ability to extend oneself in time has to do with a recognition of finitude, error, weakness, and the need for others. It also has to do with self-understanding, self-criticism, and self-unification. "Self-awareness," both of individuals and the community, is, for Peck, an important condition of community. He ties this self-awareness to humility, with an understanding of limits,[55] as would Royce. Self-awareness also has to do with the self's creativity and openness to change. William James states this issue very well when he writes: "The individual has a stock of old opinions already, but he meets a new experience that puts them to a strain. He seeks to modify or he latches on to a new idea that 'mediates' between the stock and the new experience and runs them into one another most felicitously to make them admit of 'novelty.'"[56]

The second Roycean condition for true community is that there be communication among selves, communication through attentive listening to the ideas and hopes of others. Likewise, a basic condition of community for Peck is communication. He points out that the verb *communicate* and the noun *community* share the same root. "The principles of good communication are the basic principles of community-building."[57] However, Royce goes much further than this in developing a theory of communication that is central to community building. Community, for Royce, is the product of interpretation, and I believe that his theory and method of interpretation is significant and valuable for building genuine individuality and community today.

Interpretation involves a mediation between two minds, ideas, hopes, persons. Thus, for example, I am mediating the mind and thought of Royce—accessible through a set of signs contained in his works—to the minds of my audience. Three items are brought into a determinate relationship by this interpretation: (1) I, the interpreter, who must seek to understand both Royce and you, my audience; (2) the object, Royce's thought; and (3) a mind to whom the interpretation is addressed. The relationship is non-symmetrical, that is, unevenly arranged with respect to all three of the terms. If the order of the relationship were reversed, it would change the process. Thus, if you were to write a response to my interpretation of Royce, you would become the interpreter and a new triadic interpretative relationship would result.

Royce sees interpretation as a temporal process; each of the terms of the relation correspond to the three dimensions of time: past, present, and future. Thus, what Royce wrote in the past, I am at present interpreting to you for your future interpretation. The process is irreversible, partial, and yet ideally infinite. Once I have spoken, what I have said cannot be revoked. Even if I take it back, it still has been said. This adds caution and care to what we say. We want to say what we "mean." And we want to be aware of the impact of our words on others. Parents, for example, often harm children with their words.[58] My words cannot be revoked, but what I have said is also not the final word, for there will be further interpretations, more opportunity for dialogue. Royce, in fact, believed the process of interpretation to be potentially infinite, unless interrupted or stopped for arbitrary reasons. Indeed, the interpretation of Royce's thought has been proceeding now for over a hundred years. This temporal dimension of interpretation, like the ability of self to extend in time, denotes openness, development, and the possibility for creation as well as healing.

Interpretation is by its very nature a community-building process. It takes selves outside of themselves and creates new "unities" or "harmonies."

First of all, in order to interpret Royce to you, I had to take my past ideas of Royce, compare them with my present ones, and then achieve a new understanding to convey to you. In achieving this new view, a new union of ideas, I have transcended my past self. I have added to my and the community's stock of ideas. By attending to my interpretation of Royce, you, too, open yourself to a transcending of your old self and to a new unity of ideas. Notice that action, openness, and risk are involved in interpretation, as well as an element of loyalty, of faithfulness or care.[59] To interpret Royce to you, I had to choose to re-immerse myself in Royce's thought, and I committed myself, hopefully, to be loyal to whatever truth I found therein. Further, in opening myself to Royce's ideas, to his self, I risked having my ideas changed. Peck's notion of permeability of selves to each other is certainly appropriate here. A further risk, in conveying Royce's thought to you now is that I can be wrong and you or the community can rectify my error. By attending to my interpretation of Royce, your openness also subjects you to the risk of error in your understanding and to the risk of having your ideas changed. If the attempt at interpretation is successful, new meaning will come forth, for each of us will have achieved a new unity of ideas and we will have established a shared understanding of Royce.

There are a number of crucial elements in interpretation. They are: (1) respect and regard for each self and idea involved; (2) the will to interpret, which involves (a) a sense of discontent and dissatisfaction both with partial meaning, that is, a narrowness of one's view of things, and with estrangement from others as carriers of meanings and ideas; and (b) an aim to unite selves; and (3) reciprocity and mutuality. Respect and regard for selves and ideas involves both self-respect and respect of others. Both are necessary if one is to risk openness to change, to error, that interpretation requires. Additionally, interpretation requires humility as well as a willingness to understand, in the words of William James, what is "significant to the other."[60] It invokes tolerance, patience, sympathy, and kindness; all, along with humility, are traditional virtues. Interpretation also involves an affirmation of the ethical principle of equality, a commitment to treat each individual as equal in having an opportunity to contribute to the process. It would also involve providing conditions to allow the ideas and contributions and lives of each self to be affirmed.

The will to interpret incorporates the attitude of humility as well as the elements of respect. Respect is again affirmed in the requirement of mutuality and reciprocity. This requirement also asks for a more active commitment, namely, to reach out to others, to seek genuine communication, and to engage in attentive, open listening. The will to interpret also involves a willingness to have one's ideas tested and compared against the ideas of others; to risk, as indicated above, error and change. One is reminded of the *love* of logic expounded by Charles S. Peirce, namely, the altruistic willingness "of each individual to sacrifice what is personal and private to him alone in order to follow the dictates of an impersonal method that involves the free exchange of ideas and results."[61] Both Peirce and Royce saw this attitude exemplified in science and both took the community of science as a model of community. It must, however, be clear that both philosophers emphasized attitude or spirit as well as method. As I shall argue in the last section of this chapter, liberalism fails in this regard; it advocates the formal procedures of the free exchange of ideas without acknowledging the equal need for the attitude of respect and commitment to equality of regard and opportunity of participation. Dewey also fails to the extent that he advocates the application of the scientific method in education, politics, and social reform without giving significant attention to the need to embed it in genuine community and the desire to seek communal unity.

Indeed, Royce's third condition of community is that unity actually be achieved. Through the process of interpretation, each of the individuals involved comes to share a common past and/or a common future, that is, it becomes a community of memory and/or a community of hope. As a temporal being, like the self, the community brings forth an embodied ideal; as in the case of the self, this achievement involves deeds done and ends sought. Royce defines a community as a "being that attempts to accomplish something in and through its members."[62] Like the self, the community is a plan of action. Thus, the communitarians are correct to see community as necessarily involved in action—hopefully, moral action. However, it should be genuine communal action and not imposed action on individuals. Together individuals determine acts and then act.

The fourth condition of community identified by Royce is a recognition of cooperative efforts, the recognition that without the contribution of each person the goal would not have been achieved, the deed would not have been accomplished. This manifests genuine recognition of and respect for the individual. The community, like self, is both communal and individual, both one (guided by common idea(s)) and many (the individual members).

Royce declares "a community does not become one . . . by virtue of any reduction or melting of these various selves into a single merely present self or into a mass of passing experience."[63] In a true community, there must be shared understanding and cooperation, a genuine intersubjective interaction and sharing.

This clear recognition of both the individual and the community is spelled out in the six subconditions Royce outlined for the existence of true community. In discussing these I shall draw on the fine paraphrase of these subconditions provided by Frank. M. Oppenheim.[64] The first subcondition is that each individual must direct his own deeds of cooperation. Participation in the community on the part of each member must be conscious and voluntary. The second subcondition emphasizes the mutuality and respect involved in a genuine community. This condition is that each member should observe the deeds of fellow members and seek to stimulate, encourage, correct, and enjoy those acts, as do the members of a fine orchestra. A jazz performance provides an even better analogy. Good jazz simultaneously requires unity and a great deal of individuality. By definition, jazz improvisation requires close adherence to harmonic progression while permitting, even demanding, melodic and rhythmic originality.

The third subcondition of community also concerns both respect—self and other—and mutual harmony, which to say that each individual must know that without this interacting of co-working selves, the community could not accomplish its aim. There must be mutual appreciation of the efforts of every member and a clear understanding that only by coordinating efforts can the community achieve its goals. Only by each playing his part and his instrument can a musical composition be performed. With this subcondition I am reminded of Jessica Benjamin's description of the sophisticated, interactive facial play of a parent and child. She speaks of both being attuned to one another's gestures and likens this reciprocity to the unison and oneness achieved in music and dance. It is revealing for our later discussions of self and family that Benjamin sees this interactive facial play as prefiguring successful adult erotic play.

The fourth subcondition of community deals with the temporal and open-endedness of genuine community. It is that members see present cooperative acts as linked to the community's life and hopes. There must not be neglect of the past nor exclusive preoccupation with the now. A genuine community is evolving and future oriented; it weaves a story. The story or narrative aspect of self will be discussed in the chapter 3, but with regard to the story-weaving aspect of community, Peck observes that myth making seems to be a common aspect of true community and that this trait reflects a "collective creative genius of genuine community."[65] Another aspect of genuine community's future-moving character and of its nature as an interpretive community is its openness and its inclusiveness. In chapter 4, on loyalty, we will discuss Royce's maxim of loyalty to loyalty, which is a call to increasing community and inclusiveness, but it is clear that for Royce, true communities must be always reaching to extend themselves. Peck declares, "Exclusivity is a great enemy of community."[66]

The fifth subcondition of community requires that each member concur in accepting each self as a fellow member. Combined with the condition of inclusivity, this can make for difficult, tragic conditions for a community. It truly requires reaching out of self and opening self and the community. A genuine community is one that dares to be vulnerable, to suffer guilt, and to engage in healing and atonement. Peck, in his book, describes a situation where a group had to struggle long and agonizingly with a very disruptive "evil" member. Eventually, the member was asked to leave. The group then had to deal with its guilt for becoming "exclusive." Peck sees this recognition of guilt and failure as essential to genuine community. He writes:

> Without this sense of failure and accompanying guilt, a community would, in fact, cease to be a community. It would have degenerated into exclusivity as a way of being. If it no longer agonized over the question of whether or not exclusion of a member might represent scapegoating, it would become prone to scapegoating. To be in true community means to be in constant pain and tension over the problem of human evil.[67]

Royce, in his book *The Sources of Religious Insight*[68] as well as in *The Problem of Christianity*, deals with sin and treason to the community. He argues also for a form of "communal atonement." The sinner or traitor must be reconciled, says Royce, both to himself and his community. It is not just a matter of love and forgiveness. Love must be restored, but it "will be the love for the member who *has been a traitor*, and the tragedy of the treason will permanently form part in and of this love."[69] The deed is done; the past can be transcended, incorporated, but it cannot be revoked. Further, the triumph over the treason can only be accomplished by the community, or on behalf of the community, through a servant member who acts, so to speak, "as the incarnation of the very spirit of the community itself."[70] A creative deed is performed that unites and transforms the treason into the present and future life of the community. Of this deed, Royce writes: "*The world, as transformed by this creative deed, is better than it would have been had all else remained the same, but had that deed of treason not been done at all.*"[71]

It should be obvious at this point that Royce was fully aware of the realities of actual human life and community and that he knew that community and common consciousness were hard to come by in the midst of social alienation. He was thoroughly cognizant of original sin, expressed in the tendencies toward narcissism and isolation and toward the betrayal of ideals. He writes:

> The failure to sound to the depths the original sin of man, the social animal and of the natural social order he creates—such failure, I repeat, lies at the basis of countless misinterpretations, both of our modern social problems, and of the nature of a true community and of the conditions which make possible any wider generalization of the idea of community.[72]

Communitarians and liberals alike fail to acknowledge the hard facts of human nature. The liberals assume rationality and knowledge will lead to virtue and community vis-à-vis "enlightened self-interest." Communitarians assume that a declaration of humanity's social nature is sufficient to overcome the individualism of liberalism. The communitarians also do not deal with the distinction between "genuine community" and other inadequate or dangerous communities, nor with community's tendency toward exclusivity, intolerance, and sin. John Dewey, as indicated earlier, places, as do the liberals, too much faith in "formal method" and ignores the need for the "right spirit." Further, Dewey, too, does not deal with evil. John McDermott's observation on Dewey's thought, in fact, applies also to communitarians and liberalism, namely, that they have "an undeveloped doctrine of evil, the demonic, and of the capacity of human beings *en masse* to commit heinous crimes against other beings."[73]

Royce did have an understanding of the hard realities of human and community life. After all, he grew up in a rough mining town in gold-rush California. More of this will become evident as we discuss his views on loyalty, provincialism, and "dangerous pairs" in the next chapter. Further, although we cannot discuss the details of Royce's metaphysical thought in this context, it is clear that the reality of evil, of suffering, and of the tragic in life play a crucial role in his philosophy. In his lectures on metaphysics in 1916 he assures his students that "the encounter of human selves is the most important moral aspect of the world."[74]

However, though Royce was fully aware of the tendency of individuals toward isolation and narrowness, toward sin, he was not a cynic of the mocking sort, who gives up on social and individual change. He believed, with Jefferson, that deep within the human psyche is a desire for wholeness, for relationship, intimacy, and an ability to want to comfort and help others. He argued that true human fulfillment could only come in community. Many contemporary psychologists are finding evidence in the very young of feelings of compassion, of co-feeling, and are struggling with the conditions that allow this to develop into adult moral behavior. In the chapter 3, we will discuss Royce's views on psychic and moral development, because, as we have seen "genuine individuality" and "genuine community" are crucially interrelated, each develops in interaction with the other.

I believe that Royce's views on community and self have much to offer in dealing with contemporary problems including the questions raised by communitarians—what, for instance, is a family, a home, a practice, or profession. Later chapters will deal with these questions, seeking to apply Roycean insights to the issues. In closing this chapter, however, we turn to some brief observations on Royce's views on the individualism-community issue as they relate to the contemporary debate between liberalism-communitarianism. Only some of the issues will be addressed in this section while others will be discussed in the chapters on loyalty and self and moral development.

Communitarianism—What Community, Whose Practice?

At the heart of liberalism as a political, social theory is the notion of the individual as constituted prior to all social interaction, free and equal, with the capacity to make rational choices, and with certain basic natural rights. To maintain their natural rights, these rational individuals voluntarily give up some of their freedom and enter into a "social contract" to create a political authority capable of preserving these rights and restraining transgressors. In creating the social contract, individuals obligate themselves to abide by the decisions of the majority; though the power of government is limited to the terms of the contract and is subject to the continuous review by the citizens involved. The primary role of government is to protect the rights that belong to individuals prior to the political organization of social relations. Liberalism, notes Dewey, is highly individualistic. "Primacy is given to the individual over the state not only in time but in moral authority."[75] The emphasis is on individual freedom, particularly from government, exemplified in the right to challenge and resist authority, and on individual rights. Additionally, liberalism stresses formal procedures to allow open expressions of citizens' voices and to prevent suppression of individual differences. Individual freedom must be protected in the realms of thought, speech, and action, and, thus, the Bill of Rights formalizes the civic rights to free speech, assembly, and due process. Liberalism places maximum reliance on open debate and upon intelligence.

Communitarians—critical theorists such as Habermas, Dewey, and of course Royce—share an aversion to the notion of the individual as constituted prior to all social interaction. As we have seen in our discussion of Royce's views, the individual, though self-made, is clearly also a social product. MacIntyre, for example, argues that the individual self is situated in and constituted by tradition, by a historically rooted community. Tradition does not necessarily imply "prejudice," as liberalism would see it, nor does having a tradition prevent criticism of it. Indeed, some communitarians argue, "intolerance flourishes most where forms of life are dislocated, roots unsettled and traditions undone."[76] "Further, for communitarians, morality and a sense of a good life is necessary for human development and communal living. Good takes priority over rights. Further, a sense of the good is provided by community, and human moral development occurs in historical, communal contexts. Humans, argues MacIntyre, are tellers of stories and engaged in narrative quests. They learn about good as they seek their story and the good. Tradition or community is essential to the individual quest for good because tradition is a "historically extended, socially embodied argument, an argument precisely in part about the goods which constitute the tradition."[77] MacIntyre also criticizes liberalism's emphasis on the pursuit of external goods, especially property goods, and he develops a notion of "internal goods" and a concept of a "practice." A "practice" is essentially a community engaged in a particular activity with an emphasis on goods "internal to the practice," namely, "standards of excellence and non-material rewards of excellence that command the allegiance of every accomplished participant in a practice."[78] "Virtues" are, then, acquired human characteristics, such as justice, truthfulness, and courage, which enable persons to pursue and receive internal goods and to resist corruption of practices by institutions that seek external goods and give them priority over internal goods.

The essential criticism of liberalism by communitarianism is that the individual is not constituted prior to social construction but is constituted in and out of social context. Secondly, it is agreed that the primary concern for human beings is the quest for a good life, and this can only be achieved within a social context of practice or tradition. Royce would basically concur with these ideas. Dewey adds a telling criticism of liberalism that is related to these issues and that concerns the assumption that civil liberties will take care of themselves:

> The only hope for liberalism is to surrender in theory and practice, the doctrine that liberty is a full fledged, ready-made possession of individuals independent of social institutions and arrangements and to realize that social control, especially of economic forces, is necessary in order to render secure the liberties for the individuals, including civil liberties.[79]

Dewey sees that institutions and their pursuit of external goods also corrupts democratic processes.

Although the communitarians and Dewey recognize the corruptibility of practices and civic processes, they fail, I believe, to come to grips fully with this manifestation of human failure and evil. Again, they do not have a doctrine of evil, nor can they deal with community evil and guilt. MacIntyre believes that the virtues will help resistance to corruption of practices, but it is hard to see how this will work and why the particular virtues MacIntyre cites, such as justice, truthfulness, or courage, would be those human characteristics more likely to allow resistance. Indeed, critics find MacIntyre's discussion of 'virtue' weak, and the argument for their curative or preventive role not substantially developed.[80] What is 'virtue'? How is it developed? Why is truthfulness more important to communal development than humility? We shall discuss Royce's understanding of virtue in the next two chapters.

Further, as indicated earlier, communitarianism does not deal with the notion of "genuine community," that is, it does not struggle with the question of "wicked traditions," or "wicked practices." One is reminded here of Jeffrey Archer's *Honor among Thieves,* which examines that very proposition. In his book, *Whose Justice? Which Rationality?* MacIntyre develops a notion of the "rationality of a tradition," which appears similar to Popper's notions about "good scientific theory," namely, that a tradition is most rational and most trustworthy if it is "progressive," if it overcomes crises in the most inclusive and creative way.[81] In this regard, a 'wicked' tradition or practice would seem to be one that does not progress or contribute to the reproduction of the practice or tradition. Besides resting on a false presumption of equating rationality with goodness, an issue that will be discussed in chapter 3, this seems highly unsatisfactory. The mafia has "progressed" in many ways by becoming more sophisticated in its brutality and illegality. If one is to argue for community as essential for the good, for the promotion of rights, and for the individual, one must grapple, as did Royce, with the conditions and characteristics of "genuine community" and with the "genuine reality" of human evil.

In chapter 7, in a discussion of "medicine as a practice," we will use Roycean ideas about interpretation and community to discuss "practice" and goods "internal" to practices. Rather than MacIntyre's "rationalistic progressiveness" as a criteria for "good" practice, we will discuss Royce's concept of "loyalty to loyalty," which invokes, among other things, a commitment to develop "community" as a more fruitful and satisfactory way to develop a notion of "good" practice. Harkening back to our discussion of the will to interpret, we are led again to an attitude or "spirit" component as necessary in addition to formal procedures. This returns us also to Dewey's concern for the corruption of democratic practices by the overriding of civic rights. Rights, I will argue, represent "community will" in that they need for their fulfillment a commitment that they be honored. The community must agree to their validity, and there must be a "spirit" to the law as well as the letter of the law. Communal context is also important in interpreting and applying a concept of rights because the individual never stands alone, but always in context. Rights are not absolute but must be interpreted relative to the context of those persons involved. But in invoking communal spirit I am also invoking the Roycean conditions of "genuine community" which include respect for person, mutuality, and reciprocity. In a "genuine community," "rights" might well be inappropriate and not at all required. Scott Peck states the issue well when he writes: "In a genuine community there are no sides. Conflict can be resolved, members have become skilled at listening and understanding, respect each other's gifts and limitations, celebrate each other's wounds, are committed to struggling together rather than against each other."[82] However, human communities can only strive to be "genuine," and always are prone to error and evil. Further, individuals have different loyalties and belong to different communities, and these can come into conflict. In this context, rights are probably necessary tools and ideals to keep communities and individuals striving toward the ideal. They should not, however, break apart communities and place individuals in adversarial relations as they now do. These issues will be discussed more thoroughly and concretely as we move through the coming chapters.

It should be more than clear at this point that the individualism-community tension is a profound and important one not only for American thought but for human life in general. In this chapter, we have merely begun the discussion with Royce's thoughts on "genuine community," what it is, how it develops, and how it is to be maintained. We turn in the next chapter to genuine individualism," to Royce's concepts of self, of person, and of moral and social development.

In looking toward Roycean ideas on the human person and the "genuine individual," we do not, however, leave behind the notion of genuine community. We close this chapter therefore with the idea of community as the "safe" place for human development and fulfillment. Again the words of Scott Peck, who has himself found "healing" and "fullness" in community, are appropriate.

> Community is a safe place precisely because no one is attempting to heal or convert you, to fix you, and to change you. Instead, the members accept you as you are. You are free to be you. And being so free, you are free to discard defenses, masks, disguises, free to seek your own psychological and spiritual health, free to become your whole and holy self.[83]

3

The Enlightened Individual

"Apart from our relationships with others, there would be no moral necessity."
—Piaget

"The function of the modern novel . . . has been to give us a sense of the individuality of our lives . . . best understood in terms of our ability to interpret the content of our general rules in responce to particular situations."
—D. H. Lawrence

"The moral ideal . . . may be stated thus: Be humane and reasonable at once."
—Josiah Royce

Individuality, Selfhood and Personhood

JOSIAH ROYCE, I have claimed, was a philosopher who had the courage to tackle the dual issues of "enlightened, genuine individualism" and "true/genuine community." Further, he recognized that the task of building authentic individuality and that of developing fulfilling, moral communities were tasks inextricably bound together; worthwhile individuality and community arise out of their mutual interaction in a creative, ongoing, infinite process. Chapter 2 was primarily devoted to the community building task; now we must give attention to the equally important issues of individuality, selfhood, and personhood.

Philosophers, of course, have long been concerned with the question, What is a person? Today, however, they are joined in this query by behavioral scientists, whether they be social theorists or those concerned more with psychosocial behavior; by legal and medical scholars, by educational theorists, and by concerned members of the public. One reason for this broad-ranging attention to the question of personhood is that modern technology has stimulated a host of legal, medical, ethical, and policy problems, as well as the other problems of gestation, birth, aging, and death, all of which involve clarification and decisions about the meaning and application of the concept of 'person'. In addition, psychotechnologies including drug therapies, psychosurgery, behavioral modification, and more traditional psychotherapy have become increasingly important with rising incidences of mental illness as well as antisocial and violent behaviors. In order to deal adequately with medical and mental illnesses, society must grapple with the question, What is a person? Further, as indicated in chapter 2, contemporary American society is often called the "therapeutic society," namely one obsessed with self-health and almost overwhelmed with numerous competing answers for a fulfilling individual life. No public philosophy can ignore these issues, since the state of the "public health" is preeminently a social and public concern.

Further, the social, political, and moral philosophies that have been dominant in American thought and life are increasingly under attack by, for example, Alasdair MacIntyre and by other philosophers such as Richard Rorty and Bernard Williams. Specifically targeted are the social, moral, and political views that emerged from the post-enlightenment, namely liberalism, utilitarianism, and Kantianism. MacIntyre, for example, declares these views "bankrupt" and ill-adjusted to the modern world.[1] More importantly, their stories about the individual, their understanding of self and of person are claimed to be inadequate for social-political and ethical theory.[2]

As we discussed in chapter 2, rampant individualism is under attack by communitarians but also by other social, political, and philosophical theorists, because it places emphasis on the self-made, self-reliant, self-interested human subject and elevates the autonomous individual who enters into contractual agreement as the keystone of societal arrangement as well as the focus for rights and moral respect.[3] Michael Sandel, Michael Walzer, and Bernard Williams lead a group who criticize Utilitarianism for taking the preferences of individuals as given and regarding attempts to maximize satisfaction of these preferences as good. Further, utilitarianism too easily allows for overriding one person's claim to happiness by the priority of its greatest happiness principle.[4] And, finally, Michael Slote, Alan Donagan, Alan Gewirth, and other ethicists find Kantianism wanting, especially its focus on the individual as a self-legislating, morally responsible ethical agent and upon universal, impartial ethical principles.[5]

In concert with these expressions of dissatisfaction with traditional social-political and ethical philosophy are the criticisms of theories of self and moral development. Freudian psychotherapy has been the subject of much of the criticism. It is seen as legitimizing, in theory and practice, an extreme form of egoistic individualism that subverts all values other than satisfaction of the isolated individual's purely arbitrary preferences.[6] The authors of *Habits of the Heart* frame their charge against Freudianism saying, "The therapeutic idea posits an individual who is able to be the source of his own standards, to love himself before he asks for love from others. The therapeutic attitude denies all forms of obligation and commitment in relationships. . . ."[7] Also subject to criticism have been traditional theories of moral and social development. At the center of this dissatisfaction is the theory of moral development presented by Lawrence Kohlberg, although Erik Erikson's view is similar and also implicated.[8] For Kohlberg and Erikson human moral development is movement from a highly egotist, self-centered point of view in infancy through a development of a "conscience," under the tutelage of society via authority, threat and fear, to a higher and authentic moral understanding based on universal moral principles and particularly on the concept of justice. These "ego theorists" are perceived as overemphasizing the growth toward self-independence. These theories are countered by those who find the foundations of morality present in early childhood in the infant's responsiveness to the feelings of others and the young child's appreciation of standards.[9] These theorists, including Carol Gilligan's work on an ethics of care, emphasize an "inter-subjective view" that sees the human person growing out of, in, and through relationships to an ability to be a "true subject meeting another subject."[10]

It will be my contention in this chapter that Roycean views on self and person and on moral and social development provide an excellent foundation for dealing with this complex set of criticisms of traditional moral and social-political views, as well as with the vexing questions raised by contemporary psychobiological technologies. Royce's views on self and personhood are especially fruitful for dealing with issues of personal identity and worth in birth, aging, and death as well as in self-breakdown, mental or physical, because Royce argued that the concept of person must be understood in relational, developmental, and contextual terms. The question, What is a person? is misleading from a Roycean point of view, because it implies that the search is for a static thing when the question ought to be, What is personhood? This query suggests a process, degrees of achievement, and the possibility of loss and stagnation as well as healing and recovery. Further, unlike most approaches to self and person that are reductionistic, that is, positing a single essential characteristic of the authentic self—mind, brain, or gene, for instance—the Roycean view is holistic. The self is a process having public, physical aspects—material, neural, genetic, behavioral aspects—social, cultural, psychological, political, ethical, and private, inner aspects: sensual, emotional, mental, intentional.

Personhood, for Royce, must be understood in relational terms. A necessary condition for one's sense of being a person is being-with-others; the ascriptions of 'personhood' are, in a most fundamental way, ascriptions by others, and even one's own ability to know oneself is heavily dependent upon interaction with others. This is not to suggest that self-contribution is not essential; it is. Meaning is also self-ascribed; intentionality and autonomy are rightful aspects of a 'person'. However, the development of individuality and autonomy is also dependent on social circumstances and others. And, one's very knowledge of oneself is ultimately relational and communal. Self-consciousness, for Royce, as we have seen, is developed vis-à-vis interaction with others. Self-knowledge is achieved through a communal process called interpretation, a triadic, communicative process with self and between self and others.

Finally, Royce wrote and lectured on personal, social, and moral development.[11] For Royce, one acquires the marks of personhood: one can continue to develop one's personhood, and aspects of personhood can be lost or never even achieved. 'Person' is an open-ended concept involving both temporal and historical elements. It is also contextual. Conceptions of persons have varied historically and geographically, and views others have of one's person can vary with time and place. As for moral development, it too depends on the subtle interaction of self and others. A moral sense, a conscience, is innate, based on natural, human tendencies, but it is also derived from training, experience, and private reflection.[12] 'Conscience', Royce argues, is a complex, collective mental reality as well as a seeming conflicted one. It gives two sets of advice at the same time, namely, "Live for the general good" and "Always be true to your own rational higher self."[13] Indeed, to harmonize these two motives or maxims, is, says Royce, "the great problem of life."[14] With this approach to morality, it should be obvious that Royce's views offer an interesting base from which to develop a compromise position to the universalist—particularist debate in contemporary ethical theory and to the Kohlberg—Gilligan debate in moral development theory. Further, Royce argues for a view of the self as a "plan of action" and he also sees an important role for "habits" in moral action and behavior.

The Self as Natural, Embedded, Complex Being

Royce, like Peirce, James, and Dewey, is decidedly anti-Cartesian in his views of the self. He writes: "Whatever the Self is, it is not a Thing. It is not, in Aristotle's or, in Descartes' sense, a Substance."[15] The human self and/or person is a complex phenomenon, not rightfully reduced to any one of its aspects. It should be seen as having various physiological and psychological aspects united and interrelated in complex and individual ways. In his *Outlines of Psychology*, Royce discusses various aspects of the physiological and how these interact with mental elements of the self:

> The expressive physical functions, acts, gestures, words, habits, etc.) in which our mental life gets its outward representation and embodiment, are all of them, as physical events, *determined by physiological processes that occur in our nervous systems.*[16]

However, Royce is clear that attention to complexity, not reductionism, should be the mode of approach for anyone who desires to understand the human self as fully embodied. He declares, "Psychology is by no means a branch of neurology."[17] Physical expression, for Royce, is broad and complex.

> . . . *any physical expression of mental* life which we can learn to interpret, becomes as genuinely interesting to the psychologist as does a brain function. A pyramid, a flint hatchet, a poem or dance, a game or a war, a cry or a book, the nursery play of a child or the behavior of an insane person, may be a physical expression of mental life such as the appreciative psychologist can both observe and more or less fully comprehend.[18]

Royce sees the psychologist combining various methods of study: interpretation of the multivaried physical expressions of self; examination of causal, determining physical processes; and "introspection," or mental facts directly observed by the individual psychologist. Royce argues that introspection must work in conjunction with the other methods and that comparison must be made between the individual psychologist's introspective results and those of others.[19]

Royce's holistic and sensitive approach to the complex nature of the human self is exhibited in numerous other ways in his *Outlines of Psychology*. For example, he sees the old "faculty" approach to study of the self—which divided self into will, intellect, and emotion—as not useful and too simplistic. These terms are general, says Royce. 'Will', for example, refers to the "*whole significance of our conscious life*, viewed as our conscious response to our environment, or as our mental attitude toward our world."[20] Likewise, 'intellect' refers to a "certain significant aspect of our power to have knowledge of the world."[21] If one looks at emotion, even at a single one like grief, what we see, argues Royce, is "the enormous complexity of the conditions upon which it depends."[22] For Royce, the moods and emotions have in common the feature "that, when we are conscious of them, we are aware, not only of feelings but of images, general ideas, thoughts, and external objects."[23]

Finally, Royce refuses to place singular emphasis on either heredity or environment/nurture in the development of the human self. Each plays a significant role. Thus, about the emotions for example, Royce writes, "Some of our emotions . . . are principally due to heredity; but others are very much molded in early lives." Growth of self in all its aspects, as we shall see, is for Royce a central idea. In fact, in 1911 he recognized what is clear to neurologists today, namely, that even brain development occurs under the influence of environment. He writes:

> As a fact, the brain of man which seems to be provided at birth with all its neurons, develops for a long time after birth, and especially during the first seven years of life. Constantly new connections, structural and functional, form, among its various parts. The formation of these connections is determined not merely by the inherited tendencies of the organism, not yet wholly by the laws of habit, but *by the circumstances of growth*. These circumstances are

unquestionably affected by the actual conduct of the organism in question.[24] (Royce's emphasis)

Royce's understanding of the human self counsels us not to ignore any
of its multiple and interrelated aspects. For example, in his *Outlines*, Royce
interweaves and interrelates human imaginative capacities with the sensory
capacities. He holds that mental imagery is dependent both on sense perceptions as well as motor responses to the environment. Deprivation of environment, then, would presumably lead to deprivation or stunting of the
imaginative capacity. Royce, in fact, argues that "*the training of the imagination cannot occur apart from a fitting training of the senses.*[25] Further, he disagrees with any attempt to divorce the sensory life from or to devalue it
against the "higher" intellectual life. In a most stimulating and provocative
way, Royce provides us with a new notion of the value of the sensory life to
a full and authentic self:

> On the contrary, sensory experience plays its part, and its
> essential part, in the very highest of our spiritual existence.
> When we wish to cultivate processes of abstract thinking,
> our devices must therefore include a fitting plan for the cul-
> tivation of the senses. . . .[26]

Royce thus faults the Puritans for their fear of attractive sense experiences
and argues that because of this, Puritanism, in some of its forms, seems to
have tended toward the impoverishment of religious experience. Royce concludes, "*whatever be the form of religious training, it ought deliberately to make
use of a proper appeal to the senses.*"[27] We shall comment further on this claim
by Royce in the next chapter, on loyalty, especially in connection with the
need of a community for ritual.

Not only does Royce integrate the sensory and the imaginative, but he
also integrates the imaginative with conduct. "*The whole normal life of our
imagination,*" says Royce, "*has almost intimate connection to our conduct.*"[28]
Also, Royce, like many contemporary psychologists, recognized the importance of "play" and the "play attitude" to human development, whether for
children or adults.

Play, for Royce, is significant to the development of *a person's* abilities to
integrate and to *the person's* ability to experience joy and find fulfillment in

integrative experiences. Play not only brings together sensory, motor, intellectual, and imaginative elements of the self, but it also synthesizes habit and originality. Habit is an essential aspect of human self, its growth, and its activity. There is, says Royce, a great orderliness in the human brain. This orderliness is due to the great law of habit. Royce writes, "*The brain tends to do the sort of thing that it has already often done.*"[29] The tendency to form habits is natural to human life and is a tendency we share with all of nature. However, there is equally in human nature a "plasticity." Habit and spontaneity are, for Royce, integrative, interactive components of human experience. And in play, these two aspects of the self come together in an important way. Combined with "repetitions of ancestral activities" and the habits and rules of play is a deep human restlessness, a feeling which exhibits itself in a desire to achieve both a unity of experience and a sense of uniqueness, of "placing" one's own "mark" on the experience. In play we see, says Royce, a seriousness, a persistence, an intensity, and an insistence, "an *insistence upon trying over and over again the playful activity until it wholly satisfies his own ideals.*" In this perseverance lies 'originality', the "*initiative which the child may himself be said to contribute to the organization of his playful functions.*"[30] The restlessness related to originality is also an expression of the human individual's need to distinguish self from others, and to contrast environment to self. This restlessness is also, says Royce, the foundation of individualism and social inventiveness. Royce writes: "*the persistent tendency to establish a contrast between one's social activities and those of one's fellows lies at the root of the social tendency called Individualism. . . . Social inventiveness depends upon individualistic restlessness.*"[31]

This desire of humans to imitate one's fellows as well as to be in contrast with them was discussed in chapter 2, but will be expanded on in a later section of this chapter. In Royce's view, role playing, drama, and literature, make significant contributions to human development. They are valuable, in Royce's view, for developing a key aspect of human intellectual growth, namely, the ability to grasp things in a holistic way, to "increase in our power to perceive simultaneous variety and to bring it into relation to successful variety."[32] The role of habit, of holistic grasping and "imaginative play," will be discussed further in the section on moral development in this chapter.

Royce's 'self', then, is a complex affair. It is a certain totality of aspects and facts—a number of which we have already discussed. In addition to genetic, neurological, sensory, motive, feeling, imaginative factors, all of which

play an important role in human development, the human self is in continuity with nature. Royce believes that there are, in fact, four characteristics
common to both nature and conscious human life, namely, tendencies to
(1) irreversibility, (2) communication, (3) formation of habits, and (4) evolutionary growth.[33] We have discussed the importance of habits in human
life, and we shall soon discuss the other three characteristics. Further, Royce
argues for an affinity of human conscious life with nature: ". . . the vast contrast which we have been taught to make between material and conscious
processes really depends merely upon the accidents of the human point of
view."[34] He says, "we have no right whatever to speak of really unconscious
Nature, but only of uncommunicative nature."[35] Such a view of the relation
of human self and nature has a number of benefits, some of which will be
explored later in this book. For example, such a view of nature allows exploration of an approach to nature and technology different from the more traditional one of human control and conquest of nature. It would fit with
Evelyn Fox Keller's notion of "dynamic objectivity," which "actively draws
on the commonality between mind and nature" and which seeks to recon-
stitute the subject-object relationship in science and knowledge seeking to
permit concord and similarity between knower and known.[36] Such a recon-
struction of the subject-object relationship is also, as suggested in the previous chapter, essential to proper moral development and an overcoming of
the narcissistic personality. This will be discussed at greater length a little
later.

Further, this Roycean understanding of the affinity and continuity of
human life with nature allows that a study of other conscious organisms may
lead to valuable insights about the human self, including those about health
and wholeness. It also leads us to a view of self and human life as an evolutionary, open-ended process. This is, indeed, Royce's direction, as we shall
see.

In bringing to a close our examination of Royce's view of the self as complex, as naturally embedded, and as embodied being, it is not a surprise to
find that he fully acknowledges our common-sense experience of an empirical self. We experience our self as an empirical totality, as do others. "The
first concept of the human self," says Royce, "like the concept of Nature,
comes to us, first as an concept founded upon a certain class of experiences."[37] The empirical self is constituted by a complex of both public and
private experiences, a set of facts. Among such facts are the predominantly

corporal ones, such as countenance, body, clothing, and physical actions—facts that both self and others may observe and comment on.[38] Royce grants importance to bodily continuity and the role that a sense of body plays in self-identity. He argues that if these bodily facts radically change, so must the self.[39] When applied to today's technological, ethical issues of birth, death, and aging, Royce's view is much more fruitful than the contemporary reductive views that ignore almost totally the role of a sense of body in an adequate understanding and sense of self. Roycean insights in this regard will be applied to concrete situations in our chapter on medicine.

In addition to the public facts of the empirical self, there is, for Royce, a set of inner, private facts of equal empirical status and importance for the self:

> In addition to the external or corporeal self of the phenomenal world, there is the equally empirical and phenomenal self of the inner life, the series of states of consciousness, the feelings, thoughts, desires, memories, emotions, moods. These again, both my neighbor and myself regard as belonging to me, and as going to make up what I am.[40]

Behaviorists, of course, persist in ignoring consciousness and states of consciousness as aspects of self, much to the detriment of a holistic and fruitful understanding of the human self, of human development, and of human health and human breakdown. Royce, as has become clear, believed strongly in a totally holistic approach to what he perceives as a complex, human self.

Royce, like the phenomenologists and others, also stressed the intentionality of human consciousness, namely, the goal-focused, meaning-focused human view of the world. According to Royce, mental acts are always directed toward objects and also intend the object as having such-and-such meaning, as viewed in such-and-such a way. Human perspective is contextual. The view is always from a "point of view." An example of this crucial aspect of human consciousness, for Royce, is the role of selective attention in all acts of consciousness. Attention selects only a few from the numerous impressions impinging on our sensibilities; many impressions slip through our consciousness without being retained or having any effect. Attention even modifies the quality of our impressions. Thus, notes Royce, "Attention seems to defeat, in part its own object. Bringing something into the field of knowledge seems to be a modifying, if not a transforming process."[41]

If I see the world from a particular point of view, as is strongly suggested by the intentionality of human consciousness, the only way I can transcend my narrowness and subjectivity is by checking things out with my fellows and with nature. Indeed, as we have seen, and as we shall now discuss, for Royce, knowledge both of self and of external world is grounded in social interaction. The means that the human self is, then, essentially a relational and social being.

Person as Social and Relational

Royce, along with many contemporary psychologists, believes that being-with-others is essential to the emergence of personhood. Royce argued that self-consciousness arises out of a social contrast between the self and the not-self, between what is mine and what is not mine. Royce describes the coming to self-consciousness in these words:

> Nobody amongst us comes to self-consciousness, so far as I know, except under the persistent influence of his social fellows. . . . the Self of the child grows and forms itself through Imitation . . . his self-consciousness, as it grows, feeds upon social models. . . . His playmates, his nurse, or his mother . . . appeal to his imitativeness and set him the copies for his activities. He learns his little arts, and as he does so, he contrasts his own deeds with those of his models, and of other children.[42]

Contrast and imitativeness are both necessary, in Royce's view, for adequate self-development. He continues:

> *Now contrast is, in our conscious life, the mother of clearness. What the child does instinctively, and without comparison with the deeds of others, may never come to his clear consciousness as his own deeds at all.* What he learns imitatively, and then reproduces, perhaps in joyous obstinacy, as an act

that enables him to display himself over against others—
this constitutes the beginning of his self-conscious life.[43]

And we recall, from above, that contrast between the activities of self and those of others "*lies at the root of the social tendency called individualism.*"[44]

To see how contemporary are Royce's views on the origin of the sense of self, we recall the work of Jessica Benjamin from the last chapter. She presents what she labels as an intersubjective view of human development, the view that individuals grow in and through relationships to other subjects, subjects that are different and yet alike. Royce speaks of the interaction of similarity and difference, assimilation, and differentiation in developing the human self.[45] Benjamin argues that for proper self-development there must be a balance of tension between self-assertion and self-recognition. Two independent and yet interrelated selves need to recognize each other. The recognition is reflexive. It includes not only the other's confirming response but "how we find ourselves in that response."[46] The subject says, "I am, I do." The response is, "You are, you have done."[47] Mutual recognition, argues Benjamin, "is a crucial category of early experience."[48] It is a double recognition—of the human baby as an "active participant" in experience *and* of the independence of the mother. According to Benjamin, "The recognition the child seeks is something mother can give only by virtue of her independent activity."[49] Royce's view of the development of self-consciousness, in conjunction with Benjamin, has important implications for family and education, implications which we shall draw out in later chapters.

Benjamin and Royce also agree that contrast between self and other is the foundation for individualism. For Benjamin, "As one traces the development of the infant one can see how recognition becomes increasingly an end in itself—first as an achievement of harmony and then as an arena of conflict between self and other."[50] Breakdown of the necessary tension between self-assertion and mutual recognition results, argues Benjamin, in either domination or submission.[51] Royce foresaw the twin dangers of rampant individualism or strident collectivism.[52] Both Benjamin and Royce believe that the right social context, that of genuine community, will lead the self toward harmony and affinity and genuine interaction and relationship between independent selves. The human self takes pleasure in "being attuned," in being in harmony. Indeed, to seek to negate the other or control the other, argues Benjamin, is to negate ourselves as well. This is the "paradox of recognition."[53] She writes: "The need for acknowledgment that turns us back to dependence on the other brings about a struggle for control. But if we fully negate the other by trying to control his identity and will, we have negated ourselves as well . . . the struggle must yield to mutual respect . . . mutual understanding and shared feeling, a renewed sense of connection with the other."[54] This recognition of the "other" which is so crucial to self-recognition and respect, is, as we shall see, also crucial to moral understanding.

Self-knowledge then, for Royce, is dependent upon our relationship to other persons; so too is knowledge of the external world. Without my fellows I would have no knowledge of that which we call "external reality." Recall that each consciousness, by reason of its intentionality, is perspectival, from a point of view. To overcome our finitude and our error, we need to have a "reality check" with our fellows. In Royce's words, "Our Nature, the realm of matter and of laws with which our science and our popular opinions, have to do, is a realm which we conceive as *known or knowable* to various men in precisely the general sense in which we regard it as known or knowable to our private selves."[55] From the previous chapter, we recall that Royce argues that it is "communal experience" that distinguishes inner from outer, the outer world being the one whose presence can be indicated only by definable, communicable experience.[56] Further, spatial definiteness is important to externality because only the definitely localizable in space can be independently verified and agreed upon by a number of socially communicable beings.[57] The data of sight, touch, and sound, those data most considered "real," are indeed reliable because they are most open to social confirmation. We can grasp and see a pole together or lift a weight , but we cannot literally share smells and tastes.[58] For Royce, then, our knowledge of the external world is fundamentally bound up with being-with-others.

Further, an adequate relationship to external reality, is important to self-identity and health, as Royce recognized in his extensive discussion of delusions and hallucinations in his *Outlines of Psychology*.[59] Psychiatrist D. W. Winnicott, as indicated in a previous chapter, has written extensively on the relationship of a sense of a "false self"—that feeling of being unreal to oneself, of deadness and despair—to the proper recognition of outside reality and of dealing with objects and the play experience. For Winnicott, "One of the most important elements in feeling authentic was recognition of an outside reality that is not one's own projection . . . *an experience of contact with other minds*."[60] We recall also from our previous chapter that the "narcissistic personality" sees reality only in terms of self and indeed avoids relationship with others.

With regard to the narcissistic personality, Royce, in his outlines, discusses a personality type closely related to this contemporary psychosis, "the morbidly eccentric intellect." This person combines intellectual eccentricity and selfish narrowness of personal aim; such a person, in Royce's view, is dangerous. For this personality type, "experiences are to an extraordinary degree centered about matters which have too little social concern and too much private concern for the morbid individual himself."[61] We recall also that the narcissistic person has an inability to engage in "play" or to take an attitude of "play." Jessica Benjamin notes that a strong "anti-play attitude" develops from a "frustration" of the search for recognition which results in an aggressive stance to get a response."[62] She continues by arguing that the inability to play or relate is the result of "the failure of early mutuality," which seems "to promote a premature formation of the defensive boundary between inside and outside."[63]

Richard Sennett, in his book *The Fall of Public Man,* is also concerned with failure to play and with an inadequate notion of "inside" and "outside," "private" and "public." The repression of play, he argues, leads to the "loss of the childhood power to be sociable." In play, says Sennett, a child learns the malleability of rules and how to compensate for inequality of skills; the child suspends the desire for immediate gratification for "the pleasure of being together" and for the pleasure of begin able to "objectify action, repeat it, correct it and improve it" and thus also to experience the aesthetic "quality of expressive act."[64] Sennett claims that "to lose the ability to play is to lose the sense that worldly conditions are plastic."[65] Royce's own observations on the play experience are very much in accord with those of Sennett. The ability to "play" and the sense of creativity and "aesthetic" quality are very much related to "moral experience," as we shall see. These human capabilities are also crucial to a healthy understanding of work and leisure and technology. Finally, the "play experience," with all of its meaning for human development also lays a foundation for the argument for "ritual" in public life, which we shall present in the chapter on loyalty.

Being-with-others, then, for Royce and others, is crucial for self-knowledge, for knowledge of the external world, and, above all, for a "healthy" sense of self and external reality. Others also help us in developing our "intentionality," our "meaning-giving" aspect, because they provide us with linguistic familiarity and a grasp of the world. Merleau-Ponty once wrote: "To know the world is to sing of it in a melody of words." Things in the world take on meaning as we learn to name them and to apply these names correctly. Language, however, arises only within a community of speakers and in the context of intersubjective communication. The idea of a private language, as Wittgenstein demonstrated, is a contradiction in terms.[66]

Royce is clear about the role of language in the development of the human self. Language is, for Royce, like play in integrating the motives of imitation and the love of social contrast by which one distinguishes oneself from others. Further, language is an expression both of the child's wish to characterize objects present in his experience and to "appeal intelligibly to the minds of his fellows."[67] Further, argues Royce, making social comparison allows one to become "*very highly conscious of the details of his own acts, and of the criticisms that other people are making upon these acts, and of the feelings which these acts arouse both in himself and others.*"[68] As one becomes conscious of one's actions, one is able to adjust to objects as well as to social judgments. This kind of twofold adjustment to external and social reality results, argues Royce, in the kind of human consciousness that constitutes thinking: "*In consequence, the social conditions, under which language is acquired produce the thinking process, just because it is of the essence of the thinking process that we should become aware of how our acts are adjusted to our objects.*"[69] Being-with-others, then, seems clearly fundamental to our ability to know and act in the external world.

And "being familiar or at home in the world" is an important mark of an adequately functioning person. We have seen that the ability to distinguish external and internal, to deal with objects and others is crucial to our self-health. Failure of these abilities leads to various forms of psychosis or mental illness, whether it be narcissism or autism, which culminates in utter isolation within a private world, or other self-illness involving self-mutilation or self-induced paralysis. The latter self-illness reminds us of the important role "the body" plays in being "at home" in the world. The body is that which realizes the person in the world; it is a primordial incarnation of personhood in the world. Royce, as indicated earlier, recognizes the importance of body to self-identity. Further, the body is that aspect of my person which is public and shareable, and, thus, an understanding of my body and my appropriate behavior toward it is, like my understanding of and behavior toward things, learned through interaction with others and through language.

In this regard, one need only think of the way children are taught to "name" bodily parts and how distinctions between "private" and "public" aspects of body, as determined by culture, can lead toward regard for body and comfort with it or to a neurotic relationship to this external and yet also internal thing. Language also provides us the means of communicating what is both private and public and intimately connected with body, namely, "pain." The ability to speak about and understand pain is much influenced by others' observations about and comments on our behavior. A cry because of a scraped knee elicits communication of the following sort from others. Mother might respond, "You have an ouchy; let me put medicine on it and make it better." Another response might be, "Big boys don't cry about little hurts." Depending on these responses, a child will develop attitudes toward pain and appropriate behavior for future use. The concepts of one's bodily self and behavior in the face of pain are very much dependent on being-with-others. This will be discussed further in the chapter on medicine and health.

The Self as Contextual and in Process

The focus on the role of language and communication in self-development allows us to move to another important aspect of self and personhood for Royce, namely, his emphasis on temporality, contextuality, and process. Personal identity is something that is achieved as self acts and reacts in concert with others. Self-knowledge, self-meaning is something that comes gradually and, indeed, is never complete. Royce would be in full agreement with the following statement by Charles S. Peirce: "Were the ends of a person already explicit, there would be no room for development, for growth, for life; and consequently there would be no personality."[70] For Royce, personhood or personality is not a static thing but is, rather, time-oriented, historical and future.

A prime characteristic of personhood/selfhood, for Royce, is that it involves a continual process of interpretation—both communal and self-interpretation. He puts the matter this way: "In brief, my idea of myself is an interpretation of my past—linked also with an interpretation of my hopes and my intentions as to my future."[71] This means that self and self-awareness must be seen as a time-process; understanding or reflecting on past and future and linking them with the present self."[72] It means that selfhood or personhood is open-ended and, since Royce saw interpretation as potentially an infinite process, the meaning of self can continue to develop both for the self and for others. The self is, in essence, a potentially deep and complex sign that can grow richer in meaning, and, indeed, further meaning is always possible. Peirce captures this aspect of self as a "process of interpretation" when he writes, "No son of Adam has ever fully manifested what there was in him."[73] The same notion of self was involved in the comment of Alfred North Whitehead when he claimed that all philosophy is a footnote on Plato. Who is/was Plato? What is the content of his thought? All of this is continually being reinterpreted. Thus, who I am or was as a person is an open-ended matter; it is a matter of time, context, and history. Joseph Margolis provides a nice summary of the Roycean notion of self as open to endless interpretation when he writes, "Once admit that persons are texts, have or are histories themselves; it becomes quite impossible to fix the ontological or intentional closure of their careers and natures—*even after their physical death.*"[74] This has important implications for handling "death" in today's complex health-care scene. Further, the belief that self/personhood is open-ended and always in development also allows us to deal with situations in which a measure of personhood or selfhood is never achieved or is lost, as in cases of severe retardation or the "persistent vegetative state." These issues will be addressed more fully in chapter 7.

Another aspect of self as process of interpretation, of course, is that the "meaning" and "value" of self is *significantly* dependent on others. This returns us to the essentiality of relationship to self-development and selfhood and also to the need for a mutuality of self-recognition. There are certain predicates or ascriptions that are appropriate to the self and to person and others that are not. Ascriptions that are object-appropriate, which fail to take full account of self as subject and agent or are denigrating of self, must be dealt with as inappropriate and even unethical. Some of these "false" predicates are obvious, like those expressing definite prejudice—*nigger,* or *gook;* others are more subtle and need to be reexamined, like *patient, insane,* and *sick.* Above all, care must be taken that our interpretation of others be fair and appropriate to human subjects.

The emphasis so far, in dealing with Royce's notions of self and person, has been on being-with-others and on process. What, then, about self-contribution and about notions of personal unity, personal uniqueness, and "authentic individuality?" First of all, being-with-others is a necessary condition for attaining selfhood/personhood, but it is not sufficient. The individual also can and does play a significant role in achieving selfhood. Indeed, others and self constitute together the sufficient condition for this result. As indicated, self-consciousness begins in contrast-effect, in obstinacy, in a distinction between self and not-self. Although I model others' behaviors and understand others' attributions to me, I begin, if authentic individuality is to result, to add my own little touches. I add my special mark and I begin to understand myself as different, unique and individual. In fact, one of the reasons body is so intimately tied with self is that it distinguishes me from others; it provides a unique self-identifier.

Subjectivity, self-knowledge, and self-action are necessary to one's sense of person and one's development as a person. For example, as already indicated, Royce holds "intentionality" to be one of the fundamental attributes of a person. Intentionality refers to the ability of persons to invest their action with meaning. Persons, as already discussed, engage in meaning-seeking, meaning-conferring activity. Persons see the world from a particular point of view; their selective attention focuses experience, meaning, and relationship. Persons are contextual, that is, they have their "own" context, and this is what makes them unique. We also remember, however, individual perspective explains why they need others to correct error and ignorance. Nevertheless, one's context, one's perspective is a significant aspect of the self's uniqueness and complexity.

This contextual aspect of the self has been highlighted in our contemporary scene by the new attention being given to the differences that ethnic, racial, cultural, and sexual perspectives make to interpretation of experience and meaning. Royce was sensitive to this issue. For example, he wrote on race relations, and on language as important to "provincial" identity. We will discuss these aspects of Royce's thought in the section on multi-culturalism in the chapter 6. However, regarding understanding the self, or the mind of another, we note Royce's caution about the "inevitable dangers and difficulties" of the method, in psychology, of studying *the expressive signs of mental life.*" He is quick to point out that the facts studied are numerous, complex, and "easily misjudged," especially in the case of minds markedly different from our own. To illustrate this point, he uses sex differences:

> A good example of this difficulty is the common failure of
> even very intelligent men to understand a good many
> among the expressive functions of women, or the similar

failure of women to comprehend a great many among those of men. The barrier of sex will probably prove a permanent hindrance, in some important directions and regions, to the progress of the scientific study of the mind, so far as that study seeks to make the mental life of one sex fully comprehensible to psychologists who belong to the other.[75]

The self, then, is perspectival and contextual, and to ignore this is to do damage to the human subjects with which we deal.

Another aspect of self-contribution to the process of achieving self-hood is in the contribution of aesthetic organization or unity. Recall the joy of the child in play who seeks to mold the game or role to his/her own idea or ideal. Good actors play a role; but they also play it in a "unique" way. The self as interpreter can and should exercise an active narrative role in reflecting on one's experiences and weaving them together into an informed autobiography. Each person/self writes one's own story. Usually, and especially if authentic individuality is sought, the self provides a unique story line. Through this story line one begins to develop a "character," which is a set of ideas, ideals, and habits expressed regularly over a period of time. Personal identity is found, then, in the consistency of what one does and thinks. It is found in our actions, our words, and our habits. This is, in a sense, the "meaning" we convey to others and presumably to ourselves.

This appears correct, for, at least in part, we are identified by our manifest behavior and habits. For example, we note "he is a punctual person"; "she is a reckless driver"; "he cares for his family." Our digression from habitual behavior causes puzzlement and concern in others. Often the response is "he/she is not his/herself." We are also identified with the roles we take on in life—especially in terms of uniqueness and individuality—with the "manner" in which we assume these roles. "He is a careful accountant"; "she is a creative architect"; "he is a loving father"; "he is an inadequate parent." Again, if our manner of assuming a role shifts, there is an assumed change in self. This has to do again with interpretation, both that of self and other, as well as with one's individuality and uniqueness. It should be obvious that self-interpretations of character and role and those of others do not necessarily coincide. This makes for conflict; it can result in severe social maladjustment and/or mental illness. Further, given the contextual, complex, and unique nature of self, interpretation can only be inferential. It is thus probable and open to error. Thus, we can be mistaken about ourselves and others and who they and we are. We must be cautious, Royce reminds us, of reading the expressive signs of mental life. Finally, the self is open-ended, and, thus, a change of basic habit is possible; one can become a "new person," as did Paul in his experience of religious conversion. The role of habit in selfhood is, for this reason alone, an important one for the area of health, both mental and physical.

A self or person, therefore, is engaged in developing a meaningful life-narrative for self and others. This is expressed in character, through habitual action. Another important aspect of this form of human intentionality is the person or self as the focus of moral attributes and as a source of value and values. A person is a remembered past and an intended future: goals have been pursued or will be pursued, and value judgments are made about what has been done or thought and what is worth seeking, doing, thinking. Part of my uniqueness, and, for Royce, the most valuable part, is my life-plan, my set of values and ideals that distinguish me from all my fellows. Royce emphatically asserts: *By this meaning of my life plan, by this intent always to remain another than my fellows despite my divinely planned unity with them—by this, and not by the possession of any soul-substance, I am defined and created a self.*[76] For Royce, the human quest for selfhood and unity is a profound psychological fact; humans hunger for and need a life-plan.[77]

This emphasis on a life-plan by Royce is especially interesting in light of similar emphasis in recent works on ethics. For example, Jonathan Jacobs connects the concept of "virtue" with constructing a personal narrative. "Being virtuous," says Jacobs, "conduces to constructing a followable, lucid personal narrative."[78] Alasdair MacIntyre also connects "virtue" with "personal narrative."[79] However, MacIntyre's views are founded on an Aristotelian teleology that implies a fixed end for human nature. Royce's view is of self, person, and human nature as open-ended and in process. He writes: "The true or metaphysically real ego of a man . . . is . . . the struggling but never completed expression of his coherent plan in life, the changing but never complete partial embodiment of his ideal."[80] Jacobs's account remains thoroughly individualistic, taking no real account, as Royce does, of the role of the social context and others in self-development. Jacobs also is thoroughly Kantian in placing the emphasis on self-determination. Virtue and vice, he claims, are self-imposed. This, of course, fails to take into account human finitude and sin and one's social context.

Royce also sees a key role for will in constituting individuality and uniqueness. He asserts, "I am a Will, a will which is not there for the sake of something else, but which exists solely because it deserves to exist."[81] However, Royce is also clear that what one finds within self is a chaos and conflict of wills. Passions, desires, wants all "speak too volubly with an incoherent babble of voices. I have no innate unity of life plan."[82] The only way one can become a unified self, as we have seen, is in a social context and with the help of one's fellow human beings. Royce continues:

> I myself, in so far as I have yet to learn my ideals, am dissatisfied with my inner situation. . . . It is I, then, who as a social being, continually require myself to look for guidance to my social world. My comrades, my teachers, my rivals, yes, even my enemies teach me what it is I want. Through imitation I at length learn self-mastery. Through social docility I come to attain my independence. My very freedom, in so far as I ever attain such freedom, will be due to the fact that I am able to learn through social contact with others, what it is I myself want to be.[83]

Thus, for Royce, moral autonomy develops within a social context; again, like the development of self, of individuality, this process involves a delicate balance of originality, self-will and contrast and social confirmation and supplementation.

Moral Development: Balancing the Universal and the Particular

The development of the self into a moral being was, for Royce as we have see, a significant concern. It is also a contemporary concern and one that takes us to the heart of a heated controversy in ethical theory today. The controversy is framed in several different ways. We can see the matter as a conflict between universalism/impartiality and particularism; between ethical theories that stress "impartiality, impersonality, justice, formal rationality, and universal principle, on the one hand, and, on the other, those that stress the personal, the moral self, and the other as "radically situated and particularized."[84] Michael Slote looks upon the controversy as a "schizophrenia" in ethical theory when he observes, "Modern ethical theories, with perhaps a few honorable exceptions, deal only with reasons, with values, with what justifies. They fail to examine motive and the motivational structures and constraints of ethical life. They notably fail to do this, they fail as ethical theories by not doing this."[85] These ethical theories not only fail but lead, says Slote, to "moral schizophrenia," for they split one's motive and one's reasons.[86]

The type of ethical theory being faulted by Slote is Kantian deontological ethics, placing the stress on acting from sense of moral duty, which is to say, from self-legislated universalizable moral principles. Moral action is impersonal, that is, universalizable for all persons regardless of their particularity, without regard for their self-interests. Bernard Williams has faulted Kantian ethics, as does Slote, for excluding emotions from moral motives and for impinging on personal integrity. Kantian morality, argues Williams, would ask us to help another person out of a sense of duty, out of principle, and not from a feeling of care or concern about that person. This leads, says Williams, to a devaluation of our emotions and an estrangement from our basic projects and intimate commitments. It ends up, claims Williams, alienating us from ourselves and what we value.[87] Michael Slote expands his criticism of impartial, universal ethics, which recommends always seeking the impersonally judged overall-best state of things, by arguing that it defies common-sense morality that allows "agency-favoring" actions, such as saving one's mother rather than a stranger, and even allows agent-sacrificing actions, that is, actions in which the agent sacrifices self or allows harm to self, even when it leads to less-good results overall.[88]

What is at issue here is both a certain view of the moral agent and self and how that agent regards others in taking moral action. In the Kantian view, the emphasis is on a rational self who obeys laws or principles generated from within and who sees the appropriate moral action as one that is universal or generalizable toward others. Those who argue against this view, the particularists, argue that the moral self and the others to whom that self acts are radically situated and particularized. Moral action, they argue, has an "irreducible particularity of agent, the other and the situation." Further, the moral agent approaches the world of action bound by ties and relationships, integral to one's person, and that must be taken into account. Finally, emotions, it is argued, play a role in morality, indeed, morality "necessarily involves an intertwining of emotion, cognition, and action, not readily separable."[89]

A final aspect of this contemporary controversy is a conflict between two theories of moral development, those of Lawrence Kohlberg and Carol Gilligan. Kohlberg represents the impartialist view that stresses a rational self that reaches moral maturity by moving out of an undifferentiated unity with the world and others, toward an independent and individuated existence. Moral maturity is gained by first internalizing social moral rules, which often embody threat and punishment, and then moving beyond other-societal moral legislation to self-legislation, i.e., to obeying laws or principles generated from within the self. Thus, Erik Erikson, another impartialist, in *Insight and Responsibility*, writes:

> I would propose that we consider *moral rules* of conduct to be based on a *fear of threats* to be forestalled. These may be outer threats of abandonment, punishment, and public exposure, or a threatening sense of guilt, of shame, of isolation. In either case, the rationale for obeying a rule may not be too clear; it is the threat that counts. In contrast, I would consider *ethical rules* to be based on *ideals* to be striven for with a high degree of rational consent to a formulated good, a definition of perfection, and some promise of self-realization.[90]

Lawrence Kohlberg distinguishes conventional morality, which is based on fear, from post-conventional morality:

> . . . the postconventional level . . . is characterized by a major thrust toward autonomous moral principles which have validity and application apart from authority of the group or persons who hold them and apart from the individual's identification with those persons or groups.[91]

In the post-conventional stage, moral action is action from self-legislated principle, impartially applied, that is, without regard to one's own self-interests. Moral action is impersonal, universalizable for all persons regardless of their particularity. Postconventional morality is Kantian dentological ethics, namely, actions from universalizable moral principles.

Carol Gilligan, on the other hand, stresses the moral agent and the situation in terms of its particularity. She also stresses relationship and an ethics of care. In reflecting on the difference between her view and that of Kohlberg, Gilligan sees it as a matter of two conceptions of what is relevant to the moral domain, two notions of the emotions and of the relations of emotions to morality. Further, she argues, one is dealing with two different moral imperatives:

> Two moral injunctions—not to treat others unfairly and not to turn away from someone in need—define two lines of moral development, providing different standards for assessing moral judgments and moral behavior and pointing to changes in the understanding of what fairness means and what constitutes care.[92]

Lawrence Blum, also reflecting on the controversy, argues, as do some others, for finding an appropriate place for each of these concerns, each of "these voices" in an understanding of human morality. He asserts a vision of a "final mature morality which involves a complex interaction and dialogue between the concerns of impartiality and those of personal relationship and care."[93] It is here that the view of Josiah Royce enters the picture. A century ago he framed the issues in human morality precisely in the manner of Gilligan and Blum. In the last of a series of twelve public lectures delivered at Harvard University in 1893, he tackled the difficult issue of the development of that human moral sense called "conscience."[94] The conscience, he says, gives us two sorts of advice at the same time: "It always says to us, *Be humane, be self-sacrificing*, be devoted to a will existent beyond your own. It also always says to us, *Be lawful, have a rule in life, have a plan, be consistent.*"[95] Royce also refers to two motives of conscience. The first, he says, is essentially about sympathy, open-mindedness, "sensitiveness to the needs of our fellows, recognition of the facts of life, realization that our brother has needs." The second motive, on the other hand, demands "conformity to principles of conduct," "reasonableness," and "suppression of private for relatively disinterested motives."[96]

Royce also asserts that ideally these two motives or principles ought to be harmonized. He writes: "It is necessary, but endlessly difficult to be true to both these calls at once." In fact, says Royce, the variety, the manifoldness, the fallibility of our conscience and its dignity is grounded in the fact that "as conscientious beings we are required by our moral nature to accomplish a two-fold task." This task is to "Be humane and reasonable at once."[97] In spelling out the meaning of this dual task, Royce follows paths argued by both particularists and impartialists. To be humane, in Royce's view, is to "consider all the interests that are going to be affected by your acts so far as you can possibly realize what these interests are." Further, one must "not be blind to the other live beings about you. Consider what they wish as well as what you wish."[98] This shows a concern, on Royce's part for the particularity of the moral situation. On the other hand, Royce also calls the moral person to have a "reasonable rule of action," to be concerned for "justice" and "legality." Royce, then, seems to be aiming toward Blum's goal of morality that embodies a complex interaction between the concerns of impartiality and those of care.

How, then, does Royce guide us in a morality that seeks to be both "humane and reasonable?" First of all, unlike some moral-development theories, Royce believes both dispositions, namely, reasonableness and sympathy, are human capacities, present in childhood and capable of developing into a mature morality, "the predisposition to be suggestible and reasonable at once. . . ." This predisposition is indeed, not as an innate idea but as a tendency inborn in us."[99] Royce even suggests that it is a product of evolution. "It is doubtless due to the "spontaneous variation" that has made the human brain, as a product of evolution, a possible thing."[100]

It has been a long-standing belief of Western thought that the human is "rational animal." Kantian and utilitarian ethics both assume rationality as central. Kohlberg and other moral-development theorists describe rationality as a specific human capacity with a developmental history. However, Western psychology has been seemingly antithetical to giving any central place to altruistic behavior or concern for others in human personality. Martin Hoffman notes that "The doctrinaire view, present in both psychoanalysis and behaviorism, has been that altruistic behavior can always be explained ultimately in terms of instrumental self-serving motives in the actor."[101] Hoffman, however, disagrees with this view and claims that *altruism*, "any purposive action on behalf of someone else which involves a net cost to the actor," is an innate capacity of the human self.[102] Hoffman reports examples of young children engaging in seeming altruistic or other-oriented acts. One child, at fifteen months, first offered his own teddy bear to comfort a friend, then sought out the other child's blanket to provide comfort.[103] Hoffman, in his research, finds evidence of sympathetic distress as well as tendencies toward helpful action in young children. He also finds "guilt responses to inaction" and an ability of a child to "take another's role."[104]

Lawrence Blum, citing Hoffman's work as well as that of Edward Mueller[105] argues that neo-Kantian views of morality fail to give sufficient attention to altruistic responsiveness as a basic human motivation and, further, that they fail to "give moral significance to the phenomenon of childhood responsiveness."[106] Interestingly, Royce also cites examples of sympathetic responsiveness in children:

> Fairly early examples of truly moral motives based upon this primitive sympathy appear, however, in such small but significant acts as those of a three-year-old child that voluntarily and spontaneously . . . suddenly foregoes the pleasure of even beginning to eat its candy until it can bring the candy, perhaps some distance to you, to offer you the first bite.
>
> . . . In such a deed there is, so to speak, one of the first flutters of the wings of the sympathetic conscience. . . . The process of social self-enlargement is under way. This social self-enlargement, which is present even in childhood, makes me consciously treat my neighbor as part of myself.[107]

The important point about altruistic response is that it need not and does not simply flow from our adherence to a principle of caring for others. Blum, for example, argues that responsiveness usually involves both cognitive and affective dimensions of the self. The cognitive aspects may be nothing more than a cognitive grasp of another's condition. Further, altruistic caring can be a spontaneous and direct response to a particular person and situation. For the particularist, concern and care has *prime facie moral* value; this is not so for the impartialist perspective.

Further, the impartialist view requires the agent to abstract himself from his individual interests and particular relationships; he must adopt an impartial standpoint, favoring no person over any other. This leads, argue the particularists, to notions that are counter-intuitive to common-sense morality. It leads to the possibility of acting to save a stranger from a fire rather than one's mother. It leads to acting to help a sick friend out of duty, coldly, and without care for that friend. It seems, says Slote, to deny "self-other asymmetry," sacrificing self or remaining indifferent to one's own pains, even when this leads to less-good results overall. Why should someone not sacrifice himself to save five others?

Royce, in concert with his understanding of the human self as complex, contextual, opened, sees the moral situation and moral conscience as equally one of sympathetic care and of considered principle. As we have seen, the moral will is conflicted; motives of both duty and fairness and humane concern are present, and they manifest themselves in various ways and often are at war with each other. In his work on conscience, Royce follows this conflict of motives through the developmental process.[108] Like contemporary moral theorists he believes the conditions provided for moral development are crucially important. Gilligan, for example, traces the interaction of feelings of inequality and attachment in human development to explain how this interaction leads to two lines of development; one emphasizes detachment from others, justice, shame, and guilt; the other emphasizes empathy, paying attention to the other, experiencing and taking the needs and feelings of others as part of oneself. She poses the important question of the conditions of development: "If altruistic feelings are natural and present in early childhood, what experiences might be present in the lives of those who lose these sensibilities?"[109] Gilligan, like Blum, recognizes that neither the ethics of impartialism nor the ethics of care is satisfactory alone:

> If the persistent error in care reasoning is vacillation and lack of clear judgment resulting in a tendency to include all possible ways of seeing, the persistent danger in the justice reasoner is moral arrogance, the irrational faith in the infallibility of judgments from principles rigidly applied to a situation.[110]

Royce also is fully aware of the "particularity of the moral situation." He writes: "Our moral consciousness must tell us not only that there is in general a right and a wrong, but also that in this individual case *this* is right and *that* is wrong."[111] However, he also recognizes that neither humanness nor principle, care nor justice alone fits the complexity of human moral situations:

Conscience is not satisfied either by loving conduct that is capricious, or by well-ordered conduct that is inhuman. . . . The man who, without any special reason, squanders his means upon chance gifts to a crowd at a public festival, appears to us so far kindly, but he also appears immorally whimsical. . . . The man who should persistently neglect his own family in order to give happiness to the family of the stranger would in vain plead his benevolence as an excuse.[112]

Royce firmly believes a morality is possible that blends in a interactive and ever-changing way the impartialist-principle-justice oriented view and the particularist-care-responsiveness-others point of view. One must first recognize that human moral situations will always be complex and opaque; that humans are fallible and blind. Human conscience is a developmental notion, both for individual and in general. Narrowness of view can continue to be broadened; sympathy and responsiveness can grow. The key to moral maturity, as for authentic individuality, which includes moral maturity, is authentic community and the process of interpretation. In *The Problem of Christianity*, Royce turns to an important aspect of human moral behavior, the doctrine of love and how that is to be actualized. Though we know we are to love God and our neighbor, the question, says Royce, is *how*? How can I be practically useful in meeting my neighbor's needs?

What is sure about love is that it indeed unites the lover in spirit to God's will. What constitutes, in this present world, the pathos, the tragedy of love, is that, because our neighbor is so mysterious a being to our imperfect vision, we do not know how to make him [our neighbor] happy, to relieve his deepest distresses, to do him the highest good.[113]

The answer is community and the interpreting acts that go on in authentic community. That which can make the loving of our neighbor less mysterious and difficult is community: "a community when unified by an active developing purpose, is an entity more concrete, and, in fact, less mysterious than is any individual man. . . ."[114] In community we can come to know each other, to see what others' needs are. I need not ask, Who is my neighbor," for my neighbor and I are members of one and the same community. And in that community, self-interpretation and other-interpretation broadens our understanding of each others' needs, broadens our sympathies and loyalty to our community and to universal community, and spurs us to expand both our concern and our application of our principles. Interpretation and loyalty expand our understanding of both justice and care.

We turn now to this work of interpretation and Royce's concept of the principle loyalty to loyalty.

4

Loyalty, Patriotism, and Enlightened Provincialism
Building Community in an Individualistic World

"To love the little platoons we belong to in society is the first principle of public affectons."
—Edmund Burke

"Persons only become human in association with others, but not all associations liberate human powers."
—Peter Manicas

"Every generation has to accomplish democracy over again for itself."
—John Dewey

The Need for Social Solidarity

A CENTRAL ISSUE for the United States today, and a crucial one for any public philosophy, is the building of some "sense of community, of common commitments and goals." Bryan S. Turner, political scientist, writes, "the problem of social order and social solidarity is at the forefront of political problems."[1] There is, in the United States today, a deep cynicism, suspicion, and even animus about government and other major social institutions. For example, voter apathy is high and the best voter turnout is usually for negative action against government, to veto bond initiatives, for instance, or to enforce term limits. Further, business downsizing has elicited deep distrust of many corporations because of loss of job security and per-

83

ceived disregard for commitments. Educational institutions, at all levels, face declines in funding, calls for accountability, and reform. The various professions also—especially medicine and law—are focal points of much public criticism and pointed humor. Further, even intimate relationships and commitments appear under attack. Contentiousness, violence, or litigation seem pervasive among neighbors, and among husbands and wives, children and parents, teachers and pupils, and professionals and clients.

Yet, as always in this country, there is a deep longing for community, a cry for relationship and a search for meaning and for common values. The work of Robert Bellah and his associates has already been cited. They have issued a call to Americans to see themselves as part of a political whole, a commonwealth, and for institutions to become "community enhancers."[2] Communitarian Etzioni asks that we "*enhance the community and its moral voice.*"[3] Finally, we find business executive Carol Kinsey Goman urging corporations to take seriously a "loyalty factor" as "good business," helping individuals to find "a rewarding sense of belonging" in a time when there is a "profound feeling of isolation."[4]

The philosophy of Josiah Royce offers a good foundation for tackling the problem of community building in American today. This is so because in his *Philosophy of Loyalty* and *The Problem of Christianity* Royce sought to develop a philosophical and ethical viewpoint that is person-centered yet that stresses community and community building.[5] He develops a concept of loyalty in which loyalty helps center and create a unique self but also helps self transcend private advantage and develop a commitment to community building and overcoming the tendency of communities to seek exclusivity. Royce, in fact, interprets human sin in terms of self and community isolation. Thus, unlike communitarian thought, Royce is able to address the issue of "wicked communities" and "wicked loyalties"; he is well aware that the moral voice is not always the communal voice. He also addresses the problems of conflicts of loyalties and of "blind allegiances," and "dangerous patriotism."[6] Further, because he takes seriously the role of religion in human life and sees religion as a "communal" as well as an "individual" phenomenon, Royce is able to deal with a contemporary problem identified by various thinkers, namely, "the lack of authoritative myths" and rituals to "identify for the community the commitments and meaning of our national life."[7] And, as indicated at the end of the previous chapter, Royce sees community association also as a basis and guide for benevolence and acts of service, especially in generating common interests, sympathy, and an under-standing of each other's needs. This fits well with a new emphasis on "vol-untary associations" as a means of dealing with and countering the welfare state. Royce's "enlightened provincialism" is also in concert with the com-plementary stress on "voluntary associations" as "mediating structures" in building human relationships and connections to centers of power.[8]

Loyalty: A Key to Enlightened Self and Moral Relationships

The discussion of community building, particularly of creating moral re-lationships and genuine community must begin, for a Roycean perspective, with the concept of loyalty. In his *Philosophy of Loyalty*, Royce declares, "*In loyalty, when loyalty is properly defined, is the fulfillment of the whole moral law.*"[9] Royce is not alone in his assessment of the pivotal role of loyalty in dealing with genuine social relationships and common social bonding. In his 1993 book on loyalty and moral relationships, George P. Fletcher writes: "Loyalty is the beginning of political life—a life in which interaction with others becomes the primary means of solving problems. . . . In personal re-lationships, loyalty expresses the relationship's assuming an external force, holding lovers or friends in a bond that transcends temporary disaffec-tion."[10] Fletcher connects 'loyalty' with the historicity of the 'self', with "shared histories," and with friendship, as well as with other forms of loyal bonding. Royce, in fact, developed an ethic based on the principle of loyal-ty to loyalty, which not only addresses the issue of relationships and genuine community but which provides a ground for mutual self-empowerment via social interaction, allowing individuals to develop unique life-plans and skills, as well as courage to make moral decisions in situations of great com-plexity and uncertainty.

Royce, however, is quite clear that 'loyalty' must be properly defined be-fore it can function as this grounding moral principle. He uses the term "en-lightened loyalty" to indicate the notion of loyalty he has in mind. Royce then offers us the following preliminary definition of loyalty, "*The willing and practical and thorough going devotion of a person to a cause.*"[11] The first aspects of enlightened loyalty for Royce are that it is voluntary and person-al. "The loyal man's cause is his cause by virtue of the assent of his own will."[12] Royce is fully aware of the strong connection in ordinary usage be-tween loyalty, social relations, roles, ranks, and stations. Indeed, for Royce, imitation and social training play a fundamental role in training individuals to "enlightened loyalty." Social institutions such as fraternal organizations and athletics are, as we shall see, important training grounds for loyalty and can be instances of enlightened loyalty.[13] However, "enlightened loyalty" involves personal reflections and choice as well as personal evaluation. Involved is a cause that one personally values, and adoration and affection usually are a part of such loyalty.

Royce would clearly agree with Andrew Oldenquist, who speaks of loyalties as having the character of self-dependent normative judgments, containing uneliminable egocentric particulars. For Oldenquist, "When I have loyalty toward something I have come somehow to view it as mine. It is an object of noninstrumental value to me in virtue (but not only) of its being mine. . . . People care about the objects of their loyalties . . . ."[14] Indeed, loyalty, for Royce, plays a key role in self-identity and unity. Being loyal to a cause helps unify a life: it brings one's own will to self-consciousness; it helps one become morally aware and autonomous. "My duty is simply my own will brought to my clear self-consciousness. That which I can rightly view as good for me is simply the object of my own deepest desire set plainly before my insight. . . . Your duty is what you yourself will do insofar as you clearly discover who you are and what your place in the world is."[15]

Fletcher also sees loyalty as essentially personal and closely tied to one's sense of self. The way we draw the line of our loyalties, argues Fletcher, defines ourselves as persons: "In acting loyally, the self acts in harmony with its personal history."[16] The very personal nature of loyalty relates to the fact that "loyalty" connotes a sustaining, steadfast devotion, a fundamental unwillingness to exit or betray a loyalty. For Fletcher, "The fundamental element in loyalty is the fact not present—the counterfactual conditional statement that if the competitor appears and beckons, the loyal will refuse to follow."[17] A minimal demand of loyalty is maintenance of the relationship. Loyalty, as eminently personal, also can lead to guilt and shame: guilt at betrayal by self, shame at betrayal of cause. We will discuss both disloyalty and unworthy causes later on in this chapter.

In sum, then, loyalty is highly personal, involving choice, affection, and a sense of self. However, it is, for Royce and others, also transpersonal. Oldenquist speaks of "loyalty" as a third category of normative discourse. It is not an egoism because self-interest is transcended; nor is it impersonal because loyalty depends on viewing a thing as one's own.[18] Royce speaks of loyalty as a union of the personal and the objective. If you are loyal, says Royce, your cause is viewed as something objective—something that is not your private self; it is beyond your own private advantage. Yet, the cause is loved "because of its own value, which it has by itself even if you die."[19]

Moreover, loyalty is essentially social. If one is a loyal servant of a cause, there are possible fellow servants. Loyalty tends to unite persons in one service and, thus, it has an impersonal or superpersonal quality. Further, even with two individuals, two friends, or loyal lovers, the loyalty is to the tie, the union, their love, which is more than both of them viewed as distinct individuals.[20] The focal point of loyalty, argues Fletcher, is "a relationship-based entity that transcends the individuals who constitute it." Further, the relationship stays with them: "the aspect of relationships that matter is that they enter into the individual's sense of identity," into their biography.[21] As we shall see, the ethics of loyalty, for Royce and for Fletcher, unlike that of classical liberalism, takes "relationships as logically prior to the individual."[22]

Loyalty, then, brings about a union of the personal and the superindividual or superpersonal. Contrary to opinions of certain readers of Royce,[23] however, loyalty to a cause does not imply loyalty to an abstraction. Royce argues instead that one must choose forms of loyal conduct that appeal to one's own nature. He speaks of the cause fascinating one and stirring one to rigor: "Loyalty . . . depends upon a very characteristic and subtle union of natural interest and of free choice. . . . Loyalty has an elemental appeal to my whole organism."[24] Loyalty, for Royce, is not an abstract affair, but rather highly practical. It is, as we shall see, a guide to everyday action and something that must and does result in decisive action.

Further, loyalty is natural and a basic need for human beings. Fletcher speaks of loyalty as "characteristically human."[25] Carol Kinsey Goman writes, "*Loyalty is basic to our nature as human beings—a potent force that can be brought forth for the good of all.*"[26] Interestingly enough, a series of surveys of employees about motivations for loyalty show that 85 percent of the respondents believed loyalty to be an integral part of their beings, "Just the way I am."[27] Royce is clear that loyalty is to be found in "all orders of society," and all kinds of examples of loyalty may be found "amongst the lowliest and amongst the loftiest of mankind." In Royce's view of loyalty, "all sound human beings are made for it and can learn to possess it and to profit by it."[28] Loyalty is not only natural but, for Royce, something all human beings need:

> . . . loyalty is for the loyal man not only a good, but for him
> chief amongst all the moral goods of his life, because it fur-
> nishes to him a personal solution of the hardest of human
> practical problems, the problem: 'For what do I live? Why
> am I here? For what am I good? Why am I needed?'[29]

Loyalty, as already indicated, provides self-unity. It also brings one's own will to self-consciousness and thus allows moral autonomy. For Royce, as well as many others, it is a profound psychological fact that the quest for self-hood is a fundamental concern for all persons. What is desired is self-possession or a cohesive life-plan. I need to learn to have and create a will of my own to become an autonomous being, a moral being. But, as we seek a life-plan, we become aware of a fundamental paradox of human life, called by Royce the paradox of moral autonomy and social dependency, or of the "inner" and "outer." My plan must be my *own*; I must justify to myself my own plan of life, yet left to myself, I can never find a plan of life. Contrary to popular opinion, a person has no innate autonomy, no innate moral autonomy. What one finds within oneself is a chaos and conflict of wills, an in-coherent babble of voices.[30] Thus, as has been made clear in earlier chapters, and as we know from experience, the only way we can become a unified self is in a social context and with the help of one's fellow beings.

In my social life, I get access to various models and plans of life. Through imitation of the will of others, I begin to learn the nature of my own will. I learn customs and devices of self-expression. Through social contact, imita-tion of models, and my divergence from others I begin to develop a life-plan. But loyalty helps bring all of this to fruition; it unites inner and outer, the individual and the social. It is personal and transpersonal. Royce puts it this way: "To sum up so far—a self is a life insofar as it is unified by a single pur-pose. Our loyalties furnish such purposes, and hence make us conscious and unified moral persons."[31] Loyalty constitutes what Royce calls "conscience," the flower of the moral life.[32] Conscience is that "ideal of life which consti-tutes your moral personality."[33] It is the sum of those loyalties that define oneself as a person. It is the spirit of the self.

Thus, from a Roycean point of view, there is truth to Fletcher's claim that loyalty is an important aspect of our historical self. It is, for him, par-tially a set of obligations "implied in every person's set of defining familial, institutional and national relationships."[34] Loyalty involves a sense of shared histories. By the mere fact of my biography, I incur obligations towards others; "loyalties circumscribe communitarian circles, all the members of which take others within the circle to be objects of their concern." Again, by acting loyally, one acts in harmony with one's sense of self. "Actions of standing by one's friends, nation or people reveal that identity."[35]

Royce also recognizes this close connection between a self's history and one's loyalties. One serves causes such as one's natural temperament and social opportunities suggest. Family, community, friends, country will be served partly because I find it natural and interesting to be loyal to them. However, enlightened loyalty requires more. One cannot permit one's choice of special causes to remain a matter of mere chance. One's life of loyalty must form a system and a harmony and thus one must ultimately face the problem of the conflict of loyalties and the questions of betrayal and of unworthy causes. Loyalty for Royce is essentially a matter of spirit embodied in the principle *loyalty to loyalty*.

Is Loyalty a Good?

Royce categorically holds that loyalty is a supreme good. However, he is well aware that some causes to which men give their loyalty are evil. This leads him to focus on loyalty as an attitude, a devotion to the building of genuine relationship and community. The principle of *loyalty to loyalty* becomes the main criterion of causes:

> Insofar as it lies in your power, so choose your cause and so serve it, that, by reason of your choice and of your service, there shall be more loyalty in the world rather than less. And, in fact, so choose and so serve your individual cause as to secure thereby the greatest possible increase of loyalty amongst men.[36]

Royce's principle of loyalty to loyalty has been much misunderstood, so we will try to clarify its meaning through various examples he himself gives of enlightened loyalty, as well as by drawing on other aspects of his developed philosophy. A good place to begin is with Royce's analysis of sin and guilt.

Human sin is both individual and social: it is fostered by both individual and social conditions, and it manifests itself both individually and socially. The first condition for human sin is our finite-infinite nature. This is manifested first of all in the finitude of our consciousness. *"Our finitude means, then, an actual inattention—a lack of successful interest, at this conscious instant, in more than a very few details of the universe."*[37] The finitude of consciousness is not itself sin, but the condition of sin. Because of this condition, Royce believed we are called upon to do two things if we wish to overcome sin and be fully moral human beings. First, we must intensely develop our power of response to the universe around us, to maintain as much openness as possible. Secondly, we need to recognize that full truth and reality are still to be discovered.

Human sinfulness can thus manifest itself in two ways. The first is what Royce calls the sin of irresponsiveness, which is a deliberate choosing to narrow our focus, to circumscribe our field of attention. The second form of sin is the sin of pride, the lack of humility about our limited grasp of truth and reality. Indeed, these two forms of sin are two sides of a coin. Paul Ramsey, in the spirit of Paul Tillich, describes this dual nature of sin as absolutizing the finite or the finite absolutizing itself. "Irresponsiveness to the greater world beyond is but a negative side of inordinate responsiveness to one's own present interests."[38]

In the *Philosophy of Loyalty*, Royce speaks of the inevitable illusion of perspective that he also called "natural selfishness":

> Whether he takes account of the physical or the natural world, every man inevitably finds himself as apparently occupying the center of his own universe. The starry heavens form to his eyes a sphere, and he himself, so far as he can see, is at the center of that sphere. Yes, the entire and infinite visible world, to be even more exact, seems to have its centre about where the bridge of your own nose chances to be. What is very remote from us we all find it difficult to regard as real in the same warm and vital sense in which the world near to us is real.[39]

The illusion of perspective distorts the true nature of things. Each of us interprets and sees the world differently, and values and loyalties alter with point of view. However, these different interpretations all have, argues Royce, some basis in the truth of things. This is why we must respect the loyalties of others and the values and beliefs accompanying these. They contain some elements of the truth. The error is to exalt the loyalties as all encompassing. The goal is to broaden loyalties and perspectives. In *The Urbana Lectures*, Royce argues for several procedural principles that he believes constitute the "moral attitude." One of these is the principle of harmony, which essentially prescribes maximum reconciliation of all conflicting values at a minimum cost, through compromise or redirection of each. In other words, other things being equal, the harmonization of conflicting interests results in more value being realized than is the case when conflict persists. Royce puts the matter as follows:

> If matters can be so arranged that A's will and B's will can cooperate with each other and help each other, instead of hindering each other, then the new and transformed situation possesses more objective value than the old situation. That is, a state of things in which A's will cooperates with B's will is better, other things being equal, than the situation in which A's will conflicts with B's will. And this again is an objective truth about the world of values. For the conflict, if it occurs, can end at best in the success of only one of us. The peace and consequent cooperation of both of us would by hypothesis accomplish what we are both seeking and this would be an objectively valuable result, and would possess at least the value which both of us give to our own distinct purposes.[40]

Royce's principle of loyalty to loyalty means to work for the harmonizing of conflicting loyalties so that broader truth and value may be realized.

Returning to the topic of human sin and our finite/infinite nature, it should be clear that, for Royce, the infinite dimension of human nature is manifested in our very possibility of self-transcendence and in aspiring to goals and ideals that transcend self and time. Self-actualization, as we have seen, is for Royce an ethical task, and self-actualization requires self-transcendence, a goal outside oneself whereby life can be unified. Further, to achieve self-actualization, I, of course, need self-knowledge. But gaining such, for Royce, is again plagued by narrowness of view and the sins of irresponsiveness and pride:

> Nothing is more obvious about the natural course of our
> lives than is the *narrowness of view* to which we are usually
> subject. We are not only the victims of conflicting motives,
> but we are all too narrow to know that this is true. For we
> see our various interests, so to speak, one at a time. We for-
> get one while we are living out another. And so, we are
> prone to live many lives, seldom noting how ill harmonized
> they are. . . . And, if as our naturally complex and often
> conflicting motives determine, these our various lives are
> out of harmony with one another, we constantly do irrevo-
> cable deeds that emphasize and perpetuate the results of
> this disharmony. . . . We thus come to spend our days
> thwarting ourselves through the results of our fickleness,
> yet without knowing who it is that thwarts us. . . . The
> deeper tragedies of life thus result from this our narrowness
> of view.[41]

In light of this, as we now know so well, we and our fellows need to transcend ourselves and to gain insight into ourselves.

> The social world is wide, even if it is still full of conflict. It
> broadens our outlook at every turn. A man corrects his nar-
> rowness by trying to share his fellow's point of view. Our
> social responsibilities tend to set limits to our fickleness. So-
> cial discipline removes some of our inner conflicts, by
> teaching us not to indulge our caprices. Human compan-
> ionship may calm, may steady our vision, may bring us into
> intercourse with what is in general much better than a
> man's subliminal self, namely, his public, his humane, his
> greater social self, wherein he finds his soul and its interest
> writ large.[42]

Conflicts of loyalties can be clarifying and lead to an increase of loyalties and
values.

However, this is not the whole story. Our very social nature and our need
for others also can lead to sin. First, the social order can encourage one to
give in to the collective will and become a "they" as part of the crowd, rather

than a unique self. One can refuse to take responsibility for one's own existence, to be a self. This self-loss, says Royce, engenders a deep sense of guilt.
It is a deep betrayal.

> Now, the sense of guilt, if deep and pervasive and passion-
> ate, involves at least a dim recognition that there is some
> central aim of life and that one has come hopelessly short
> of that aim. . . .[43]

There is another form of betrayal and sin, namely, the sin of spiritual self-assertion, the sin of pride, of absolutizing, of withdrawal into self-sufficiency.
This error can be committed both by individual and group. For the individual, it is to follow one's own self-will and to betray the group, to belie one's
need for and dependence on a group and to deny the mutual interdependence involved in a community. Part of the meaning of the principle of loyalty to loyalty is the understanding that loyal relationships are an essential
part of one's being as a human person, understanding that genuine, loyal relationships are crucial to self-development, to self-unification. It gives support to the fact that true moral autonomy and freedom grow out of and are
dependent on genuine loyal communal relationships. To desire self-sufficiency is betrayal of the self:

> No one can rationally say: 'Loyalty can no longer bind me
> because from my deepest soul, I feel that I want my indi-
> vidual freedom.' For any such outcry comes from an igno-
> rance of what one's deepest soul really wants.[44]

For Royce, the worst sin is betrayal of our loyalty. A traitor is one who
has had an ideal and has loved it with all her heart, soul, and mind and
strength, but who has been deliberately false to her cause. The betrayal here
is not only against self, but against fellow servants of the cause who have
placed trust in the relationship and in the loyalty pledge. The sense of community is profoundly injured. Further, because the bonds of loyalty are in-
tegrally a part of the selves involved, betrayal does not dissolve the bond
between member and group. The tragedy of the treason becomes part of the
history of the bonded community. Royce speaks of atonement for treason in
terms of a creative deed done by the community or someone on behalf of the

community that "makes the world better than before the blow of treason."[45] These acts of atonement and healing must be specific and concretely relevant to the situation. For example, if a lie is the act of betrayal, an act of truth and openness must occur that increases the sense of trust in the community.

The sin of pride and self-sufficiency can also be committed by the community, and this constitutes one reason why loyalties may be questioned and/or broken. A community may portray itself as the ultimate goal, worthy of the ultimate loyalty. In doing so, it betrays the goal of loyalty to loyalty and engages in the sin of absolutizing the finite. Such a community and cause is evil or in error and must be corrected. Further, a community may demand a loyalty that is ultimately anti-community. The principle of loyalty to loyalty is, for Royce, the main criterion for testing false or unworthy causes. Destruction of loyalties and communities is evil, and causes or communities that require this should, says Royce, be justly opposed:

> A robber band, a family engaged in a murderous feud, a pirate crew, a savage tribe, a Highland robber clan of the old days. . . . Men have loved such causes devotedly, have served them for a lifetime. Yet most of us would easily agree in thinking such causes unworthy of anybody's loyalty.[46]

Royce is especially concerned in *The Philosophy of Loyalty* to argue that the true conception of loyalty has been obscured by viewing the warrior as the most typical representative of rational loyalty.[47] Leo Tolstoy, for example, argued that war, which is an evil, was the inevitable consequence of patriotism and, thus, that such a form of loyalty was an evil.[48] Royce recognizes truth in this belief and urges enlightened loyalty and enlightened patriotism:

> We all think too often of loyalty as a warlike and intolerant virtue, and not as the spirit of universal peace. Enlightened loyalty, as we have now learned, means harm to no man's loyalty. It is at war only with disloyalty, and its warfare, unless necessity constrains, is only a spiritual warfare. It does not foster class hatreds; it knows of nothing reasonable about race prejudices and it regards all races of men as one in their need of loyalty. . . . Enlightened loyalty takes no delight in great armies or in great navies. . . . It has no joy in

national prowess, except insofar as that prowess means a
furtherance of universal loyalty. . . .[49]

Enlightened patriotism for Royce, is one that sees nation building as community building within the nation as *unum pluribus*, and as building international alliances and community via an insurance scheme. These issues will
be discussed shortly. And indeed, the patriotism described by Tolstoy, for instance, as "the exclusive desire for the well-being of one's own people" would
be seen by Royce as exemplifying the sin of pride and thus as *not* a true loyalty.

    One aspect of patriotism and the warrior spirit that Royce does find im-
portant to enlightened loyalty has to do with the "spirit of courageous action" described by James in "The Moral Equivalent of War."[50] In *The
Philosophy of Loyalty*, Royce argues for two inseparable characteristics of true
loyal conduct: decisiveness on the part of the agent and *fidelity* to decisions
once made, insofar as the later insight does not forbid the continuance of
such fidelity.[51] One who is loyal, argues Royce, cannot play Hamlet's role.
Following James in *The Will to Believe*,[52] Royce says that indecision that
would itself practically amount to a decision to do nothing would be a failure to be loyal to loyalty. One's choice of loyalties and causes is always fallible, but to be loyal one must courageously act. The guiding principle must
be: "*Decide, knowingly, ignorantly if you must, but in any case decide, and have
no fear.*"[53]

    Royce's call to be loyal to loyalty is a call to each person to work active-
ly to achieve a coherent life-plan and to build community and relatedness
where she is and where she can. It is a call to critical courageous faith and
humble awareness that what we take to be worthy of our loyalty may be for
this time and place, but not for all times and places, and it may even be a
mistaken loyalty. Royce provides two tests for these ideals worthy of our loyalty, true self-fulfillment and the expansion of genuine community.

    Royce gives an excellent concrete example of practiced loyalty, both in
the *Urbana Lectures* and in *The Philosophy of Loyalty*.[54] In January 1642 a
conflict occurred between Charles I and Parliament. Charles had resolved to
arrest certain leaders of the opposition party. He had sent his herald to the
House to demand the surrender of these members. The Speaker of the
House forbade their arrest without their consent, appealed to the ancient
privilege of the House that gave that body authority over its members. Thus

a conflict between the House and the royal prerogative was initiated. The King resolved to assert authority and the next day went in person to the house, accompanied by his soldiers. He demanded of the Speaker indication of the persons whom he wished to arrest The Speaker of the House at once fell on his knee before the King and said, "Your Majesty, I am the Speaker of the House, and being such, I have neither eyes to see nor tongue to speak save as this House shall command; and I humbly beg your Majesty's pardon if this is the only answer that I can give to your Majesty."[55]

What does this example illustrate for us about Royce's understanding of loyalty. First, conflicting loyalties are clearly the case and the conflict is unique to the individuals and situation. No mere application of abstract principles can resolve the situation. Imagination and creativity are involved in fulfilling obligations of loyalty. Royce writes, "Custom, procedure, convention, obviously were inadequate to define the Speaker's duty in this most critical instance. . . . The Speaker's words were at once ingenious and obvious. They were in link with the ancient custom of the realm. They were also creative of a new precedent."[56] Secondly, there is self-consciousness of the act of loyalty; there is decisiveness and courage. The decisiveness and self-consciousness are interrelated; the cause is a specific one that the loyal servant has freely chosen. There is complete identification of self with the cause—the Speaker declares that he has no eye or tongue except as his office gave to him. The loyalty is to a concrete community that helps define the person's identity.

Thirdly, there is humble acceptance on the part of the Speaker of the possibility that his loyalty may be limited, fallible, and even mistaken. There is, says Royce, a beautiful union of formal humility and unconquerable self-assertion. There is about the loyal act a "personal dignity."[57] Finally, the Speaker also speaks for the principle of loyalty to loyalty, for broadening the scope of loyalty, because he reminds the King of the common loyalty to the peace of the realm. This loyal act combines self-fulfillment with a courageous reminder of the need to broaden loyalties and understanding. The servant of enlightened loyalty seeks not the disparagement of loyalty to the King nor exaltation of loyalty to the House, but a broadening of the scope of loyalty by calling upon loyalty to a wider community.

This brings us to the question of training for or teaching loyalty and of somehow building broader loyalties.

Training for Loyalty: Enlightened Provincialism

Previous chapters have dealt with Royce's understanding of "genuine individualism" and "genuine community" and with the conditions necessary for developing such. These discussions will be assumed in what follows. Indeed, in dealing with the topic, "Training for Loyalty" in *The Philosophy of Loyalty*, Royce asserts that teachers must avoid trying to awaken any particular sort of loyalty before a proper basis is laid, namely, one that involves "rich development of social habits" and a sufficient age. He writes: "One must obtain the material for a moral personality before a true conscience can be won. Conscience, as we have seen, is the flower and not the root of moral life."[58] This reminds us of our previous discussion of crucial conditions in mother-child relationships, of the importance of play, and especially of a supportive communal situation of communication, mutuality, and trust. We will address these issues even more specifically in our discussion of family, in chapter 5.

Turning to the specific issue of loyalty, Royce focuses on three basic conditions for fostering enlightened loyalty that are often neglected: (1) the process of idealization; (2) the influence of personal leaders, and (3) the perfecting of loyalty through grief and sacrifice in the service of a cause. Further, he identifies aspects of loyalty already present in childhood and adolescence that need to be encouraged, rather than inhibited. Among these are sympathy and truthtelling. Royce makes two very important points in this regard. Truthfulness, in childhood, has its own casuistry and form of crude loyalty, and this should be respected. He writes: "The parent or teacher who trifles with the code of honor of children by encouraging the talebearer, or by even requiring that a child should become an informer, is simply encouraging disloyalty. He outrages the embryonic conscience of his young charges."[59] Secondly, notes Royce, children are very much aware of expressions of loyalty or disloyalty toward them, even if they do not yet clearly understand their own duty. Thus, in dealing with children, one must be scrupulous about expressing loyalty toward them. These issues relating to childhood resources will be expanded in the chapter on family.

For the adolescent and even younger children, Royce identifies two forms of loyalty that though subject to abuses and excesses, nevertheless are important training grounds for enlightened loyalty, namely fraternal organizations and athletics. Again, Royce cautions that harm may be done in over-hasty development of fraternal groups and fully formed athletic organizations among the young. These tend to hinder natural groupings of the young as well as the spontaneity of play. Because of young age and lack of development, it may also lead to the abuses of mischief and too much passion. Fraternal organizations can foster "genuine loyalty" and community if there are safeguards against exclusivity and the sin of pride. Athletics can foster "fair play" and commitment to excellence, bodily and intellectual. The abuse of athletics Royce finds aptly centered in what he calls "absurd social prominence" and "extravagant publicity."[60] Much more attention could be given to these forms of loyalty, and some discussion of them will occur in our chapter on education. There we will draw on the work of Michael Novak, who argues that sports are liturgies of "enhumanment" and a proper form of loyalty.[61]

We turn now to the three basic conditions identified by Royce for fostering loyalty. The first two are closely interrelated—the influence of personal leaders and the process of idealization. Loyalty, as we have seen, unifies the personal and the superpersonal; it involves profound self-identification and self-transcendence. And models and imitation play a crucial role, for Royce, in self-development. Royce describes how personal leaders and transpersonal cause are inseparable in the training of loyalty.

> The cause comes to be idealized partly because the leaders so vigorously insist that it is indeed ideal. On the other hand, the leaders become and remain personally efficacious by reason of the dignity that the cause confers upon them. Were they considered apart from their cause, they would seem to be merely ambitious propagandists seeking gain or notoriety. . . . Yet if they did not speak for the cause, and so give it the life of their personal enthusiasm, nobody would be taught to regard their cause as ideal. The cause thus needs to become incarnate, as it were, in the persons of the leaders; but the leaders get their personal influence through the fact that they seem to be incarnations of the cause.[62]

A number of points are being made here. First, Royce is stressing that loyalties must be specific, concrete, and personal. They must be embodied, that is, demonstrably believed in by a concrete person and clearly efficacious in a specific life. Carol Goman, in discussing loyalty in a business organization, states that a CEO's main responsibility is to provide "visionary leadership," to communicate the mission of the organization, and to demonstrate by action her own belief in the goals, her own concrete loyalty.[63] Role models are effective in human relationships, as Royce well knew, because they represent "life-plans in action." Royce's statement implies several addtitional points: cause and leader and/or loyal servant become intricately interrelated; betrayal on either side leads to dishonor for the leader; a leader who dishonors a cause casts profound doubt on self and varying degrees of doubt on the cause, depending on its value and strength. These are easily illustrated. I only cite Jim Bakker's betrayal of his religious cause. And, of course, loyal servants can be raised to higher levels of human dignity by their service to a worthy cause. Again, countless examples of such instances can be cited.

The third condition of training for loyalty that Royce identifies is the perfecting of loyalty through labors and sacrifices in the service of a cause. In this connection, Royce discusses loyalty to what he calls "lost causes," those that have failed to be realized in the visible world of history but that survive as an ideal. A prime example of such, for Royce, is the religion of Israel, together with its successor Christianity. Through a historical evolution, the loyalty and cause become refined, universalized, and intensified. A lost political ideal transformed into a prophetic theory of the divine governance of human affairs and into the doctrine of the universal future triumph of righteousness. Loyalty for a lost cause, argues Royce is attended by both grief and imagination. Grief transforms into a stimulating sense of need, and imagination provides visions that can be translated into deeds. Further, loyalty to lost causes brings into focus what Royce terms "loyalty as a moral attitude, and whatever is eternally valuable in religion." This "moral attitude" is at the heart of Royce's point: "One begins, when one serves the lost cause, to discover that, in some sense, one ought to devote one's highest loyalty to causes that are too good to be visibly realized at any one moment of this poor wretched fleeting time world. . . . Loyalty seeks, therefore, something essentially superhuman. . . . In its highest reaches it always is, therefore, the service of a cause that was just now lost—and lost because the mere now is too poor a vehicle for the presentation of that ideal unity of life of which every form of loyalty is in quest. . . ."[64]

There is, for Royce, a clear link between loyalty and religion. However, one must be clear what this means. Royce wrote three major works dealing with religion, *The Religious Aspects of Philosophy*, *The Sources of Religious Insight* and *The Problem of Christianity*.[65] I have written on Royce's understanding of religion on other occasions and thus will only bring essential features of that view to bear on our discussion of loyalty.[66] Two important themes emerge from Royce's first two works on religion: that religion unifies the emotional, practical, and theoretical sides of human experience and that the essential postulate of any religion is that *"man needs to be saved."*[67] Salvation, in Royce's view, involves three essential elements or components: an ideal goal that centers and fulfills self; the belief that human beings need help less they fail to achieve this aim, and a vision of that which will fulfill the need for help. Royce sums up these three elements as follows:

> The religious experience of the individual may concern three objects: first, his Ideal, that is, the standard in terms of which he estimates the sense and value of his own personal life; secondly, his Need of salvation, that is, the degree to which he falls short of attaining his ideal and is sundered from it by evil fortune, or by his own paralysis of will, or by his inward baseness; thirdly, the presence of the coming or the longing for, or the communion with something which he comes to view as the power that may save him from his need, or as the light that may dispel his darkness, or as the truth that shows him the way out, or as the great companion who helps him—in a word, as his Deliverer. The Ideal, the Need, the Deliverer—these are three groups which the individual experience, as a source of religious insight has always undertaken to reveal.[68]

In *The Problem of Christianity*, Royce expounds on his salvation theme through a sympathetic analysis of a specific religion, namely, Christianity. And though he sees Christianity as a religion of "the Master," taught and lived out by a person who serves as an exemplar to his followers, he refuses to found the essence of Christianity on opinions of the founder's person or the details of his life. Rather, the essence of Christianity is that it regards the "Beloved Community" as the true source of the salvation. Essential to Christianity is "the idea of a spiritual life in which universal love for all individuals shall be completely blended, practically harmonized, with an absolute loyalty for a real and universal community, God, the neighbor and one church."[69]

Loyalty and religion are crucially linked, for Royce, because religion, in its true form, embodies the principle of loyalty to loyalty; it seeks universal community, an ever-broadening circle of loyalty and fulfillment. It exemplifies "ultimate concern," as Paul Tillich has so well argued, commitment to that which is ultimate and fulfilling. But ultimate concern for Tillich, as well as for Royce, is tied to the *Protestant Principle*, a critical guard against idolatry, against the sin of absolutizing the finite. Again, it is the call to critical loyalty and humble awareness that what we take to be worthy of our loyalty may only be so for this time and place, but not for all times and places and may even be a mistaken loyalty. Religion involves loyalty to a "lost cause" in the sense that full embodiment is not expected now, and imagination, faith, and courage, as well as critical refinement, are called for in one's loyalty. It is the spirit of loyalty, the search for genuine community that is important. Thus, in *The Problem of Christianity* Royce writes: "*Look forward to the human and visible triumph of no form of the Christian church.*"[70]

The Roycean link between religion and loyalty is, I believe, an important insight and one that is recognized by contemporary discussions of loyalty. Fletcher, in his 1993 examination of loyalty strongly urges that the state not interfere with or intrude on the loyalties of its people, if this can be avoided. He is especially concerned about the free exercise of religion. Like Royce, Fletcher sees loyalty as embedded in community practice; religion, if properly practiced, is an important form of community practice:

> . . . in order for a claim of higher loyalty to be plausible it
> must be embedded in a community practice. There must
> be others who hear the same voice, and there must be, in
> recited legends or in a written texts, some objective mani-
> festation of what the higher power demands of loyal fol-
> lowers. . . .[71]

Like Royce, Fletcher sees religion as guarding against the sin of idolatry via the community. Religious loyalty is loyalty to a group as well as to the divine voice. A congregational conception of religion mediates against the excesses of individuals who think they hear the voice of God. Fletcher is, like Royce, clear that genuine religion involves humility.

> . . . the foundation of the religious life is the acceptance of
> a higher power in the universe, and that acceptance, in
> turn, entails humility as a condition of the religious life.
> Humility requires that one hear the voice of God not as a
> self-proclaimed prophet but as one member of a congrega-
> tion that tests its visions over time.[72]

Religious loyalty, then, is an important element of loyalty, and religious
affiliation can provide an important training ground for loyalty. Much religious emphasis today in America is on an individualistic notion of religion,
on the individual search for salvation. Such a stance is self-defeating because
it encourages the belief that one can achieve one's own salvation; thus, the
danger of the sin of self-sufficiency, of pride, is a real one. It also misses the
critical humility that can be provided by a genuine religious community that
guards against self-proclaimed prophets. Religious liberty needs to be seen in
this light. Thus, Fletcher argues that "the correct interpretation of the free
exercise clause, then, would defer to religious loyalties only if they are founded on a system of beliefs embedded in community practice and tested and
refined within a community of believers."[73]

Royce, however, would caution against communal pride and exclusivity
and would demand the further test by the principle of loyalty to loyalty.
Fletcher seems to recognize the need for a test of broader loyalties when he
writes that "there are limits to society's capacity to defer to intragroup loyalties of families and communities . . . the autonomy of private groups . . .
must yield to society's commitments to racial and gender justice. . . ."[74]
Royce held that there must be careful balancing of various group loyalties
and broader loyalties, and he recognized, as does Fletcher, that there are psychological needs, as well as societal needs, for "smaller" loyalties, for a set of
concentric circles of loyalties.

The Little Platoon: Enlightened Provincialism

In 1977 in *To Empower People: The Role of Mediating Structures in Public Policy,* Peter Berger and John Neuhaus put forth a public policy/research
manifesto in which they argued for the development in the United States of
"mediating structures" that would help provide meaning and structure for
individual existence, as well as provide a more sure foundation for demo-

cratic society.[75] Such "mediating structures" would help individuals feel more at home in society as well as make political life more meaningful. "Mediating structures" were defined as *those institutions standing between the individual and his private life and the large institutions of public life.*"[76] These institutions, identified as neighbor, family, church and voluntary associations, would give the private life of individuals a measure of stability while at the same time transferring meaning and value to the megastructures of government, business, education, and the professions.[77]

Berger and Neuhaus in their book and the contributors to a companion book[78] expressed concern about the vitality of democratic life. The fear was that the political sphere, if too detached from the values and realities of individual life, would become deprived of its moral foundation, delimited by lack of consent.[79] James Luther Adams, in *Democracy and Mediating Structures: A Theological Inquiry,* ties together mediating structures and the separation of powers, and he notes that Hitler defined totalitarian society as "one lacking effective mediating structures that protect the self-determination of individuals and groups."[80] In chapter 2, we discussed the concern of Alexander Hamilton and James Madison to develop a theory of equipoise for the government of United States, namely, the balancing of powers to protect against the tyranny of the state. However, there were also important drawbacks to dispersal of power in America, namely, fragmentation of sovereignty and loss of interest in government and democratic participation. Hamilton, for example, was concerned that government at a distance would lead to both the dilution of patriotism and cynicism.

Royce also, as has been indicated earlier, was much concerned about this set of problems. He addressed both in the context of his philosophy of loyalty and in his theory of enlightened provincialism. In the *Philosophy of Loyalty*, Royce distinguishes two types of social consciousness, the provincial and the 'self-estranged." The provincial type belongs to provinces and smaller communities, and here "the social mind is naturally aware of itself as at home with its own." The world of the "estranged social consciousness" is that of the Roman Empire or the state of Louis XIV where "nobody is at home." In this world "loyalty passes into the background or tends to disappear altogether."[81] Royce found the United States of his time to be in a state of "estranged social consciousness." The nation needed, argued Royce, to be trained in the spirit of loyalty to loyalty; what was needed most for the people was "*to help them to be less estranged than they are from their own social order.*"[82] The proposed method of training Royce suggests is to develop and increase a new and wise provincialism.

Although Royce sketches elements of this notion in his *Philosophy of Loyalty*, it is most fully developed in his *Race Questions, Provincialism and Other American Problems.*[83] "Wholesome provincialism," involves "possessing a set of customs and ideals and a love and pride which leads the inhabitants of the province to cherish as their own, these traditions, beliefs and aspirations."[84] Royce is clear that "province" stands for no determinate political or legal division of a country, nor does it necessarily imply any sense of opposition to city or nation. Rather, the term "enlightened province" is meant to apply to any group that constitutes itself a "genuine community." Thus, these would be groups where there is communication among unique individuals who learn to share a common past and future, who cooperate together in common deeds, who encourage and stimulate each other's acts and growth, who share in and identify with the ongoing life of the community, and who know that without the effort of each person the community could not achieve its goals. A "wise province" is like a fine orchestra—constituted of many musicians, each playing a part on a unique instrument—that performs well a beautiful piece of music.

Likewise, a "wholesome province" constitutes a genuine bond of enlightened loyalty. It is a loyalty voluntarily assumed; it embodies both a personal and transpersonal "cause"; it is self-fulfilling at its level for those involved; it is a bond, a relationship profoundly damaged by betrayal because it is part of shared histories and personal biographies; it is a relationship of mutual trust; and it eschews exclusivity, being open to the call of higher loyalties and to the harmonization of loyalties. A "wise province" is imbued with the spirit of loyalty to loyalties.

By advocating "wholesome provincialism," Royce was arguing for the need to encourage community building and loyalty on a grass-roots level, for establishing community loyalty, pride, and identity at personal and specific levels, so that both self-expansion and community expansion might occur. Royce understood what social scientists are discovering today, namely, that openness to novelty in the environment increases to the extent that individuals and groups feel a sense of confidence and security in their own identities. Royce, along with Edmund Burke and Berger and Neuhaus would argue that larger loyalties are built from smaller ones. Burke wrote, "To love the little platoons we belong to in society is the first principle of public affections."[85] Mediating loyalties and structures are needed in the task of building universal community. Royce dealt extensively with the notion of mediation in his doctrine of interpretation and in his work, *War and Insurance*.[86] In the next section of this book, we will discuss mediation as well as mediating structures or concrete examples of possible "wise provinces," namely, the family, the profession, and the educational community.

5

The Family
Building Individuals and Community

"Because of its central position in both our individual and personal development, as well as its role in our cultural and social articulation, the family often takes on the additional burden of being scapegoat to our fears."
    —Ned L. Gaylin

"Too hasty concern for replacing the 'dying' family may, in fact, bring about its untimely death."
    —Mary Jo Bane

"A family is a group of people who love and care for each other."
    —common definition in a Yale University study

"The family is a unity of interacting personalities."
    —Jetse Sprey

"The concept of motherhood is of central importance in the philosophy of both African and Afro-American people."
    —Barbara Christian

"I am annoyed that we lack a history of fatherhood."
    —Thomas A. Laquer

PUBLIC PHILOSOPHY, as defined earlier, involves addressing crucial issues of public concern, as well as the major question of what it means to be a responsible participant in "forms of life that are the common concern of many diverse communities."[1] This chapter and the two that follow deal with three such "forms of life": the family, education, and medicine. These are certainly areas of human life of central concern to numerous individuals and multiple communities in this time in the United States. All three have been perceived as in a state of "crisis" and each has been subject to a wide range of criticisms. Further, each has impact in a profound way on the life of almost every individual living in this country. Because of their centrality as social institutions of "public import," they should function as good testing ground for the applicability and validity of Roycean insights.

In dealing with each of these three areas, my focus will be on their possible function as "enlightened provinces," as "genuine communities," which can build individuals and communities capable of self-expansion and of acting on the principle of loyalty to loyalty. They shall also be viewed as needed "mediating structures" capable of mediating between individuals, between individuals and communities, and between community and community. Finally, as institutions that impact profoundly on the lives of individuals and the projects of communities, they become prime candidates for the working out of a Roycean resolution of the tension between individuals and their communities so evident in the thought and life of the United States.

This chapter focuses on family as a concept, as an institution normally charged with crucial social roles, such as child care and child socialization, and as an entity undergoing changes often seen as "near-crisis" events. However, from a Roycean point of view, the family will also be seen as the "original community," the "formative crucible," and as "the basic symbol of ethical life."[2] Given that the family is a finite and fragile human institution, the question, of course, to be asked in this regard is, What conditions must be present and/or provided to help actual families play these kinds of roles in a way that leads to individual and communal fulfillment? The later section of the chapter will attempt a partial answer to this question.

The Family as an "Entity in Question"

From a number of points of view, the family, at least in the United States, is perceived as in a state of crisis. In 1970, in his book *The Death of the Family*, David Cooper declared that the family is "a lethal chamber, destroying human personalities."[3] Christopher Lasch speaks of the family as "besieged."[4] Many, for example, believe that the family's stability as an institution is clearly declining or certainly shaky at best. To demonstrate the "instability plight" of the family, this group cites among its pieces of evidence, the increasing divorce rate in the United States, the tripling since 1960 of the illegitimate birth rate, and the fact that 15 percent of American children live in single parent homes, many of them in poverty or precarious economic conditions. Another aspect of this "instability crisis" is the increased incidences, or at least increased visibility, of spousal violence.

Another perception of the American family is its "profound failure" in terms of child care and socialization. A dramatic illustration of this aspect of the American family is provided by this set of facts:

One Day in the Life of American Children

3 children die from child abuse.

9 children are murdered.

13 children die from guns.

30 children are wounded by guns.

63 babies die before they are one month old.

101 babies die before their first birthday.

202 children are arrested for drug offenses.

307 children are arrested for crimes of violence.

340 children are arrested for drinking or drunken driving.

1,234 children run away from home.

5,314 children, in all, are arrested for these and like offenses.

7,945 children are reported abused or neglected.[5]

Political theorists of varying schools bemoan the decline of the family. Robert Nisbett is concerned about the loss of authority in contemporary society and argues that the weakening of family authority causes revolts against it.[6] Others see the decline of family authority as threatening to democracy as a political system. The family, in this view, is crucial to socializing individuals with the "capacity to give authoritative adherence to the background presumptions and principles of that society" [a democratic political society].[7] Politicians in recent years have voiced their concern for the family by calling for a restoration of family values. However, the concern for the political import of family is somewhat ironic given a fair amount of evidence for the lack of public support of families. Political theorist Jean Bethke Elshtain, for example, writes, "Located inside a wider ethos that no longer affords clear-cut moral and social support for familial relations and responsibilities, young people, unsurprisingly, choose in growing numbers to postpone or evade their responsibilities."[8]

Among the facts that could be cited to demonstrate the "failure of social support for families" is this additional list of horrific per-diem statistics:

27 children—or about a classroom—die from poverty.
145 babies are born at very low birthweight (less than 3.25 pounds).
480 teenagers get syphilis or gonorrhea.
636 babies are born to women who had late or no prenatal care
801 babies are born at low birthweight (less than 5.5 pounds)
2,255 teenagers drop out of school.
2,868 babies are born into poverty.
100,000 children have no homes to return to.
1,200,000 latchkey children come home to houses in which there is a gun.[9]

The issue of lack of moral support for "family" is, of course, a complex one. However, part of the weakening of moral support is certainly centered in the view of "family as an institution serving as an oppressive harmful structure, spawning domestic violence and child sexual abuse." Some of the hesitation about entering family relationships, cited by Elshtain, is related to this but also to the many feminist critiques of family as an oppressive patriarchal institution. This critique certainly raised serious questions about fatherhood and male power, about abandonment by men of families and family responsibilities. In the late 1970s, there were also devastating critiques of motherhood and even a call for the dissolution of family and parental relationships. In *The Mermaid and the Minotaur*, Dorothy Dinnerstein declared mothering to be "disastrous to society."[10] Others declared mothering "noxious to daughters" and the cause of subsequent unhappiness.[11] Individuals were told that their liberation depended on technological freedom from biology and biological sex and that they should become true individuals without ties. Parental relationships were oppressive and contradictory to individual fulfillment.[12]

For many persons, then, the family in the United States seems to be in serious trouble. There are, however, some who view this situation somewhat differently. Psychologist, Ned Gaylin, believes that the so-called family crisis is symptomatic of general fears about a social milieu that is awry and in great flux. He writes: "Because of its central position in both our individual personal development, as well as its role in our cultural and social articulation, the family often takes on the additional burden of being scapegoat to our fears."[13] Gaylin argues that the family is, in fact, the most permanent of all social institutions, "throughout human history." Gaylin notes that the family has accommodated through economic, political, religious, and technological cataclysms, modifying itself and adapting but continually surviving as "an identifiable and indispensable social unit."[14] Mary Jo Bane also believes that the staying power of the American family has been grossly underestimated. The American family, she argues, is neither lost nor in crisis. There is, she contends, no foundation for widely held beliefs that the family is unable and unwilling to care for the young. This is as much a myth as the myth of the decline of marriage. Although the divorce rate has increased, at least 75 percent of divorced persons remarry.[15] Both Bane and Gaylin argue that instead of declaring the death of the American family, we should be calling for a re-evaluation of social policies so that these may better accommodate familial priorities and be supportive of successful family practices.[16]

The Question of Family; Rethinking Family

In a Roycean attitude of finding elements of truth in various viewpoints, I too would argue that one must be cautious about premature declarations of "the death of the family." The concept of family inheres in a basic stability, expressing a crucial human relationship and need. Indeed, the scapegoating and fear referred to by Gaylin, I would submit, identifies a real concern for the type of social unit and set of human relationships that family represents. To deny the failure of so many families is to hide one's eyes, but to cry "crisis" is also to belittle the adaptability of family and the many good things that are occurring today in attempts to build families, things like the new idea of "chosen" families.[17] We shall discuss this shortly when we turn to the issue of defining *family*. First, however, in noting the stability aspect of family, one must also highlight change and, above all, avoid the impression of one model of family structure.

A number of recent feminist writings suggest, in fact, that the attacks on the validity and "feasibility" of the American family stem, in part, from imposing a reductionist mind set on the issues of family, a single model of family that embodies false definition and expectations. In an excellent volume entitled, *Rethinking the Family*, Barrie Thorne outlines five themes that she believes central to a "feminist rethinking of the family."[18] Four of these themes are central to our own discussion of family. The first theme is that "there is no monolithic family, no natural biological functional, timeless family structure."[19] Historical, anthropological, and cross-cultural studies of family reveal a multitude of family structures. To speak of *the* family is to belie this fact. To assume that one structure, one set of relationships is appropriate to varying times, cultures, ethos, and circumstances is to assume that time, place, ethos, culture, and circumstance make no difference to human projects. It is to assume, in Roycean terms, that one "form of loyalty" is the best; it is to absolutize the finite. Exalting a single family model is to impose a value judgment on varied human efforts to adapt their caring to difficult and different circumstances.

The invalidity and dangers of a single focus model of family can be illustrated in several ways. Judith Stacey, for example, in a study of white working-class families in the Silicon Valley argues that the Archie Bunker, white working-class stereotype is inaccurate and morally dangerous in portraying a false expectation for both males and females, especially by painting this class as "racist" and "reactionary."[20] Indeed, in her own study, she found a variety of family patterns of marriage, divorce, and rearrangement, including divorce-kin networks of former spouses and relatives. Only 11 percent conformed to the model called "the modern family," namely, male breadwinner, female housewife, and children.[21] She writes: "Family arrangements found among blue collar people in the Silicon Valley are at least as diverse and innovative as those found in the middle class."[22] Stacy believes that the supposed model of the "modern family" has stereotyped and made life difficult for African-American women as well as white working mothers, both of whom have crafted untraditional kinship-family structures: "African-American women and white, working-class women have been the genuine postmodern family pioneers, even though they have suffered most. . . ."[23]

Patricia Ann Collins argues that feminist and family theorists have failed African-American women in their failure to challenge the controlling images of "mammy," "matriarch," and "welfare mother," and in their neglect of essential aspects of African-American families.[24] She argues that one must honor these mothers by "developing an Afrocentric feminist analysis of Black motherhood."[25] In her excellent analysis, Collins argues that "the institution of Black motherhood consists of a series of constantly negotiated relationships"; it is an institution that is both dynamic and dialectic.[26] Collins highlights five themes relative to "Black motherhood." One is the centrality of "blood mother," other mother, and women-centered networks, that is, networks of aunts, grandmothers, sisters, cousins. These networks, incidentally, do not negate male roles; indeed, contrary to much belief, fathers may play a central role in the family.[27] Another crucial theme for understanding this revolutionary form of family is that of socialization for survival. Collins provides us with the following statement by Gloria Wade-Gayles:

> Black mothers do not socialize their daughters to be "passive" or "irrational." Quite the contrary, they socialize their daughters to be independent, strong and self-confident. Black mothers are suffocatingly protective and domineering precisely because they are determined to mold their daughters into whole and self-actualizing persons in a society that devalues Black women.[28]

Collins and others argue that part of the socialization for survival for Black children is the dominant theme of "providing a better chance," a vision of transcending, accompanied by an affirmation of the value of work as part of an ethic of caring and personal accountability.[29] Collins, in her analysis of Black motherhood, ties in the network of other mothers with community and political activism. She also sees motherhood as a symbol of power because "Black women's involvement in fostering African-American community development forms the basis for community-based power."[30] Finally, she deals with the "costs" of Black-motherhood, which include isolation, stifling of creativity, and much work and sorrow.[31]

The excellent literature on African-American mothers, as well as Stacey's Silicon Valley study, highlights several important aspects of family that cannot be neglected. One of these concerns the myth of family boundaries. This, in fact, is another of the five themes identified by Thorne as part of feminist rethinking of the family. The nuclear family model, Thorne argues, is a "distorting ideological construct, that 'maps' the function of 'nuturance' onto a collectivity of specific persons (presumably nuclear relationships) associated with specific spaces ('the home') and specific objective bonds ('love')."[32] The extensive "other mothers" and black-women's networks and the ex-family networks in the Silicon Valley belie a set of "fixed family boundaries" and "sets of relationships." The concept of fluid or extended family boundaries has ramifications also for our images of children. Black-mother networks, for example, challenge the assumption of children as private property.[33]

Another example of family boundary extension today that adds to our move toward openness is the phenomenon of gay families. In her book *Families We Choose*, and in an article, "The Politics of Gay Families,"[34] Kath Weston sees gay families as evidence of the adaptability of the notion of family and as a transforming of the discussion of family issues.

These families challenge the supposed monolithic model of family and its key elements: the question of boundaries, the issue of choice, the primacy of concepts of reproduction and procreation, and notions of mothering and fathering. Boundaries in gay families are fluid; there is "eclectic composition" and "little differentiation of erotic/nonerotic ties." Gay family networks are, says Weston, "friendship" networks, open to choice and thus more democratic. Because of the "choice" aspect, Weston argues, gay family networks are able "to encompass dissent and difference without denying difference."[35] The concept of choice brings us back to Elshtain's analysis of family and the question of authority in a democratic society. There is, says Elshtain, a vexing lack of congruence between political and familial modes of authority. The family is not, at least from a traditional view, voluntary. Elshtain writes, "A strong version of the liberal ideal of 'free' consent from birth was deeply problematic, given the nature of human infants."[36] Later in the chapter, we will deal with the issue of freedom and choice in the family. The very question nevertheless challenges any set notion of family.

The whole challenge of the primacy of the notion of reproduction raised by gay families, as well as new forms of reproductive technologies is another issue to be addressed later. However, Weston's summary of the challenge presented by gay families is worth quoting:

> Gay families have not incorporated the chronological succession implicit in the Anglo-European notion of genealogical descent. Although chosen families can incorporate biological symbolism through child-bearing and adoption, the children raised in gay families are not expected to be-

come gay or form gay families of their own. Following the principle of choice, the kind of families these children establish should depend on their own sexual identity and whether they establish families at all should be left to their discretion.

. . . chosen families do not directly oppose genealogical modes of reckoning kinship. Instead they undercut procreation's status as a master term imagined to provide the template for all possible kinship relations.[37]

This brings us to another theme Thorne identifies as part of feminist rethinking of family, which we also find central to an analysis of family, namely, the glorification of single concepts of motherhood or fatherhood.[38] Nancy Chodorow and Susan Contralto explicate a "deadly" notion of motherhood that they believe has dominated feminist and nonfeminist writing and that they call the "Fantasy of the Perfect Mother."[39] This fantasy involves the concept of an "all-powerful mother," a sense of mother as totally responsible for the outcomes of their mothering.[40] This concept leads to two dangerous tendencies. The first focuses on aggressiveness and omnipotence in the mother-child relationship leading to the conclusion, cited earlier, that mothers are "noxious to their children" and that "mothering is disastrous for society."[41] In fact, argue Chodorow and Contralto, certain themes emerge from this prong of the mother fantasy: (1) the blaming of mother as destroyer; (2) the extreme expectations of maternal sexuality leading to an assumed incompatibility between motherhood and female sexual fulfillment; (3) the link between motherhood and aggression and death; and (4) an emphasis on the isolation of mother and child.[42] This exemplification of the fantasy of motherhood is summarized by Chodorow and Contralto as follows: "Mother and child are both seen as victims. . . . Having a child can kill a woman or make her into a murderer. . . . Mother and child seem caught in a fantasized exclusive and exclusionary dyad where frustration and rage hold sway."[43]

The other consequence of "the fantasy of motherhood" is the image of "maternal perfectibility." Again, the emphasis is on the total responsibility of mother. This image of the perfect mother comes from the nineteenth century but remains dominant for many today. The ideal mother "guarantees both morally perfect children and a morally desirable world."[44] Mother is to make the home a "haven in a heartless world."[45] The mother-child relationship becomes central to the development of the child, but even more for the benefit of the whole society. Children must have good mother care; maternal deprivation is noxious to good moral development. Thus, mothers are urged to "stay home full time."[46] Further, it was assumed that good mothering came naturally, with a little help, of course, from experts like Dr. Spock.[47] This image of the perfect mother, like the negative image of all-powerful mother, idealizes motherhood, expects too much and emphasizes an isolated mother/child dyad.

Both images are distorted and dangerous. They are reductionistic, deterministic, and absolutizing of the finite. They project narrow and unrealistic images and expectations about mother and mother-child relations. These images ignore the role of others, including males, in nurturance. We need to reenvision the family and to rethink the notion of fatherhood. Sarah Ruddick examines the "official story" of fatherhood, which includes contradictory and distorting elements.[48] On the one hand, this story tells us that fathers are necessary ingredients both of childhood and good-enough mothering. Heterosexual mothers will sacrifice much to keep "barely good enough fathers" in the house. Psychoanalysts claim that children without fathers are "trapped with a preoedipal . . . maternal dyad."[49] Yet fathers, says the official story, are depressingly absent—dead, lost, or gone. They rarely assume a full share of the emotional work and the responsibility of child care. Fathers neither apologize nor worry if their jobs, hobbies, sports, fatigue, or personal ambition keep them from their children.[50]

Ruddick acknowledges elements of truth in this official story and that the history of fatherhood is inseparable from economic and domestic power. But, she argues, "we can't afford a fatherless world"; we must transform fatherhood.[51] The emphasis must be on attitude and relationship and on parenting or "mothering" as a gender-inclusive, genderless activity of child tending in which men and women engage.[52] Reminiscent of gay families and their challenge to the primacy of reproduction, Ruddick argues that female birthgiving is "neither necessary or sufficient for good enough mothering."[53] Mothering must be seen as a chosen project, one which is the case only if "she or he acts upon a social commitment to nurture, protect and train children."[54] Likewise, male procreation must come to be seen "as a chosen activity through which men create for themselves responsible and responsive ways and occasions for donating sperm."[55] In refashioning the concept of fatherhood and in concert with the emphasis on choice and commitment, Thomas W. Laquer reports on the case of a lesbian family in which one of the female partners was designated "father" on the birth certificate and was called by the court "the psychological father." In commenting on this case, Laquer writes: "What matters is that, in the emotional economy of her relationship with her lover and their child, she was the father, whatever that means, and enjoyed the rights and bore the obligations of that status. She invested the required emotional and imaginative capital in the impregnation, gestation and subsequent life to make that child in some measure hers."[56]

David Morgan, in arguing for a new approach to family theory and to the issue of fatherhood, wants to overcome the reduction of the father question to only two issues, namely, the marginality of men in families and the uncertainty of the parameters of fatherhood. He provides an excellent summary of these two issues and also gives us a good foundation for an expanded discussion of fatherhood and family. He identifies a number of issues worthy of extensive discussion.

First, there is a broad range of roles, statuses, and positions men may have in families: househusbands, stepfathers, adolescent fathers, widowers, grandfathers, brothers, and uncles, to list a few. Secondly, as indicated, the word *family* has a range of meanings, and distinctions are also important, such as those between *household* and *family*. Finally, in dealing with the issue of the role of men in families, the focus must not be just on domestic relations but must include consideration of other issues, such as work.[57]

We will have to rethink and refashion the concept of family and the related notions of motherhood and fatherhood. In doing so, we will reconsider some themes of this section. First, there is no monolithic, natural, biological, functional, timeless family model or structure. Secondly, neither fatherhood nor motherhood need be glorified, but, rather, there must be an emphasis on choice and commitment to particular kinds of attitudes and activities. Thirdly, family boundaries must be perceived as open and fluid, spanning biology, time, and place. Related to the question of boundaries is a fourth theme, namely, a refusal to dichotomize family and individuals on the public/private spectrum. Such a splitting isolates families and individuals from their necessary social context and ignores how the public impinges and intrudes on family and how family and individuals negotiate and bargain with social, economic, and political structures and systems of race, gender, ethnic, and class oppression to forge self- and family identities.[58] And underlying the deep ambivalence in discussion about family is the theme of individualism and community. Barrie Thorne writes: "The tension between individualism and community is basic to the politics of family change." Linda Gordon also highlights this individualism/community tension when she writes: "The task of feminism is to defend the positive gains of individualism and liberal feminism while transcending the capitalist-competitive aspects of individualism with a version of loving egalitarian communities."[59]

With these themes in mind, we turn now to a Roycean analysis of the family—with its possible function as "original community" and its formative crucible for building selves and communities.

The Family as "Formative Community"

Family life in the United States is being rethought, reformed, and refined. In July 1989, the high court of the State of New York expanded the legal definition of family in order to recognize "domestic partners" and to extend the privileges of rent control to gay couples. The court decision included this statement: "It is the totality of the relationship as evidenced by dedication, caring and self-sacrifice of the parties which should, in the final analysis, control the definition of the family."[60] The emphasis here is on the quality of the relationship and the commitment to that relationship. To make this even clearer, Judge Vito Titone provided four "judicial" criteria for determining what constitutes a family. They were: (1) the exclusivity and longevity of the relationship; (2) the level of emotional and financial commitment; (3) how a couple has "conducted their everyday lives and held themselves out to society;" and (4) the "reliance placed on one another for daily family services."[61]

This definition, it seems to me, appears to be going in the right direction in terms of the four themes of the previous section. It also fits with the Roycean perspectives on family that we now will explore. What, then, is meant by designating the family as "an original community, a formative crucible." First, as should be clear from our previous chapters, for Royce, individuals and communities need each other. Stable, unique selves develop out of a genuine communal context. Family, as original community, should provide the conditions that initiate the development of genuine unique selves. Royce, as we have seen, believes the human self-development process is crucial, as well as a complex and delicate one. We, of course, agree. What, then, does this process entail? First of all, there must be a commitment on the part of the community and the individuals in it to this process and a sense of loyalty to this cause. Sarah Ruddick states the point nicely when she writes: "We must create institutions and practices where men or women, whatever their personal coupling and connections, might join together in a collective commitment to nurture and cherish the procreative promise of their children."[62] This is the commitment we have seen as central to Black motherhood.

As a form of loyalty, this commitment takes individuals beyond themselves, for the loyalty is to an external cause, worthy in its own right. It is also, we recall, always a personal and internal commitment. Royce is clear that loyalty, if genuine, must be a matter of choice, must involve one's own project, one's own deep sense of self. Loren Lomasky, in developing a theory of rights, provides an interesting and new perspective on family that I believe helps clarify the Roycean notion of loyalty to family and to self-development. First, Lomasky develops a concept of self that he believes necessary to any person as a "rights-holder," namely, of self or person as "project pursuer." Lomasky defines *project* as "those ends which reach indefinitely into the future, play a central role within the ongoing endeavor of the individual and provide a sufficient degree of structural stability to an individual."[63] This understanding of self is, of course, very close to Royce's concept of self as "a plan of action." Using this notion of "project pursuit," Lomasky goes on to argue for family as the foundation for the development of a moral community and for grounding rights. First, he notes that having children is often an "integral part" of persons' projects. Loyalty to the cause of the genuine selfhood of one's children would, for Royce, if it is genuine, need to be of this "personal nature." It needs to be a matter of choice and commitment.

Secondly, Lomasky argues that personhood, in the sense needed for rights-holding and project pursuant, cannot be impersonal, for it involves respect and valuing; this, in turn, calls for recognition as a particular person. We recall that for Royce, love is the recognition of the unique individual, that is, this and no other. Lomasky writes:

> . . . the epistemological requirement for valuing particular persons is the ability to identify and reidentify them as distinct individuals. A can recognize and respond to value for

> B only if A is able to pick out the distinct individual that is
> B. . . . [A] continuous history is required. . . . Thus, the pos-
> sibility of ongoing social relations with individuals who are
> perceived as self-identical over time is a necessary condition
> for according them rights. . . . The establishment of net-
> works of social relationships among persons provides the
> raw material from which moral community is fashioned.[64]

Lomasky's thesis is that intimate association provides the firmest possible
epistemological basis for appreciation of individuality. The family is, argues
Lomasky, the earliest and most enduring pattern of intimate association.
Thus, the family, as the original moral community—one which "involves
complex and overlapping relationships in which people stand to each other
as distinct individuals"—is a crucial foundation for a "rights respecting
moral community;" it establishes children as "distinct project pursuers."[65]

Family, as original community, then, is a necessary "formative crucible"
for creating genuine individuals. In previous chapters, we have discussed various aspects of the formative conditions for genuine selves. Among these are
the need for interactive communicative processes that allow a subtle blend of
imitation and creativity, contrast and defiance; accommodation and nonaccommodation. Recall the work of Jessica Benjamin with her emphasis on a
balance of tension between self-assertion and self-recognition and upon mutual recognition and mutual independence. The child must be recognized as
an active participant in an experience, and the person, in the mother role, as
independent person. Benjamin asserts, "the recognition the child seeks is
something only mother can give by virtue of her independent activity."[66]
The family must function as a genuine community that loves and respects
the self of each as of unique worth, recognizing that the contribution of each
is essential to the overall project of the family. Children and parents must
treat each other as valued, unique selves.

This emphasis on respect of each as a genuine individual is fully consistent with Royce's notion of family as an important form of loyalty. First, as
indicated, loyalty involves choice and personal commitment. This, in turn,
requires some sense of self as a project pursuer and the commitment to family as part of one's own project. Secondly, loyalty is not, for Royce, either
self-sacrifice nor pure benevolence. Loyalty requires independence, decisiveness, courage, concern for self as project pursued. And it is commitment to

a particular cause, to the particular good—in this case, to the development of this particular individual child.

In emphasizing family's responsibility for engendering genuine individuals, one must not forget Royce's equal stress on its community-building function, on its embodiment of the principle of loyalty to loyalty. It must be concerned to urge each self to expand and transcend its limited, finite perspective. The sin of pride, of rampant individualism, of limited perspective was, for Royce, a real danger for any community, including the family.

In this regard, family therapist Gaylin argues that there are three tropisms that dominate our contemporary American ethos and thus help create the present dilemma of family. These work against families. All three are related to Royce's concern for overcoming self-isolation. The first is the notion, which Gaylin finds dominant in much behavioral science, particularly in Freudian psychology, of a natural opposition between the human individual's freedom and society.[67] Royce clearly opposes this view with his understanding of the mutuality of genuine individualism and genuine community. Gaylin's two other tropisms are procentism (our preoccupation with the immediate) and egocentrism (our self-centeredness).[68] This is why, in Royce's view at least, family needs to be concerned about self-expansion and self-transcendence.

Royce advocates two interrelated approaches to self-expansion that address Gaylin's tropisms directly: to see self and community as process and as story maker. The Roycean self, we recall, is an "interpreter," a story maker who weaves together her "story," a unity of past, present, and future, which is coherent, yet open-ended and ongoing. Likewise, the community allows members to transcend their individual stories by building a common story, common memory, common values, and common hope. Storytelling, myth, play, and ritual are, for Royce, crucial to self-identity and self-transcendence. Stories and play allow self to assume roles, to identify with others while also forging a self-identity. Play, for Royce, we recall, unifies the various aspects of self while also relating self to "common" rules.

Douglas Gunn, another family therapist, is much in concert with Royce's views when he argues for family identity creation through role activity and storytelling.[69] Gunn cites the work of Erik Erikson to point out two crucial aspects of identity formation, namely, a feeling of well-being with oneself and a feeling of acceptance in the community.[70] Likewise, argues Gunn, a family needs a sense of identity, a feeling of well-being with oneself as well a context in the wider community.[71] Further, says Gunn, family-identity cre-ation, particularly through family storytelling "impinges upon all members of the family." It is a particular manner and style of parent-child interaction, teaching concepts of right, wrong, responsibility, and proper interaction with other people.[72]

The storytelling, advocates Gunn, also benefits adults, for it builds kin-dred relationships, as do family rituals.[73] It expands time and space by in-volving various generations of the family, including those who are dead. It builds trust in kindred, thus making personal resources available to family members. The importance of kin, even "fictive kin" such as Black other-mothers, has already been hinted at in our earlier discussions of Sili-con Valley ex-family networks, Black-American networks, and gay families. "Kin building" is an important part of family identity building, as well as supplying a supportive network. It also plays a role in self-expansion because it brings individuals into contact with a wide range of perspectives and even conflict of views.

In an interesting study of Italian-American families in Northern Califor-nia,[74] Micaela D. Leonard discusses the extensive kinship work done by women of all class, such as visits, letters, phone calls, sending cards and pre-sents, and organizing holidays. This work, she says, is characterized simulta-neously by cooperation and competition, guilt and gratification. Further, these kin-centered networks are sources of power, sites of emotional fulfill-ment, and, at times, "vehicles for actual survival and political resistance."[75] Kin building certainly is a form of community building, as well as identity building, and steps need to be taken to value and support such work, even though it is not wage labor. Modern technology, the computer and linked communication networks, for instance, can contribute to this type of kin building. For example, a number of grandparents are maintaining contact with grandchildren through e-mail and the WorldWideWeb Networks. Videotapes and phone conferencing are other ways of building kinship. This is especially important today when families are geographically separated.

In addition to storytelling and kin work, Gunn identifies some other family identity-creation activities, including photographing events and link-ing them to stories; identifying mementos, like watches and furniture, and giving them a story; and presenting tradition as rituals and as distinctive ways of doing things. In summary, Gunn writes: "The key to such a family identity lies in transforming the bric-a-brac of the past—the genealogies, rituals, and anecdotes—into a family story that unites the present generation with its past and that reveals patterns, themes, and motifs by which a family can recognize the unity of its life.[76] To have one's own story also adds to family value and meaning. Families, churches, and schools should encourage "family narrative" and the sharing of the narrative within family and with others. Daycare centers, especially for latchkey children, might find this a valuable exercise for building a sense of identity and self-worth for these children and their families. Employers could also encourage this through "family bulletin boards" and other events, thus strengthening family as well as breaking down the false public-private dichotomy of home and workplace.

Royce was well aware of these aspects of building family identity and self-expansion. He himself was concerned about telling his own family story, and he encouraged his mother to do this also.[77] As indicated earlier, he gave high priority to literature, play, and storytelling in children's lives. He was also an extensive letter writer with a large network of family members and friends.[78] As we know, Royce was keenly aware of the importance of religion in establishing family identity and community, as well as self-transcendence.[79] A main family ritual in the Royce family was daily family Bible reading. He was also aware of the key role of ethnicity and language in cementing identity, as well as expanding self through multicultural experiences. We will discuss this aspect of Royce's thought in our chapter on education. Again, sharing family stories with different racial, cultural, and ethnic bases, in a school or work or church setting, could help build tolerance and understanding.

Before moving on to family, as "interpretive, mediating community," I would like to make three summary points. First, because of the centrality of storytelling, myth-making, and ritual to self- and family identity, it is imperative that those who deal with families and individuals as outside helpers respect and utilize these aspects if possible. I will discuss this point further in the sections on education and medicine. Secondly, one must also view self and family as a summative, yet ongoing temporal process, reflective of and embodying time, place, and context and yet transcending them in significant ways. This view, I believe, will be more fruitful for both understanding and supporting individuals and their families. One implication of this, of course, is that the proper unit of analysis or concern is never just the individual as isolated unit. Individuals are always both embedded and transcendent. Two recent approaches to family seem on the right track in this regard. The first is family process therapy, which sees family as a "unity of interacting personalities," as an "ongoing, open, social system" whose qualities grow "out of relationships among the parts." Family process is seen as "a complex set of interconnected positive and negative feedback loops that provide stability (*homeostasis*) and change (*morphogenesis*)."[80]

The second promising approach to family therapy and study is family-interpretive methodology, which brings a "gendered understanding" to all social and cultural life by focusing on women's different symbolic and metaphoric responses to sociohistoric changes in family life. This method focuses on women as "active participants in creating their own social realities," and on "everyday actions and underlying patterns of meaning."[81] I would suggest that this approach can be expanded to males, as well as different generations. It also seems closely related to Royce's emphasis on "interpretation" as a key form of knowledge.

A final point needs to be made about family as "formative community." *Motherhood, fatherhood,* and *family* all might be more fruitfully viewed in terms of an attitude of care and commitment. Indeed, *family* is most commonly defined as a group of people who love and care for each other. The definition of *family* by the New York court is refreshing and encouraging, given the trend of other courts, especially in surrogate-motherhood and custody cases, to define *family* in strictly biological terms.

For Royce, the type of attitude brought to a situation is a key aspect of relationships. For example, loyalty is basically an attitude, a motivation governed by the principle of loyalty to loyalty. Likewise, for family, the key is the commitment of each individual to promoting the growth of "genuine" individuals and "genuine communities." In this regard, I find much hope and support in an approach to early childhood and parent education known by a variety of terms—confluent education, filial relationship enhancement, transpersonal education, and people teaching.[82] The term *people teaching* refers to "any effort which helps children and adults learn more about their humanity and acquire the skills necessary to live harmoniously with others."[83] This method emphasizes four areas, all of which are exactly congruent with Royce's understanding of the human self and self-development. These are (1) body awareness, which includes an accurate body concept, physical acceptance, body integration and dealing with issues such as sexism, racism, age bias, birth, and death; (2) sensory awareness, especially providing experiences that nurture all sensory capabilities; (3) emotional development, which includes awareness, identification, and communication and the understanding and appreciation of fantasy and imagination; and (4) affiliation and friendship, which includes developing a perspective on human association that deals with conflict/cooperation and kindness and affection, and with forming and negotiating relationships. Solitary and group play are both emphasized.[84] This type of education should be fostered in every avenue and area possible, not only in schools but in churches, in the workplace, and at every level of human development, from young children to senior citizens.

The Family as Interpreting and Mediating Structure

There is little doubt that for Royce one of the most important tools for building self, community, and family was interpretation, a third key mode of knowledge. Interpretation has been discussed in the previous chapters, but a brief review for this context is important. There are three central elements to interpretation. All three involve a set of moral commitments. The first ethical element is respect and regard for each self and idea involved. This includes self-respect and respect for others. Thus, families need to believe in the moral worth of each member—male and female, child and elder, the average and the achiever, the handicapped and the able bodied.

The second ethical element of interpretation is the will to interpret, which involves both humility and a desire to expand self and perspective. Humility allows recognition of each person's limited and partial perspective and meaning, which, in turn, calls for expansion of self, a seeking of contact with the ideas and perspectives of others. Royce believed humans have a natural need for fulfillment and something wider. Certainly children exhibit a natural curiosity and imaginative expansion. What is needed in family is a moral commitment to provide conditions of stimulation that encourage each member to reach out to higher and broader levels of meaning: physical, emotional, intellectual, imaginative, sensory. Here, people teaching is very much on the right track.

The third ethical element in interpretation is reciprocity and mutuality, a willingness to take part in the process with trust and good faith. This involves a moral commitment to reach out to others, to open oneself to communication. The process requires both respect and trust. One willingly tries to understand what is significant to the other and tests one's ideas against the ideas of others. This is not an easy task for isolated, fearful individuals, and here is where the continual interaction of community and individual building becomes clear. Community building on a small scale leads to self-transcendence and the overcoming of fear and isolation. This is why family identity building is so important; it provides community affirmation and self-affirmation, which, in turn, leads to self-respect and a sense of security. With this, risk taking with others becomes more likely.

Family process therapy provides an interesting highlight to this key Roycean concept of interaction of individual and community with its focus on family as an interactive system and on feedback. These therapists see feedback in terms of a circular process and reflexive effects: one family member's actions have consequences that will feed back on and influence his or her own actions, as well as those of other members of the family. Thus, a positive feedback loop increases the possibility of escalating or repeating a behavior, while a negative feedback loop reduces the probability of repetition or escalation.[85] An interesting example of this notion also illustrates Royce's interpretive process: brother pulls sister's hair; sister goes to mother rather than pulling hair in return and escalating the behavior; mother asks the boy, as she pulls his hair, "See how it feels to have your hair pulled. Did you like it? Would you want your sister to do this to you?"[86] This interpretive act helps the sibling transcend the experience to a new level of meaning. The negative feedback also reduces the probability of repeated behavior on the part of the boy.

This example also helps us highlight a crucial feature of Royce's doctrine of interpretation, namely, to develop a cooperative form of mediation between what he called dyadic dangerous pairs. In *War and Insurance* where this idea is developed extensively, Royce, in a seeming reconciliation of a Hobbesian view of aggressive man and a human view of a natural human sympathy, declares that "By nature, man both loves and hates his neighbor."[87] Human individuals, says Royce, both nourish and inflame each other; one cannot do without the other; but when together there is often a quarrel, for each has a different quest or interest. Royce writes: "*the dyadic, the dual, the bilateral relations of man and man, of each man to his neighbor, are relations fraught with social danger. A pair of men is what I call a dangerous community.*"[88]

Indeed, in line with family process therapy, Royce notes that "when mutual friction once arises between a pair of lovers or of rivals or of individuals otherwise interestingly related . . . *the friction tends to increase,* unless some other relation intervenes. . . ."[89] The resolution of the tension depends, for Royce, on establishing a new and creative social tie between them, an enrichment of the community beyond the two.[90] What is needed is an inter-preter B whose task is to interpret A's interests to C and B's interests to A, thereby creating, making conscious, and carrying out a common or united will. If successful, C will create, sustain, and increase harmony between A and B.[91] In the hairpulling case, this is what the mother attempts to do. The interpreter, says Royce, has the function "*to transform the essentially danger-ous pair into the consciously and consistently harmonious triad.*"[92] Royce calls the interpreter the "Spirit of the Community."[93]

Royce was very concerned about family conflict. For example, he dis-cussed extensively, in *The Problem of Christianity*, the biblical story of Jacob's family and the familial estrangement and reconciliation of Joseph and his brothers.[94] Further, Royce clearly sees the family as a "community of inter-pretation," each member—whether father, mother, child, or, in today's changing milieu, significant others, including grandparents, gay partners, other mothers—playing the role of interpreter/mediator. Indeed, for Royce, the commitment to bring children into a family involves an act of interpre-tation, an act of loyalty, a trans-evaluation of values, a creation of a tie or bond that represents a third and creates an important triad.

Royce, in fact, uses the family's three basic relationships to talk about three species of loyalty.[95] The three basic relationships are: between friends, spouses, or lovers; between siblings; and between parent and child. These re-lationships provide the occasion for "dangerous dyads" and quarrels, for me-diation and interpretation, and for loyalty. Because we have already dealt with siblings conflict, we will begin there. Frank Oppenheim points out that, for Royce, each sister and brother are called upon to emphasize and respect the other's equal freedom and autonomy. If a brother or sister respects the in-dependence of other siblings, both will enjoy physical and psychological "free space." Both need this if each one's self-development is not to be diminished by or interfered with by other siblings. Sibling loyalty, then, is to the cause of creating adequate free space needed by the other.[96] In a family, of course, others—for example, mother, father, grandparent—could also serve as medi-ators and demonstrate loyalty to free space and to family harmony.

The loyalty involved between lovers, friends, or spouses, for Royce, is to goodness or happiness. In Oppenheim's words, "Friends, spouses, lovers, ful-fill their basic need when they share happiness continuously. Nevertheless, this kind of goodness can arise only if their love either grows constantly without estrangement or overcomes estrangements that arise."[97] In terms of lovers, spouses, friends, I prefer to think of love as "mutuality." Mutuality involves a *sharing* of each other, seeking in imaginative, creative, active ways to please and give to the other, as well as to create a harmony of interests. Like a good symphony, there is mutual harmony, support, assistance, growth, and exaltation.[98] Like Royce, John Dewey also uses the term *goodness* to describe love: "Love . . . is the resolute purpose in each to seek the others' good, or rather to seek a common good which can only be attained through a common life. . . ."[99]

As for parent-child relationships, these can result in what Royce calls "the conflict of successive generations." The loyalty needed in this case is to the bond of generations. It involves a duty to transmit and receive life, in all its levels. There must be communication and understanding of physical, affective, socio-cultural, intellectual, moral, and religious life, as well as transmission of the refined wisdom of previous generations. Parents, argues Royce, must both transmit and hopefully enhance family, as well as cultural, social wisdom.[100] Involved here again is building the "family story," but it goes beyond that. One of the roles of parents, and even of children, is also to mediate and interpret between family and society, with its various institutions, as well as between family and other families and households. In this regard, kinship networks, mostly created and used by women, as we have seen, are really the work of mediation and interpretation. This is certainly the case with Black mothers who engage in a series of constantly renegotiated relationships in order to "mold and benefit systems of race, gender and class oppression" and thus create empowerment for themselves and their children.[101]

Men and women have played mediating and interpreting roles between their families and the larger community. This history needs to be brought to visibility so that we can discover mechanisms that support and enhance successful mediation and interpretation and thus bring needed support to family growth and development.[102] In our complex society, we may need to create a group of "family advocates," concerned individuals outside of the social institutional structure, not formally employed to work with families or individuals in families, who can help families build community, create their own stories and tell them to others, who can mediate between dangerous dyads in the family as well as between family and institutional structures. Senior citizens could be trained for such a role. This would enhance their status as well as help build community and families. They could perform this role within institutions also. They could become "interpreters" and "mediators."

Interpretation and loyalty are, of course, difficult tasks requiring moral commitment and skill. Frank Oppenheim has described, in some detail, Royce's explication of what he called the "art of loyalty."[103] In his extension course on ethics, Royce used two contrasting cases of alienation between a mother and a child. One concerned an already alienated son and an up-braiding that occurred in such a sharp manner that final estrangement resulted in the son's suicide. The other case involved the discovery by a daughter of a mother's theft of funds in order to provide for her education. I recommend a careful reading of Oppenheim's discussion of this latter case.[104] Loyalty, Royce argues, always involves the search for more light without foreclosing possibilities; it requires flexibility, patience, attention to the present, enough light to move to the next step, and a determination to counter any urge for quick resolution.[105] Most important is maintaining the conditions for continuing dialogue and leaving open all possibilities so that eventual healing of the estrangement might occur.[106]

In drawing to a close, it is clear that Royce's philosophy provides many fruitful perspectives on family and family issues. Above all, we find that loyalty to family and all that it represents is a highly demanding one, requiring patience, openness, imagination, concerted action, and courage. The fulfillment possible in achieving a genuine and healthy family more than compensates for the effort, the grief, the sacrifice, for it represents a goodly portion of our own individual sense of worth, meaning, and fulfillment.

Above all, in working for 'family', whether our own or others, let us neither idealize nor condemn a form of family, but work toward families that overcome self-sufficient exclusion and conflict to become, in different measures, "genuine communities" that create "genuine, loving individuals." Arlene Skolnick captures some of my belief in this regard when she writes, "If we care about children, we need to focus less on the form of families they live in and more on ways of supporting their well-being in all kinds of families."[107] However, one can also express a hope for a brave new world such as described by Judith Stacey: "In the postmodern period, a truly democratic gender and kinship order, one that does not favor male authority, heterosexuality, a particular division of labor, or a singular household or parenting arrangement becomes thinkable for the first time in history."[108] Again, it is not so much the form as the ethical substance of the relationship involved. Further, as we move forward to the future, may our attitude be one of a deep sense of fallibility and humility, humor, patience, critical wisdom, and courageous commitment.

Education

A New Paradigm of Self and Knowing

"Everything has changed but our ways of thinking and, if these do not change, we drift toward unparalleled catastrophe."
—Albert Einstein

"The mind is meant to expand in a series of ever-larger concentric circles, taking in new perspectives to supplement and clarify the meaning of earlier ones."
—Benjamin Barber

"How are we to make the most of the new values we set on variety, difference, and individuality . . . how are we going to realize their possibility in every field, and at the same time not sacrifice the plurality to the cooperation we need so much? How can we bring things together as we must without losing sight of plurality."
—John Dewey

"The most precious moment in human development is the young creature's assertion that he is unlike any other human being and has an individual contribution to make to the world. . . ."
—Jane Addams

Education: Critique and Crisis

THERE IS probably not a more crucial set of issues for a public philosophy than those concerning education. First of all, education, like the institution of the family, shapes the lives of almost every individual and community and in profoundly significant ways. Secondly, universal public

129

education is believed to be fundamental to adequate democratic citizenship.[1] Thirdly, education is also assumed by many in the United States to be the key to individual social mobility and economic success as well as to the competitive, economic health and well-being of the nation.[2]

Yet the educational system in the United States has been under a steady critical assault for an extended period of time, with numerous books and studies calling for educational reform.[3] Already in 1971, Ivan Illich, his book *Deschooling Society*, raised devastatingly critical questions about the failure and validity of universal public education.[4] In 1983, the National Commission on Excellence in Education published a national report entitled *A Nation at Risk: The Imperative for Educational Reform*.[5]

In spite of all the criticism and scrutiny, however, the result, to many, appears fruitless. There is, in fact, a very strong feeling of deja vu in the United States about educational issues. Educators often speak in terms of "cycles," an indicator of a view of history in which there is no progress, only repetitive recurrences. The feeling of "having heard this before" is probably best exemplified in the twenty-fifth-anniversary issue of *Change* magazine. This issue features articles on education that have appeared throughout the period 1969–1994. A number of these articles present contemporary-sounding themes. In a 1971 article, for instance, we read, ". . . the combination of a general economic crisis and a sharp loss of public confidence . . . appears to have brought the whole field [education] under the most searching public, political and internal scrutiny."[6] This statement could easily have been written today.

As in the past, there is today dissatisfaction in the United States with the education system. For instance, one issue among many stirs strong voices in favor of moving away from public support of education to a system of educational vouchers that would allow parents to make choices about the schools their children would attend. Extending, or complementing, the example are private corporations now spending large sums of money on education for their employees, and even founding educational institutions.

In looking at the situation in education, I believe we need to focus on the following points. First, like the family, because of its central role in individual personal development as well as its important function in social, cultural, and economic articulation, education has, and probably will continue to take on, the burden of being the scapegoat for individual and social frustration in a time of change and turmoil. Secondly, like the family and parenting, we have placed on the institution of education highly unrealistic expectations. For example, today, we expect education to deal with dysfunctional families and parenting, the drug and teenage pregnancy problem, and the problem of escalating violence in families, particularly among youths. Thirdly, in spite of the many positive features within our system of education and the real attempts at reform of weaknesses, paradigm assumptions are distorting efforts to deal with the important issues of knowledge, pedagogical authority, and "canons" of content and subject matter. This paradigm "absolutizes the finite" as well as commits the sin of perspectivism. Further, the paradigm hinders change and leads to feelings of the "same old stuff again."

It is the prominent paradigm of education that I shall address in what follows, drawing on the insights of Josiah Royce, as well as my own twenty-five years experience as an educator and as a parent of children who have both suffered and benefited from their educational experiences. In addressing the paradigm issues, I will discuss education in terms of what I take to be its primary function, a function it shares with the family, but which it greatly supplements, namely, giving individuals the tools to be "genuine" individuals who are able to live unique, personally satisfying, functional lives in a rapidly changing, technological, and democratic society. I find the following statement of Benjamin R. Barber fairly close to summarizing what I also believe should be the goals of an educational system in our contemporary U.S. democratic society. He writes:

> The fundamental task of education in a democracy is the apprenticeship of liberty—learning to be free . . . to learn how to sculpt individuality . . . and to participate in a democratic community.[7]

Barber also lists the following skills as important to the task of learning to be both a unique individual and a functional member of a democratic community: to think critically, to act deliberately, to have empathy, to hear others, to accommodate others, to think historically, and to have virtues.[8] I, too, find these skills very important, and I will address each of these as our discussion of education proceeds.

In what follows, we will critically analyze the paradigm dominant in education in America. Then we will explicate a new paradigm that includes notions of education as building a community of learning, teaching as a process of interpretation, and the classroom as an "enlightened province." We shall also deal with some of the central issues of education being discussed today, namely "parental involvement and authority," "multi-culturalism and political correctness," "technology and new pedagogy," "assessment and accountability," and "teaching vis-à-vis research."

Education's Problematic Paradigm:
Too Thin a Self, Too Small A Human

Among the unexamined foundational assumptions of education is a view of the human self/human person that is too thin and too small, that is, a reductionistic focus on the cognitive/intellectual, competitive, atomistic, individualistic self. It is the self who is perceived as naturally free, endowed with inalienable rights against the community; a self-reliant, self-interested self who enters social relations contractually and who needs the skills and competence to play "competitive" games adequately in the real world. It is the rational economic self who sees "rational" individual behavior in terms of the "highest payoffs."[9] Involved with this paradigm of self are two fundamental aspects of our contemporary American ethos, identified in our chapter on family, namely, *proscentism* (our preoccupation with the immediate) and *egocentrism* (our self-centeredness).[10]

Closely interlinked with the traditional view of the cognitive, individualistic self is a "pale" vision of learning and knowledge seeking as an individualistic, lonely pursuit, involving mastery of neutral methodologies and skills and the passive grasping of objective truths. The passive-knowing self model has led to traditional beliefs and practices that, I believe, have seriously hampered what we take to be fundamental goals of education: building genuine individuality and community. Ultimately, that model has harmed countless students in their pursuit of worthwhile life projects. One of the practices instituted by the passive-knowing self model is the traditional lecture-textbook mode of instruction, whose goal is the transmission of knowledge as content. It has made students into note takers, memory experts, and regurgitators. It has reinforced the notion of teacher with her textbook as all-knowing expert, ruler of subject matter and classroom. It has helped lead students to boredom, rebellion, and dropping out.

The cognitive-self, passive-knowledge-seeker model also grounds the emphasis on method, means, and skills as the key to educational success. It ignores motivation, attitude, and character. The cognitive model also leads us to overvalue factual collection, statistical and technological manipulation of data, and the heuristics of cookie-cutter patterns of decision making. We are generally taught that methods are neutral, unbiased, and productive of clear, certain answers. This ignores the fact that methods and skills as used by humans are used selectively—so well demonstrated in Daniel Hough's *How to Lie With Statistics*.[11] Recent developments in the philosophy of science have clearly demonstrated that science and its methodology are products of time, place, context, and human selectivity.[12] Further, emphasis on methodology and skills means they are taught as divorced from questions of relevance, context, and goals. Yet, these questions are precisely the ones to be asked and explored if our methods and skills are to be successful in life where complexity, ambiguity, and uncertainty are predominantly present.

And this emphasis on the cognitive-passive knower armed with methods and skills leads to that third crucial aspect of our contemporary American ethos, namely *technocentrism* (our faith that science and technology can solve all our problems).[13] Sadly, the traditional model of self and knowledge also leads to our fairly unfruitful approach to computer technology in education, namely, seeing it in terms of skills practice and enhancement, and as a means of access to data and information. Such an approach blinds us to the value of computer technology as an effective community-building tool. We are ignoring the Internet's greatest attraction—for human conversation and human-to-human contact rather than for gathering information from data banks.[14]

Another consequence of the emphasis on the passive-knowing self and on the transmission model of education is a general neglect in education—not by all, by any means—of the learning process. Pedagogy has typically focused on the "how to" of transmission, that is, on the transmitter rather than on the receiver, the student. Fortunately, there are those who have and are giving attention to the learning process and who are concerned about the interface between quality teaching and quality learning.[15] Along with the transmission-lecture-textbook syndrome comes the model of teacher-authority-expert, ruler of the classroom. Communication of content and methodology is important in the classroom, but that often dictates the inordinate value assigned the knowledge-expert. Thus teaching as a process has been little studied and little valued. Likewise, moves toward assessment of teaching effectiveness or of the learning process continue an uphill battle. Unfortunately the public demand for assessment is equally mislead by the dominant paradigm, and, thus, the system continues to stress content and skills, particularly those related to competitive and economic success.

The twin models of self and knowing in education, as we have indicated, are highly reductionistic. The focus is on the cognitive self with general neglect of other aspects of the full-fledged human being. This leads to unfortunate hierarchical devaluation of important aspects of self that do have a place in education and should not be squeezed out by economic considerations or supposed priorities of time. Rather they should become an integrated part of a curriculum that stresses the intimate connection between intellectual, moral, and affective development. For example, we need to re-examine the role of play, music, dance, art, and sports in education at all levels. Rather than "frills" or "frivolities," these may be central to fuller human development, as our discussion of Royce's work has already indicated. Imagination and creativity has been stifled in too many students, as some of the "right brain" advocates have demonstrated.[16] Each of these—play, music, dance, sports—can function as self-expanders and community builders. On the sports issue, one recalls also Royce's caution about attention development, that "natural" play be allowed sufficient nurturing before actual organized athletic events are stressed. Further, the competitive, economic motive has too quickly overshadowed what Novak refers to as the "rooting" and "enhumanment" aspects of sports.[17] More will be said about that later in this chapter.

In higher education, this ignoring of the emotion/body/mind relationship has led to the traditional and unexamined split between "academic affairs" and "student affairs," a clear cognitive-personal split, which separates curricular and extra-curricular college life—the classroom from residential life, student government, fraternal life, and community service. This division is also hierarchical; it divides the "real" business of the university and "mere housekeeping," the "cognitive work of the faculty at the top and the staff's affective work at the bottom."[18] This is a subtle version of the "public-private" split in family life and in the work world. These separations appear highly questionable in light of new research indicating an intimate connection between intellectual, moral, and affective development. And, after all, human persons are not easily separated into these arbitrary splits. Research also shows that students learn faster and are more likely to continue their education when they find a "home" in academia, that is, when they find ways to link up their experiences inside and outside the classroom.[19]

An even more disturbing cognitive-personal split is between the "academic" and professional/vocational, and between "academic life" and "life." This has led, in many secondary school systems, to separate but not equal academic paths—the college-bound and those "others." Messages about personal esteem and about the value of various occupational paths or life possibilities sent by this split have caused all kinds of personal and social damage. Convinced that knowledge and method transmission were neutral and objective, it also led, until recently, to the disdainful ignoring of cultural, ethnic, gender, class contexts for learning and knowledge creation. Knowledge, as we now know, is partially a "social construction," and the knowledge seeker and knowledge learner must be dealt with as persons with "perspectives" that need to be respected and incorporated and transcended into broader perspective.

The academic-professional/personal split in higher education has taken a somewhat different but nevertheless insidious form. "Academic," conceived on the model of the cognitive-knowing self, is a knowledge-seeking life, focused on research, theory, method, and information. "Academic community" becomes "discipline community," with separation of knowledge, methods, and views of the self and human experience. Thus the self is "known" as biological, physical, psychological, sociological, or even more specifically, as genetic, behavioral, neural-chemical. Further, faculty are trichotomized into researchers, teachers, and community servers. Each activity is rewarded on the basis of its closeness to the cognitive-knower model—research as knowledge-seeking, teaching as knowledge transmission, and community service as non-knowledge-producing. Faculty, following the belief in the lecture-mode of instruction, are encouraged to be "expert" transmitters of knowledge in the classroom and passive or non-participants in students' lives. This, of course, flies in the face of the fact that students cite as the most significant influence on their lives those full-blooded caring teachers, and not content or skills learned. As Royce affirmed, and we know, it is models of thought and action that teach and influence.

Another separation in higher education encouraged by the cognitive-knower model, and parallel to the college-track/vocational syndrome, is between "academic" discipline and the "professional" schools. The disciplines, on the model, provide the "real" knowledge and methods while the professional faculty do the "applied" and "practical" stuff. Barber has argued that this unexamined split has, in fact, resulted in a "two cultures" view of the university, two "unacceptable models of education." One he calls the "scholastic-purist model," which seeks a rebuilding of the ivory tower as a neutral domain of omnipotent knowledge that is transmitted via a canon to the few. The other model Barber identifies as the "marketplace" model that emphasizes service to the market and training and research in the name of products and profit. He cites educational institutions actually created by businesses: "All American High" by Whittle Communications, Warner Cable, and Toshiba, and All-American University by Xerox, Dutch Royal Shell, and Nissan.[20] The danger of this split should be evident, but Barber's conclusion gives cause for deep concern: the split engenders, on the one hand, irrelevance and disdain for the "barbarians in our midst" and, on the other, the belief that "the profitably lived life is not worth examining."[21]

This leads us to two other unfortunate aspects of the cognitive-knowing, knowledge-transmission model of education, namely, its failure to deal with the moral self and the communal self. Involved in the model is the belief that education must pursue a "value-free" path, espousing or engaging in no form of values or ethics education. "Good citizens," it is argued, need only the neutral shells of critical analysis; "enlightened reason," it is assumed, will carry the day to "right" action. "Tolerance," we are told, requires a kind of ethical relativism, an acceptance of everyone's beliefs as valid, without attention to personal commitment, to the habits of integrity, honesty, and fairness. This view ignores the ferment in ethical theory today that questions overemphasis on rationality and on the autonomous, self-legislating individual at the expense of attention to the special relationships of human beings, such as friendship and family, and to the combination of emotional, rational, imaginative elements evident in sensitive, ethical judgments.[22] This view of the role of "values" in education also ignores the tremendous concern of the public with value issues and virtues. There is also a growing sense in America that "we are in real danger of producing a new generation of leaders who are ethically illiterate at best or dangerously adrift and morally misguided at worst."[23]

Finally, there is the communal self and the human need Royce and others identify for satisfying communal living. There is also, as indicated in earlier chapters, a cry, in America, for community building. In fact the Wingspread Group on Higher Education recently identified as a needed major outcome of education today the "ability to live in and build community."[24] Indeed, our society is multi-ethnic, multi-cultural, multi-national, a truly global and diverse society that is being pulled closer and closer together by information transmission, people flow, markets, and political actions. Yet society's integrative mechanisms are breaking down, yielding increased violence within families, communities, institutions, and nations. Any sense of the common or public good is assaulted by the pursuit of individual self-interests—reflected in the extreme by the depletion of natural resources, financial scandal, and greed. Community building and learning to live together are urgent tasks, and education as an institution must play a key role in this task.

However, education is ill-equipped to deal with this need, for its foundational model of the self and human relations is more suited to promoting power-struggle and conflict. This model portrays self-made, self-reliant, self-interested subjects entering social arrangements "contractually," bargaining for the overall best self-benefit. If the relationship does not prove to bring the highest individual "payoff," it is dismissed or quickly dropped. In education, we find the emphasis more on a competitive, success-oriented community than on the classroom as a "community of learning" where knowledge is viewed as "communal achievement" and as "success together." It does not ground "collaborative learning models" that we now find are highly effective in fostering student learning and achievement.[25] Rather, the myth of "the cognitive self who seeks knowledge as information" lends support to the cynical views of those who hold that "nothing of importance happens in the classroom" and that "one can learn it all from a text, a video, or a computer program."

It should be abundantly evident by now that I believe we need new models of the human self and the knowing process. Further, in my criticisms of education, I also want to assert that many good things are going on at various levels of education and that there are many dedicated, excellent teachers. Often, their efforts seem overwhelmed by stronger, more powerful voices, condemning worthwhile efforts to the role of the small voice crying in the wilderness. And, yet, consider the effects of those "still, small voices" in the biblical stories of Elijah, Isaiah, and John the Baptist, voices that were the heralds of profound change. The existing paradigm remains too often assumed and too little consciously scrutinized and overcome. It will be better to begin to develop and act on a new model of self and knowing so that educators may turn with "fresh" vision to the tasks of building "genuine" individuals and communities.

A New Model: Education as a Community of Learning

Royce's philosophical view gives us an excellent foundation for a new approach to self and to the knowing and learning process. Working from a Roycean perspective, I would like to suggest the contours of such a new vision.

Beginning with the human self, a more adequate view than the narrow focus on the cognitive self would portray the self as a temporal, historical, developmental, embodied subject-agent with physical, mental, emotional, social, cultural, and moral aspects, who seeks meaning in terms of an individual, personally satisfying, and functional life. Further, this self is and needs to be in relationship with other beings. Our discussion in earlier chapters, as well as a substantial body of evidence, indicates that interrelationships, interdependence, and creative interchange are necessary for healthy human self-development—for a sense of self-worth, an awareness of limits, and a sense of belonging and harmony. The relationships, of course, need to be supportive of self and to involve mutual recognition and respect. A dramatic demonstration of the tragic result of isolation from human community was the failure of the "wolf-child," a human baby raised by wolves, to develop human qualities or the ability to relate to other humans.

A form of relationship crucial to human selves is a balanced, creative interrelationship between various aspects of the self—mind, body, emotions, feelings, values. Our traditional over-stress on the cognitive self fails to take into account all of the crucial aspects of the self and even fails to grasp what "human intelligence" might mean. For example, workers in the field of artificial intelligence have discovered that computers can do well in mastering logical and rule-bound skills; computers easily master computation and deductive problem solving and fairly complex game playing. But computer experts cannot produce the diagnostic, holistic skills of human experts. In spite of advances, computers have not, for instance, achieved the true holistic playing-skill levels of master chess players. Although "Deep Blue," the chess-playing computer recently gave Gary Gasparov trouble, ultimately it failed and for lack of this holistic ability. And computers are also profoundly poor at the most common tasks, like tying shoe laces and interpreting complex linguistic phrases. These skills suggest integrative, holistic operations of the various aspects of the human self. Moreover, a recent book, *Emotional Intelligence* by Daniel Coleman, suggests that we tend to ignore a critical range of abilities crucial to coping with life intelligently. He calls this complex of abilities "emotional intelligence," which includes self-awareness and impulse control, persistence, zeal, and self-motivation, empathy, and social defenses.[26] Coleman also provides detailed guidance about how parents, schools, and others can nurture and strengthen emotional intelligence. Much of what he says sounds very Roycean.

The traditional U.S. education paradigm also has emphasized a self-interested, competitive self who strikes the "best bargains." This view belies the communal and moral aspects of human persons. Education at all levels needs to be concerned about the communal aspects and needs of the self and about community-building skills. There are encouraging signs in the educational community that more attention is being paid to the communal and moral aspects of the student's human person. For example, there is a new movement to integrate "community service" into the university and college curriculum, not as an add-on or extra-curricular experience but as a key learning experience that interacts and interweaves with classroom, research, and other curricular activities. Various evolving institutes allow students to integrate their classroom experiences with action learning and problem solving in the field and in the community. These exist at Virginia Polytechnic, the University of Virginia, the University of Washington, and the University of Iowa. At Mercy College's Institute of Gerontology in Dobbs Ferry, New York, students work with senior citizens in providing advocacy and interpretive services for the elderly as well as other needy individuals in the community. At my own university, California State University, Bakersfield, business and accounting students work with nonprofit groups, helping them better manage their activities, while at the same time learning the value of volunteer and community service. Also at CSUB, philosophy students work with a university ethics institute in providing consultation on professional ethics statements and in presenting workshops on values clarification and ethical decision making for high-school and junior-high groups as well as other student groups. At the University of Missouri, students are working with at-risk pupils in the secondary schools and with families in family-help groups and child-care support groups to foster a better understanding of parenting, prenatal care, and family-conflict-resolution techniques.[27] A whole new curricular emphasis is now emerging on "conflict-resolution" and community building in law schools and other educational settings.[28] The Mediation Assistance Program at Albany Law School is an example. A reading of Royce's *War and Insurance* would be most beneficial to such efforts.[29]

In the state of California there is a new School for Career Plan that envisions a closer integration of academic and vocational/technical education. This plan would orient students, beginning in kindergarten, to "career awareness and work values" and would provide, at various levels of education, exploration of "career pathways" and opportunities to learn not only in the classroom, but also in the practical worksite and community settings. It calls on the community, educational institutions, and the business world to work in creative, fruitful ways and to encourage an attitude of "life-long learning." It urges that *all* students must be provided certain foundational skills—"reading, writing, calculating, communicating, working with people of different ethnic and cultural backgrounds, appreciation of the humanities and the arts, scientific reasoning, critical thinking, adaptability to change, computer literacy, self-esteem and a positive work ethic."[30] This plan has admirable goals, and some creative experiments are occurring in various communities to implement the plan. The most important aspects of the plan are (1) commitment of a "community" to the full development of the human potential of all of its children; and (2) the recognition of learning as a life-long and integrative experience. Much work and thought by individuals will be needed to make such a plan work. It may even begin building "enlightened provincialism."

As for the "moral" aspects of the human self, there are, as indicated above, projects occurring in the educational community that allow students to be engaged in self-values clarification processes as well as projects that help demonstrate the applied relevance of ethical knowledge and ethical decision-making skills. In addition, there are some "ethics across the curriculum" projects underway as well as "teaching the virtues" courses in different subject fields.[31]

Another important challenge is to bring to our new educational paradigm the notion of self "as a chosen project." Royce's concept of the self is of the self as a "plan of action," a "life-narrative." Royce writes of "my idea of myself—linked also with an interpretation of my hopes and intentions as to my future."[32] The self-created narrative defines a "community of self," a meaningful life-plan, a sense of one's destiny. The self-narrative is an essential component of the notion of the self's autonomy. Respect for self-autonomy is, in many ways, respect for the self's life-narrative. We will discuss this further in our discussion of medicine in the next chapter. Indeed, the "life-narrative," as we have seen, is also crucial to a community such as the family. And, respect for the community's narrative, the family's story, is respect for its autonomy, its "self."

All of those engaged in education need to focus on a new view of the self, which is holistic and Roycean in character. This notion of self can be introduced into the classroom in various ways, through journal assignments, for instance, that ask for narrative reflection on background and past experiences in relation to present experiences and future goals. Portfolios—a student's selection of assignments from a number of pieces produced over a period of time—can be introduced, reflective of temporal and developmental progress through a course or through a major or through a high-school career. A most successful example of an educational experience that focused on the concept of "self as narrative" was a course I taught entitled, Building Bridges and Sharing Stories. The focus of the course was the theme that we each have a unique and important story that "sums" who we are, where we have been, and where we are going. A number of community leaders from various ethnic backgrounds and professions came to the class to share their stories. They were each asked to focus on crucial aspects of the past that made them who they were then. They were also asked to reflect on what they still wanted to accomplish and why. The later portion of the class focused on each student sharing his or her story with the others. The students were amazed that they had stories worth sharing. Further, the class became a genuine community of great diversity and yet shared unity.

In addition to a new view of self, there also needs to be a new view of the knowing and learning process. Royce, of course, along with many philosophers and other scholars today, believes "knowledge" to be partially a "social construction"; it is contextual, relative to time and place, and always involves a limited view of reality. It is fallible, open to expansion, and transcendence. Above all, for Royce, knowledge is best achieved via a communal process because in that manner some of the limits of one's perspective can be overcome. Further, for Royce, "interpretation," an interactive communal form of knowledge, is a third mode of knowledge, alongside cognition and perception. Scientific knowledge and those pieces of information we call fact, are, argues Royce, considered reliable because they are the product of communal collaboration and critique. Individual scholars who share research and ideas with others for critique and discussion know very well that a better product, idea, or paper is the result. Students who engage in team research projects or who work with faculty on research projects also learn the value of knowledge sought via a communal process.

Unlike the traditional passive-knower model that concerns itself with cognitive relations to things and people's assimilation of knowledge, the communal model of knowledge has as its central educational goal 'community', that is, relations between people as knowledge seekers. It seeks to assimilate students into communities of knowledgeable peers and to give them the ability to engage in lifelong learning, namely, to join various communities of knowledge at various times and places. Further, a communal model of knowledge acquisition allows for and emphasizes the process of judgment, that ability to deal with information evaluatively and contextually. Sensitive judgment fosters educated decision making and action. But judgment is not easily learned individually, but rather is developed in a group process. In groups, individuals can talk to each other and share differing perspectives. This allows unexamined biases and assumptions to come to light; it allows the broadening of perspective and more reflective judgment and decisions. One research project, for example, demonstrated that medical students who learn diagnosis collaboratively acquire better medical judgments and do so more quickly than individual students working alone.

A Roycean communal model of knowledge would also be supportive of the recent emphasis on collaborative learning, namely, "a structured, systematic instructional strategy in which small groups of students work together toward a common goal."[33] Such a strategy emphasizes *positive interdependence* and *individual accountability* as well as prosocial behavior such as active listening, cooperation, and respect for others. It also emphasizes "face-to-face problem solving."[34] Studies of cooperative learning strategies have shown it to have great potential for increasing student achievement. James Cooper, a known expert on this strategy, writes: "Analyses of cooperative learning's effects on critical thinking, self-esteem, racial/ethnic relations, prosocial behavior, and a variety of other measures have consistently demonstrated that cooperative learning is superior to more traditional forms of instruction in a majority of cases and is rarely inferior to other forms of instruction."[35]

The communal model of knowledge fosters a different notion of pedagogical authority—authority established by communal test and interaction.

The teacher is no longer an expert who transmits, but a coach or facilitator, a colleague in the learning process. More will be said about teaching short-ly. In the communal model, students are seen as active participants in knowl-edge, taking more responsibility for their own learning. Respect for persons is fostered because it allows us to see that others have important and valu-able insights and pieces of knowledge. Students can feel that they have worth and are respected for who they are. A. W. Astin in a recent study of over two hundred colleges and universities, assessed nearly two hundred variables as factors that would make a significant difference for students in their under-graduate education. He concluded that student-student interaction and stu-dent-teacher interaction were by far the best predictors of positive student cognitive and attitudinal changes in the undergraduate experience.[36]

The communal model of knowledge would indeed lead us to be inter-ested in "quality interaction" and student learning processes, because it en-courages and prizes each individual member of the community as an important contributor to the common goal. Cooperative learning strategies seek to promote active learning. It is this kind of instructional learning strategies that a communal model would encourage. And, unlike the pas-sive-knower model, which tends to use computer technology for data pro-cessing, information gathering, and skills enhancement, those operating within a communal knowledge paradigm would see computers as a means to foster "community" and a tool for active participation of the learner in the knowledge process. For example, electronic mail would be used for group discussions known as "listen" or computer conferences, as well as for inter-active communication with the teacher.[37]

The communal model of knowledge also readily accepts the notion of as-sessment and accountability, as does the scientific community. Knowledge grows via critical collaboration and communication. Feedback is the key to refinement. Classroom assessment of knowledge and its justification help to clarify goals, objectives, and content for both teacher and students. It makes the classroom a dynamic environment, and learning and knowledge acquisi-tion an active, ongoing collaborative process. Susan Numenedal writes: "Through this kind of assessment, faculty . . . will be able to find out *early* what is—and what is not—working in the changing classrooms they create. By obtaining feedback on how and how well students are learning what they are being taught, faculty will be able to make appropriate modifications to their teaching while student learning is taking place."[38]

An interesting classroom assessment technique called "the muddiest point" asks for student feedback about what is least clear in a class session. Depending on the feedback received, points can be repeated, expanded, and elaborated on or presented in a new way. This technique is also a teaching tool, for it requires students to engage in the metacognitive processes of monitoring and assessing their own learning. If the feedback is shared with the students, it can help them "improve their learning strategies and study habits in order to become more independent, successful learners."[39] Again students become communal partners in the learning, knowledge-seeking process.

We need mechanisms within the secondary and higher education experience to integrate the various aspects of the self—biological, cognitive, emotional, behavioral, neural-chemical, moral, social, cultural—as understood and taught in the various disciplines. Perhaps parallel to the human genome project we need a "human self-project." This could be an excellent focus for a General Education component in university or community college curricula or a theme integrating the secondary-school curriculum. Further, we need to do a better job of integrating so-called extra-curricular activities, student life activities, with the curriculum so that the whole student can be challenged and educated. School events that bring the arts, club activities, and curriculum together, as well as communal and parental participation, would help break down the false dichotomies in students' lives. Rather than fund-raising carnivals, school fairs could become "educational events" in which participation from family and individual could be valued as part of "learning" and "knowledge-seeking" activities. More will be said about this when we discuss multi-culturalism.

Attention should be given to Royce's remarks on fraternal groups and sports as loyalty and community-building activities. Michael Novak, for example, has argued that sports can be viewed as liturgies of the goal of "enhumanment."[40] To be enhumaned is to be rooted, identified with a team effort, with a symbol of a place.[41] It also emphasizes the body and its finitude. Like Royce, Novak also sees sports as exemplifying community, courage, harmony of mind and body, beauty and excellence.[42] They can also teach the lessons that Royce identifies in terms of "lost causes," to persist in loyalty through varying fortunes. For Novak, "To watch a sports event . . . is to take a risk. . . . The mode of observation proper to a sports event is to participate—that is, to extend one's own identification to one side, and to absorb with it the blows of fortune, to join with the team in testing the favor of the Fates."[43] Finally, there is associated with sports an unique appreciation of excellence, not the kind that is too rabid in denunciation of their opposition. Rather it is, says Novak, "a richer and more sophisticated appreciation of excellence. I have watched ovations for a player on the other side. . . ."[44] There is a respect for excellence in others. Like Royce, Novak sees sports fans as demonstrating "particular loyalties."[45] More attention needs to be given to sports in the task of educating for loyalty, excellence, harmony of body and mind. However, one needs also to emphasize Royce's cautionary words in this regard: "The athletic evils, such as they are . . . are due . . . to the absurd social prominence which newspapers and the vast modern crowds give to contests which ought to be cheerful youthful sports."[46] He also writes: "Fair play in sports is a peculiarly good instance of loyalty. . . . The coach . . . to whom fair play is not a first concern, is simply a traitor to our youth and our nation."[47] Finally, he cautions against emphasizing sports too early, lest the benefits of "natural play" be lost.

Royce's understanding of the importance of play in helping develop self and community has been discussed in previous chapters, but we need to bring aspects of this to the question of education. Royce argued for the combination of habit and spontaneity in play, and he sees in play a development of a sense of seriousness and persistence in regard to a self's own creativity and values. In play, says Royce, there is *"an insistence upon trying over and over again the playful activity until it wholly satisfies his ideals."* In this perseverance lies "originality," the initiative of *"which the child may be said to contribute to the organization of his playful function."*[48] Further, this originality exemplified in play, is, for Royce, the basis for social inventiveness.[49] Richard Stennett, in his book, *The Fall of Public Man* argues that the repression of play leads to "the loss of the childhood power to be sociable."[50] Further, in play, Stennett suggests, one is required to combine rules and spontaneity; one can "objectify action, repeat it, correct it, improve it."[51] Play, then, involves self-transcendence and self-correction, and acknowledgment of rules along with creativity. Finally, Royce believes play, as a human activity, brings together the sensory, motor, intellectual, imaginative and intentional aspects of the self. This kind of unification is essential to self-unity and to sensitive moral judgment.

In a time when play seems abandoned for competitiveness, serious attention needs to be given to these aspects of play and to the performative arts as a crucial part of the educational experience. The old model of the cognitive knowing self tends to emphasize content and cognitive-skills learning, even at an early age. Much more attention needs to be given to play and play-related activities. Related to this is the importance Royce placed on literature and storytelling as means of imaginative play and self-unifying. Literature also plays an important role in providing role-models, in teaching idealization, in portraying human action and emotions. D. H. Lawrence expresses this well when he writes, "The function of the modern novel . . . has been to give us a sense of the individuality of our lives . . . best understood in terms of our ability to interpret the conduct of our general rules in response to particular situations." Literature and language also tell the "stories" of peoples and cultures and families. We shall discuss this more as we deal with multiculturalism. Literature also gives us a sense of the self as narrative, as historical, and as temporal.

Benjamin Barber, in his recent book on education, writes, "Education is systematic story-telling."[52] He sees storytelling as valuable in several ways but especially in teaching a sense of historicity and temporality. With Royce, Barber believes that stories help people define themselves, but they do, in part, because they give us history that, in turn, is "prudence's teacher" and "wisdom's most precious source":

> History is the birthing room of our common character. We
> know ourselves by understanding our temporality, our em-
> beddedness in time, our connection to roots—even roots of
> which we have knowingly severed ourselves.[53]

Storytelling connects us with the past, individually and communally. It builds community, as it does with family identity. Literature can give us the shared wisdom of humanity; it can bring us in touch with successes and failures. It can give us "roots."

But stories can also tell us about our possibilities, about the future. Human beings are entities in process; they need a sense of openness, of an ability to risk. Our awareness of time—memory and anticipation—is one crucial mark of us as human beings. It sets the ground for our moral, responsible nature and for a sense of guilt as well as of accomplishment. One cannot redo the past, argues Royce, and thus one must accept responsibility for the irrevocability of deeds already done. One can redeem a past act through a new act of atonement, but the past cannot be changed. The sense of future thus allows the possibility of atonement; it allows an agent a sense of hope for change, and it, again, emphasizes an agent's responsibility for deeds done, for the consequence of acts performed or contemplated. The time-blind person is the procentrist person, who deals only with current needs, perhaps by consuming, by acts of immediate pleasure, by relationships that provide gain now. This person operates with a "me-now" attitude. A sense of time is a crucial aspect of a loyal, responsible project pursuer. Thus, Barber is correct when we writes: "Obliviousness to time almost always reappears as social irresponsibility. . . . Ripped from time, atomized individuals are without strings, without givens, without parents, without responsibilities—literally outside of time."[54]

A model of person that emphasizes person as temporal, historical, open-ended project pursuer would, with Barber and Royce, argue for teaching via every means possible, a sense of temporality and historicity. Literature and storytelling are obvious means, as is the study of history, especially if it is taught as a relevant, lived, open-ended experience and not as "frozen-in-time," a memorization of past deeds. Further, the history of a subject area, whether biology, philosophy, or psychology, helps students to see the field as something developed from the work of fallible, finite humans who can be models to them. It also helps students to see knowledge as social construction and the possibility of their entrance in and participation in this community of knowledge-seekers. In utilizing history and literature, in our communal model of knowledge, the emphasis is less on content and more on human action with all those implications—moral responsibility, guilt, loyalties, fears, joys, sorrows. In the communal model of knowing, it is the actions of persons with projects who combine intellect, feeling, emotions, bodily actions, values, etc., that are worth knowing, emulating, understanding, transcending. The story of interest is the story of finite, embodied, encultured, temporal, historical persons.

The Classroom and the Educational Institution as a "Wise Province"

A crucial component of the educational task, then, is storytelling and allowing stories to be told, created and recreated. In the universal public education system of the United States, a fundamental task is to tell our story as a people, or more precisely, to tell the tale of our struggle to become a people. Benjamin Barber notes, correctly I believe, that "any careful reader of

American history cannot help but notice that American has always been a tale of peoples trying to be a People, a tale of diversity and plurality in search of unity."[55]

There has been much ferment in educational circles around the issue of changing demographics. By the year 2020, we are told, "about one third of Americans will be members of minority groups, traditionally poorly served by education at all levels."[56] This has stimulated a number of studies, books, articles, and conferences concerned with identifying emergent issues of diversity. The task is to understand the concerns of minority students and to develop the best possible educational processes to enable the educational community to help students of a wide range of racial, ethnic, cultural, and religious backgrounds to learn together and to grow together into responsible, informed, tolerant persons who can live in harmony in a rapidly diversifying and changing world.[57]

Among the issues raised for education by diversity are: different communication styles of other people;[58] different motivational variables and learning styles;[59] variability in what is considered relevant or connected with cultural and everyday experience; the need to weave minority students into the fabric of the classroom and to integrate minority scholarship into the curriculum. A most important issue centers on how to build a climate of mutual respect in the classroom by facilitating the sharing and understanding of the varied worldviews of the students. Such understanding goes beyond learning about differences in food, art, music, dance, and literature because it needs to include the different perspectives on value issues—for instance, how time, family, competition, and orientation toward nature are understood. It would require teachers and students *allowing* themselves to be known as persons with unique biographies, family customs, preferences, interests, and worldviews.[60] This might require personal interaction outside the classroom.[61]

These kinds of issues are precisely those that a communal model of knowing would address, for again, it assumes the contributions to the classroom experience needed by each unique individual, including the teacher. The communal model assumes the need for tolerance, respect, and the search for means of mutual understanding and self-expansion. Our new vision of the self and of knowing would applaud the many new developments encompassed in the term "multicultural education."[62] Such an educational experience, of course, is a difficult one to organize and to bring to fruition in classrooms. It will take the imaginative skills and cooperation of many. Above all it will take the motivation and practical action of teachers, administrators, parents, and community and political leaders. The exploration and adoption of our suggested new paradigm will, I argue, be a great step forward for education in this country.

In talking about diversity and multiculturalism, I, for one, also want to include the issue of gender diversity. Gender perspective is a fundamental perspective and includes diversity within itself, as does any ethnic or cultural category. Although women do not constitute a "minority" in the minds of many, the nonrepresentation of their voices and views, throughout American history, does make it imperative that their issues be included in the new broadening of perspectives in the classroom, as well as those of the gay population and culture. What is needed is a multicultural, nonsexist educational experience.[63] Fortunately, attention is now being given to the role of gender in teaching and learning.[64]

Our nation has always been pluralistic and diverse; but many stories have not been told; these voices have not been heard. Fortunately a number of recent books have begun to make these stories known. These include: Ron Takaki, *Strangers From a Different Shore*; Gary Nash, *Red, White and Black: The Peoples of Colonial America*; Rudolfo Acuna, *Occupied America: A History of Chicanos*; Louise Erdich, *Love Medicine*; and Carl Degler, *At Odds: Women and the Family in America.*[65]

Josiah Royce, incidentally, unlike most U.S. historians, recorded and reflected on racial and ethnic conflicts in our early history. In 1886, for example, Royce, in his *California from the Conquest in 1846 to the Vigilance Committee in San Francisco* (1856), wrote about and reflected on the many racial, ethnic, even gender conflicts arising out of the attempts of diverse human beings to live and work together in the mining towns and emerging cities of early California.[66] In 1908, Royce tackled head-on the philosophical issues of these conflicts in his *Race Questions, Provincialism and Other American Problems.*[67] Royce, with his clear understanding of the subtle interrelationship and tensions of individualism and community, would have been astonished that anyone would argue for a "melting pot" notion of cultural assimilation. The human thirst for unique individuality and community could not condone, for long, a melting away of differences and identities.

Royce's views on diversity within community are, in fact, being well expressed today by Carlos Cortez when he argues for a "Constructive Multi-culturalism." According to Cortez, this view responds "thoughtfully to both powerful Pluribus and necessary Unum imperatives, as well as setting limits to Pluribus and to Unum when they become poisonous to climate and de-structive to community."[68] Pluribus, of course, represents such values as freedom, individuality, rights, while Unum extols authority, conformity, and commonality. Royce's philosophy of community and notion of "wholesome provincialism" embody the delicate balance of pluribus and unum that Cortez finds at the heart of a constructive multiculturalism.

A "wholesome province" is, of course, for Royce, a form of "genuine community." Among the conditions of genuine community are (1) interac-tive, creative similarity and difference provided by unique individuals; (2) communication among selves; and (3) a created and recreated unity in a common past or memory and a common future or hope.[69] Royce compared a highly developed community to "the soul of a man . . . it has a mind of its own."[70] In the chapter on family, we discussed how a family forges an iden-tity, just as does a self. It too, then, can become a "genuine community," a "wise province." A classroom, we would suggest, could also become such an entity, as could an educational institution. Each provides ways to build a common story, a past, a present, and a future. Shared goals and values and common effort are important to such a task. Yet individuality of contribu-tion is encouraged.

A mark of a "genuine community," a "wise province," is that the unity it achieves is an "aesthetic unity," a unity with diversity. As indicated earlier, the unity envisioned is that of a "good jazz performance, when "the basic 4/4 beat is flouted by each player through his own improvisation."[71] Individual-ity and diversity is respected, exalted, given expression, listened to, and yet at the same time each works toward a "common sound or composition." Further, each member of the combo encourages, stimulates, corrects, inter-prets, enjoys the acts and voice of the other." Each member of the class is val-ued for his or her contributions, perspective, and heritage, and yet each is encouraged to forge a communal product and a shared history. I shall com-ment shortly on the role of the teacher in such a classroom.

To understand a little more fully Royce's notion of "wholesome provin-cialism," we need to discuss Royce's views on (1) false forms of provincialism or "sectionalism," and (2) the leveling tendency of civilization.[72] False sec-tionalism is an excessive pride in one's own lifestyle and views, a fear of the strange and novel and a tendency to isolation. Royce declares, "False sectionalism, which disunites, will indeed, always remain as great an evil as ever it was."[73] Royce attributed the leveling tendency to ease of communication, popular education, and consolidation and centralization of industries and of social authorities. For Royce, this leveling results in reading the same news, sharing general ideas, submitting to overmastering social forces, living in the same external fashions. Above all, it tends to "discourage individuality, and to approach a dead level of harassed mediocrity."[74] Royce's criticism of the leveling tendency in modern industrial society would apply also to any notion of a "melting pot" into which ethnic and other differences will disappear. The essence of this "melting pot" concept was that all differences would fuse into a common cultural life and thought. Royce strongly felt that "a community does not become one . . . by virtue of any reduction or melting of these various selves in a single merely present self or into a mass of passing experience."[75]

Indeed, in talking about these two dangers of "provincialism," Royce is alerting us today to a need for constant critical attention to the subtleties of power, of the media, of institutions, of class and gender, which can inflame "sectionalism" or produce "leveling." In education, our communal model of knowing cautions us against designating "authorities" in the knowing process, whether teacher, textbook, or "canons." A "canon" is a "distilled version of the past" that has been designated by a community as "official." From the point of view of the communal model of knowing, it must be examined critically for what it can bring of value to the present time, place, and context. Further, we need to see in the canon stories about how power traditionally has been distributed *and* challenged; clearly, the canon has always been contentious and controversial and changed over time.

This brings us briefly to the "political correctness" controversy. Here, I believe, we need to think of "constructive multiculturalism" as posing limits to both pluribus and unum. "Political correctness" combines and labels a host of issues.[76] First, it is used to describe the goals of those advocating a more pluralistic, multicultural, race-, gender-, and class-sensitive curriculum. Such a view certainly is "political" because it seeks to "democratize" the curriculum, to make it genuinely a "community of learning." It is also about "power," for it is about the "canon" as just described, about voices heard and voices ignored or silenced. To label these concerns as "correct" is to assume that there is no room for respect or the voice of a "dominant" groups such as Euro white males. Such labeling portrays the advocacy for multicultural curriculum as sectionalism, which it assuredly is *not*. Rather, we need to provide conditions so that all voices can be heard. A diversity of voices, whether they be contentious or complementary, allows for a broader perspective on issues.

A second issue encompassed within the label "politically correct" is the advocacy for policies designed to minimize sexual and racial harassment on campus. This advocacy is often perceived as "witch-hunting," and, if carried out without caution, safeguards, due process, and respect for individuals, it could become just that. However, to make classrooms and institutions places where one finds conscious, self-reflective, sensitive language and behavior as standard procedure is to build "genuine communities" and "wise provinces." Indeed, the position known as "political correctness" might be better labeled "political openness" or "political diversity." What one would hope for is that these two prongs of "political correctness" will eventually result in an educated student who is capable of intellectual criticism of self-view and other's views, who can have a sensitive, sympathetic feel for the other's culture, an ability to discover common ground, and from that ground to establish common communities. This kind of education requires a communal model of knowing and classrooms that function as "genuine communities" or "wise provinces."

Teaching as Interpretation and Community Building: Jazz Improvisation

If classrooms are to become "genuine communities of learning," then teaching must itself become communal and community enhancing. I shall deal with the latter aspect of teaching first. If teaching is to be community enhancing, it must have, as one of its main goals, person-empowerment, both for teacher and student, enabling each to become self-learners and teachers of others. The teacher, then, is not primarily a conveyer of information, but rather a facilitator, setting out a structure and a process whereby students can learn from each other, as well as from the teacher. In order to have such a classroom one must help students gain skills of listening, of communicating, of critical analysis, of problem solving. There are a number of techniques that can empower students and teach these skills. For example, there are instructional strategies for teaching students to pose thought-provoking questions: by pairs working in various ways to raise questions; by small groups brainstorming questions; and by the total class generating questions from general discussion.[77] Another set of techniques empowers students by allowing them to generate examples of concepts or sequences of examples and to organize these into "example maps" that can then be reflected upon, criticized, and refined by small groups or the class as a whole.[78] These techniques and others also help students to listen and communicate. In utilizing any small-group work in a classroom, it is important to let students know that both listening and communicating are important and that a key part of good group work is stimulating and encouraging each other to participate in the process. Assessment of group activities, whether self-assessment, assessment by other group members, or by the instructor should take this into account. Further, an attitude of respect of self and other and of tolerance of and openness to diverse beliefs, practices, experiences, and values must be fostered. Of course, in such an effort, *personal modeling* by the teacher is a key element.

Creating a community of learning and knowing assumes that each individual is both a learner and a knowledge contributor. This includes the teacher but does not mean all knowledge contributors are equal, for clearly this is not the case. Rather, the learner-contributor principle values what is contributed as important to the knowledge-seeking process. An apt metaphor for a teacher in this situation is that of a midwife. A midwife is a person with skills, knowledge, and experience who lends these to and in support of others in the birthing process. The midwife does not "have the baby" but works with, encourages, and allows others to do so. Students can, in differing degrees, also perform this role for each other. Teachers need to explore ways to empower students. Group investigation and team research projects foster community, empower students, and teach the idea that each individual is a learner and knowledge contributor. A strategy known as "Jigsaw" assigns students to a group of four to six. Content to be studied is divided and assigned to each student to teach the other students.[79] This allows students to become engaged in the subject that also reinforces the notion of each as a learner and a teacher. Creativity and problem solving can be combined through "game strategies," through "imagery stimulation" in seeking solutions, and through the use of visual- and performing-arts techniques to solve problems together. For example, a problem or subject area can be explored using a class mural.[80] Games and role playing are excellent classroom techniques for dealing with multicultural material and tolerance-sensitivity building. Ba Fa' Ba Fa', for example, is an intercultural simulation that teaches students to create two cultures, each with a fictitious set of cultural values, customs, and communication styles. Through exchange and interaction among the cultures, students learn that language, stereotyping, and communication styles may influence the interaction between two dissimilar appearing groups.[81] Other such games are Star Power, Cultural Pursuit, and Power Shuffle. Power Shuffle, for example, is considered very powerful because it "allows students to share who they are without having to explain or defend themselves;" it allows students to "see their identity as uniquely their own;" and it "gets people talking and listening to one another."[82]

In seeking to make classrooms communal, we need also to focus on a new understanding of the role of teaching. We have already introduced the concept of midwife. Drawing on Royce's concept of interpretation, it seems appropriate also to see teaching as a triadic (perhaps quadratic) process and relationship involving student, teacher, content, and context. Royce, of course, would assume context as a given in interpretation and thus focuses on interpreter, interpretant, and the person to whom the interpretation is addressed. The teacher knows a content and a body of skills and methods, which she attempts to interpret to the student and/or the class. As interpreter, a teacher is always also a learner and a researcher. To be fair to the depth and complexity of the subject matter, the idea, the teacher must study the subject matter/idea carefully so as not to betray students' trust that, as far as possible, the teacher is offering a genuine and adequate interpretation of the subject.

One recalls that, for Royce, the process of interpretation does involve a "moral attitude," a will to interpret, to do one's best to bring about understanding and a harmony of ideas. Interpretation involves commitment to "know," as far as possible, one's subject, as well as one's audience. It also involves humility and the realization that interpretation is an endless process, for a subject is always open to new understanding and interpretation. It involves love of subject and a concern to share it with others. This fits well with the idea of the teacher-scholar who loves her subject and wishes to share it in love and excitement with others. It fits well, too, with the idea that learning occurs in attempting to teach others. Indeed, teaching should involve continual learning. How can I interpret the essence, development, and meaning of my endlessly wonderful subject area if I don't understand it and "know" it myself? Secondly, sharing and communication involve understanding context and audience. Otherwise, the interpretation will fail; for it will fall on deaf, uncomprehending subjects. This is one reason why multicultural understanding is important in a community of learning. The community needs to be in touch with each other, to be able to listen as well as to provide feedback. Like a good "jazz" combo, all must be "in tune," though hearing different versions of the melody.

Teaching then is learning and interactive, a role that can be taken on by any member of the community. Students become also interpreters and teachers. We learn from each other. One must see others, says Royce, as "dynamos of ideas and experiences." One person cannot grasp the complexity, diversity, ambiguity of reality; one cannot feel or see it all. Others are carriers and supplementers of meaning; they allow me to transcend self, experience, perspective. Others are endless treasuries of ideas, experiences and meanings; they provide the contrast-effects and/or the models by which I hone, refine, broaden self, ideas, and experiences.

A classroom is not just an arbitrary organization but, rather, it is a place where a community of learning, self-development, respect, and pluralism can be built. A classroom should be like a jazz ensemble or a symphony orchestra in which cooperation is a conscious act of observing, respect, interacting with the deeds and voices of each other. Each knows that without just this combination of individuals, this interacting of co-contributing selves, this piece of music, this achievement of knowledge and insight would not be possible. All the members take pride and joy in their own and the group product. The classroom is also a research lab in which all can hone their observations of human behavior and ideas and test their own behavior, ideas, and values. The classroom is a community of scholars in that student and teachers can share with each other their own lonely research endeavors and test these ideas and judgments; it is a place where knowledge and experience grows out of this interaction of cooperating selves.

With this view of teaching and the classroom, it follows that teaching is an art form. One learns through practice, experience, and interaction how to play in an orchestra or jazz ensemble. It involves developing sensitivities about the individual and unique qualities of each player, including oneself. For a lead player or conductor this involves risk, adventure, and, in the case of jazz, the skill to improvise while keeping harmony and stimulating the improvisation and harmonizing of others. And, as a good musician or conductor, it also means learning how to convey the love of the art and a feeling that these acts of teaching and learning involve self-development and self-fulfillment.

Another implication of this view of teaching is that teaching is or should be as "public" an act as research and publishing, not a private act. Teaching is personal performance, a statement of belief and action, a model to others. It is bizarre that teaching has for so long been considered a private professional act, rarely open to collegial scrutiny. Colleagues, in research and publication, serve as sources of ideas, tools, criticism. Why should it not be the case with teaching? Whoever thought that sharing among teachers about teaching would not be valuable. Lee Shulman makes the following observations about teaching that I find to be going in the right direction.

> We close the classroom door and experience pedagogical solitude, whereas in our life as scholars, we are members of active communities, communities of conversation, communities of evaluation, communities in which we gather with others in our invisible college to exchange our findings, our methods, and our excuses.
>
> I now believe that the reason teaching is not more valued in the academy is because the way we treat teaching removes it from the community of scholars . . . if we wish to see greater recognition and reward attached to teaching, we must change the status of teaching from private to community property. [83]

Teaching is "community property." It belongs to each individual in the community of learning, including students. It is valuable because it builds community and can provide self-development and self-fulfillment. Just as students can learn from each other, so can teachers. Teaching is an art form that can be practiced together; it is a subject about which we can talk, dialogue, and share. Fortunately, teaching is becoming more public and there are many new strategies being developed to allow teachers to help each other grow and develop as teachers.

One exciting method in this area is peer coaching. Peer coaching is "a structured formative process by which trained faculty voluntarily assist each other in enhancing their teaching repertoires within an atmosphere of collegial trust and candor."[84] It involves working together to: (1) create individual instructional goals and clear observation criteria; (2) provide reciprocal, focused, non-evaluative classroom observation; and (3) encourage prompt, constructive feedback on those observations.[85] A new concept is "reflective teaching" by teachers who continuously "inquire into their own teaching practice and into the concepts in which their teaching is embedded."[86] Various strategies have been suggested to aid in this reflection: portfolios, cross-cultural teaching experiences, journal writing, ethnographic studies, and reflective teaching lessons.[87]

Related to peer coaching is a method called "reflective partnerships," in which two faculty members share their teaching experiences by observing each other teach and discussing each others' actions and intentions.[88] Another strategy is case-studies. Cases are detailed, story-like accounts of classroom incidents designed to raise issues about effective teaching and learning.[89] These can be used to prompt lively discussion among teachers about teaching. All of these methods seem very Roycean in intent.

To encourage better and more reflective teaching assessment by self and others is crucial, especially assessment that emphasizes growth and interpretive connection. In evaluating teaching, the portfolio idea makes good sense because it documents these aspects of teaching, namely, growth, development of self, and concern for student development and for development of the community of learning. Peer review could be a form of teaching and learning, a further expansion of the community of knowing. And peer observation makes sense for teaching viewed as an art form, as a process, because it is best observed and judged by being experienced.

This notion of teaching interconnects teaching and research; it emphasizes interactive, cooperative learning strategies; teacher-student research, as well as applied research and teaching situations in which students interact with ideas that impact significantly on their own lives. It thus connects teaching and community service, for both student and teacher. Individualization of the classroom is called for and can be accomplished in various ways—multicultural, gender-sensitive education; personal reflection projects shared with others; interactive and personalized comments on tests, papers, etc. Teaching and learning need to be seen as personal, experiential, fulfilling processes.

Education, argues Barber, is storytelling. It is a communal and individual experience in which unique, diverse, individual stories are written, while together a common story is written.

7

Medicine as Mediating Practice

"The concept of patient-centered medicine is now widely accepted, but this has not eradicated the almost automatic initial assumption by the doctor of the superior role, with the patient occupying a position of relative insignificance."
　　—Marie Camphin and Erica Jones

"How can people be helped to develop a sense of self and self-worth (identity) that is not based on putting down or controlling someone else?"
　　—Virginia L. Warren

"Sickness . . . shatters the web of assumptions on which our lives are based. We take it for granted that our arms, legs, feet and other organs will respond to our commands. When they do not . . . we discover how much of our sense of self is bound up with our body. . . ."
　　—C. Silberman

"For Chinese thought, the body is never merely material and mechanical, but an open and flowing system of vital energy."
　　—Tu Wei-Ming

"Data from the emerging field of PNI and related disciplines increasingly indicate a mind-body continuum and discredit the anachronistic split of Cartesian dualism."
　　—Kenneth R. Pelletier and Denise L. Herzing

Medicine and Crisis and Critique

I N A FINAL test of the public philosophy outlined in this book, we turn to examine our third "form of life," medicine. At this time in U.S. history, this area of human life is clearly of central concern to numerous individuals and multiple communities. One clear evidence of this concern is the present public ferment about a new and more adequate health care system.[1] Dramatic changes are being demanded of the present health care system and numerous changes are occurring.[2]

Further, like the family and education, medicine is perceived to be in a state of crisis and is being subjected to a wide range of criticisms. These criticisms take a variety of forms. One set of criticisms focuses on the very foundation of medicine, on its metaphysical assumptions about the human person. Medicine, at least as it is practiced in the Western world, is perceived as operating with a reductionistic, outmoded view of the human being. In the words of one critic, Drew Leder, medicine has focused on a Cartesian body viewed as mechanistic and inanimate thus rendering "invisible" the psychological, social and cosmological dimensions of the body.[3] Medicine, it is said, has been operating with a classical perspective on reality leading to the view that our human bodies are isolated objects completely disconnected from our own minds and consciousness and from the rest of the world at large. Our body, from this perspective, is wholly governed by the blind laws of matter, and our mind and consciousness are ultimately explicable by the brain's anatomy, chemistry, and physiology.

This Cartesian-Newtonian paradigm, based on an incurable dichotomy of matter and mind, has been challenged by many developments in research as well as from other sources. Among the challenging areas of research are those in psychoneuroimmunology, psychosomatic medicine, psycho-social systems, and research centered in the psychological conditions of stress, depression, and bereavement. Data from these fields indicate a different view of mind-body, namely, a mind-body continuum and a complete interaction between the immunological, neurological, and psycho-social systems.[4] Larry Dossey offers a most telling comment about the inadequacy of medicine's reliance on a Cartesian mind-body model when he writes, "It is odd that medicine, which considers itself scientific in the most modern sense, utilizes a set of assumptions about the workings of the world that completely ignore many of the insights of the physics of this century."[5]

A second set of criticisms of medicine argues that its inadequate Cartesian model has led to an equally faulty notion of "disease" and that this, in turn, has led to a view of the patient as a passive participant in the therapeutic process. Such an understanding, it is believed, fails the patient and ignores valuable aspects of any healing process. Thus, for example, by splitting body from other aspects of the person, traditional medicine, it is charged, has treated "disease" (pathological changes in the body) but failed to deal with "illness" (the experience of that disease) or "illness behavior" (the patient's actions resulting from the experience of the disease).[6] Medicine, it is argued, must redirect its attention to the subjective experiences of patients and to the notion of the doctor-patient relationship itself as therapeutic.[7]

Medicine, it is claimed, has lost the "human touch" and a number of physicians have argued for ways of restoring this to medical practice. For example, "the patient-centered method," counsels physicians to "enter the patient's world to see the disease through the patient's eyes."[8] A number of studies and articles have appeared in medical journals describing and assessing ways to bring the patient's perceptions into the medical situation, including techniques of interviewing and ways of dealing with the patient receptively, with empathy and non-judgmentally. Meanwhile, there has also been an increasing demand by patients to be treated as unique persons with valid views and to be listened to by doctors.[9]

In addition to these charges against traditional medicine many have called for a serious rethinking of the traditional model of medicine in light of two new factors: (1) technology and (2) the increasing introduction of market principles and various "third parties" into health-care delivery. The increased reliance by the medical profession on technology, it is asserted, has rationalized and objectified medical judgment by making it a matter of objective evidence provided by laboratory, mechanical, and electronic devices. It has specialized the profession while also making it more technical.[10] At the same time a number of economic and political factors have impinged on medicine to add to this trend toward rationalization and deprofessionalization. Medicare/Medicaid helped increase the demand for medical care, and this spurred competition as well as escalating costs. The escalating costs have led to a call for more efficient delivery of medical services. Further, medicine has become corporatized as large medi-giants integrate health care facilities, medical services, and insurance. This also adds to the emphasis on *costs* rather than the *welfare of patients*. The introduction of DRGs (diagnosis related groups) has shifted some decision making to third-party bureaucrats, and much work in medical facilities has become routinized, being performed by less well trained people. Many physicians have become "entrepreneurs," and profit rather than altruistic care has become an increasing concern.[11] Medicine, we are told, is "gaining in efficiency, but losing the human touch."[12]

Medicine has also been accused of replicating the hierarchical class and power structures and patriarchal practices of our society, thus effectively validating these structures and participating in the multiple forms of oppression that are the result of such structures. Thus, in 1975, Michel Foucault analyzed medicine as one of those institutional domains that, under the guise of neutral investigation, engages in policing tactics and political agendas. In Foucault's view, "Individuals who enter and receive treatment within these institutions are defined not only as diseased but as deviant, as persons existing outside the bounds of social normality."[13] "Health" and "disease," it is argued, are "social value judgments," and medicine serves state and society rather than the interests of the patient.

The Feminist critiques of medicine have sounded similar themes. Thus, Susan Sherwin writes, "The institution of medicine has been designed in ways that reinforce sexism."[14] In its ascriptions of illness, for example, male dominated medicine has "declared many conditions which are normal for women as unhealthy," such as menstruation, pregnancy, body size and menopause. These experiences have been "medicalized" and, thus, male-dominated medical practice has engaged in domination and control of woman's body.[15] Further, women as patients have been treated paternalistically; their illness experiences have been discounted; they have been overmedicated with drugs such as Valium, and a vast number of unnecessary hysterectomies have been performed.[16] Feminists, along with many other groups, have analyzed and critiqued the ways gender, race, and class have affected health care delivery. The conclusion of the critique is that people's health-care needs have usually varied inversely with their power and prestige in society. "The very people with the greatest health needs are likely to find the whole system alien."[17]

Medicine, then, as a life form and institution, is perceived as desperately in need of a radical reassessment of its goals, its foundational model, and its practices. New models or sketches for medicine have been proposed: for instance, the biophysical model of George L. Engel, the "patient-centered" models in family medicine, the Aristotelian-humanistic philosophy of Pellegrino and Thomasma, as well as new approaches to the human body arising out of phenomenology.[18]

In what follows, I wish to add a dimension to this search for a fruitful model for contemporary medicine by arguing that we view medicine as a "mediating practice," one involving Roycean interpretation skills and the role of mediation—for instance, between the medical-scientific view of illness and disease and the patient's view, which includes individual and social values and beliefs. Through mediation, medicine's goal is to bring about a common understanding, and a set of healing practices. "Healing" will be understood in terms of bringing individuals to a sense of "constructive functioning living," that is, a harmony of values, beliefs, and interests with the psycho-physiological situation, a sense of self-recognition, acceptance, and control. The goal of medicine, in my view, is healing, and it involves service to the individual good of persons. The "individual good" of persons will be explicated in terms of the physical, subjective, intersubjective, social, cultural, developmental, and relational aspects of actor-agents as well as the threefold category of interests: social role interests, subjective interests, and deliberative interests, as recently developed by McCullough and Chervenak in their *Ethics in Obstetrics and Gynecology*.[19]

In developing this view of medicine, I will argue that medicine not only needs a new view of the human person, but that it also must embrace a communal model of knowledge, one which affirms the role of various "experts" in health care as well as the insight that the patient is a significant source of knowledge and information. The clinical process must be seen as an interactive inter-relational search for the meaning of the individual illness, a meaning which is temporal, developmental, and open-ended. Further, as agents of individual persons seeking "constructive, functional living," physicians and other health care workers will need to serve not only as healers but as educators and empowerers. This means that these practitioners must recognize the moral and health costs of various forms of oppression and use their healing power to empower patients as significant *contributors* to their own healing as well as *power brokers* of their own "adequate care," as mutually defined. Serving as empowering agents will require health care practitioners, particularly physicians, to develop certain virtues, namely, humility, compassion, integrity. These virtues help blunt mere self-interest, constrain the use and abuse of power, and direct one's concern to the interests of others. They also help guide the application of the moral principles of autonomy, beneficence, and justice.

Finally, as a mediating practice, medicine can be seen as working to integrate various aspects of the sciences, including the psycho/social, as well as humanistic skills and knowledge. This must be the case if medicine is to provide "health" for "whole persons." Taking this perspective may also allow a more fruitful approach to technology as well as to overcome the false dichotomy of the sciences and the humanities and the presumed opposition between theory and practice.

Body as "Machine" Versus "Lived Body"

Medicine, like so many other fields of human endeavor, has been hindered, as indicated, by its unexamined adoption of a Cartesian metaphysician framework, a framework that reduced self to a cognitive knower only tenuously related to a mechanical material body.

Royce and other American philosophers such as Peirce, James, and Dewey, clearly repudiated the Cartesian view and exposed its inadequacies. For Royce, as we have seen in previous chapters, the self is a complex phenomenon, never rightfully reduced to any one of its many aspects—physical, sensory, emotional, motivational, cognitive, imaginative, or even spiritual. Further, for Royce, the self is also a process, constantly engaged in growth, change, and self-redefinition, as interaction occurs with other persons and other forms of existence.

In medicine, in contrast to a holistic notion of self, we have a focus on the person as body, but even more problematic, a body viewed as a machine with life. Leder argues, persuasively I believe, that the Cartesian body is a dead or inanimate body. Descartes, says Leder, motivated by a paramount concern for immortality, believed the perishable body to be a threat. In his dualistic scheme, then, nature and body took on the qualities of dead matter, of a machine. Both nature and body, then, could easily be mastered and controlled.[20]

In concert with this understanding of medicine's Cartesian machine-like dead body, Michel Foucault, for example, in his own 1975 critique of medicine, notes that in the eighteenth century, classifications of disease shifted from a basis in the symptoms experienced by a living patient to a basis in the organic lesions found in corpses. The experience of illness came to be viewed not as important but rather as epiphenomenal.[21] Leder summarizes the situation in medicine as follows: "At the core of modern medicine is the Cartesian revelation: *the living body can be treated as essentially no different from a machine.*"[22] Such a view of health and disease, of course, is reductive of the person, and it ignores other subjective forces of self such as beliefs, fears, worldviews, which do usually play a profound role in disease and response to treatment. Even the phenomenon of placebos should alert us to this fact.[23]

Fortunately, the voice of the phenomenologists who advocate for an alternative model of body as "lived body" is growing stronger in medicine.[24] Royce, who also engaged in phenomenological analysis, I believe, would find this analysis of person a very fruitful and generally correct one.[25] The "lived body" view sees the person as fully and necessarily embodied and as thus continuous with nature and material reality in important ways, yet also transcendent of them by the human characteristic of intentionality, of having purposes toward and in the world. Important to this view is what Leder calls the "intertwining" of the intentional and the material. "To be human is to be the site of an intentionality which is materially determined and enacted."[26] For medicine, this means that in treating disease it must see the biological and the personal/existential as crucially interrelated in a mutually implicated and interactive way. The biological is thus encompassed in a broader framework, that of the whole individual's experience of and responses to the disease. Disease can *not* be seen merely as a mechanical breakdown of a body-machine, but must now be seen as a global sense of disorder, a disruption of body, self, and world. *Illness* means a loss of certainty, of control, of freedom to act, and of a familiar world.

Illness, from the point of view of the lived body is experienced by the ill person as a fundamental loss of wholeness. There is a loss of bodily integrity and an alienation from one's body. E. J. Cassell puts this point very well when he writes:

> Disease can alter the relation (with one's body) so that the body is no longer seen as a friend, but rather, as an untrustworthy enemy. This is intensified if the illness comes on without warning, and as illness persists, the person may feel increasingly vulnerable.[27]

Because of the human person's inescapable embodiment and the fundamental centrality of body to human life and everyday activity, illness has to do not just with a threat to body but to the whole person. Robert Murphy, whose tumor forced him to a life in a wheelchair, writes, "Disability is not simply a physical affair . . . it is our ontology, a condition of our being in the world."[28]

However, the understanding of disease in traditional Western medicine is quite different from this. Robert Veatch, in a classic piece, describes disease or illness as viewed by the Western medical model.[29] Four essential characteristics of disease as viewed by traditional western medicine are identified: non-voluntariness; organicity; healing by a class of technically-competent experts, the physicians; and falling below some socially defined minimal standard of acceptability.[30] The first characteristic, argues Veatch, draws on the notion of the "sick role" as developed by sociologist Talcott Parsons. As Parsons defined it, the person in the sick role is exempt from responsibility for his condition. More importantly, "One in the sick role is not expected to use willpower or self-control to overcome his condition."[31] The patient, then, is expected to be a passive recipient of care, not an active participant in healing or treatment.

The second characteristic, organicity, focuses clearly on the materialistic, reductionistic Cartesian body. The emphasis would be on organic, somatic causes of the illness and on appropriate treatments and responses by "organicity" experts. Any connections of body with the psychological or with the lived world, would, of course, be ignored and regarded as irrelevant. Somatic (organic, biochemical, physical, genetic) determinism would be the prevailing understanding of any disease phenomenon.[32] Veatch raises doubts about such a view of disease by highlighting the inability of the medical model to deal with borderline cases, "marginal forms" of disease.[33]

As a typical marginal form of disease, Veatch focuses on narcotic addiction. Addiction, he notes, clearly has organic symptoms experienced by an addict in withdrawal—nausea, vomiting, dilated pupils, diarrhea, and elevated heart rate, and high blood pressure. These symptoms are not unlike an influenza virus. However, narcotic addiction also produces psychological symptoms—euphoria, craving, feelings of dependency, paranoia. There are also behavioral manifestations with decided social impact.[34] At the causal level, the questions become more problematic. Are the causes of addiction organic, perhaps biochemical? What, then, about psychological theories based on the belief that there are addiction-prone personalities? Or how do we evaluate sociological theories that place the cause of addiction in the environment of the addict?[35] Veatch's analysis, then, raises doubt about medicine's disease notion. Numerous critiques of medicine's traditional notion of disease conceived in purely physical terms have given additional support to Veatch's analysis and conclusions.[36] Among these are those of Caroline Whitbeck and George J. Agich who question a functional, objective, value-neutral analysis of disease such as offered in Veatch's "medical model view" and by Christopher Boorse in his writing on the concept of disease.[37]

Like its Cartesian model of body, medicine's objective, organic notion of disease seems inadequate for dealing with the healing of complete persons embodied in a "lived world." Thus, as the phenomenologists advocate, medicine should attend those aspects of disease sometimes called "illness behavior," aspects denoting the patient's experiences and perceptions of the disease. Nurses, sociologists/anthropologists and some physicians *are* concerned about this aspect of disease, as indicated earlier.[38] A most interesting study in this regard is by a group of therapeutic physicians and colleagues in Glasgow. The abstract of their work stimulates much thought:

> The amount of treatment received by 380 patients with backache was found to have been influenced more by their distress and illness behavior than by the actual physical disease. Patients showing a large amount of inappropriate illness behavior had received significantly more treatment. . . .
>
> The symptoms and signs of illness behavior need to be clearly distinguished from those of physical disease, and better assessment of illness behavior is essential if everyday clinical practice is to fulfill the ideal of treating patients as well as diseases.[39]

In focusing on a separate, inanimate body and on a reductionistic, organic concept of disease, medicine, I believe, often fails to heal those it seeks to treat, and it does so in a number of ways.

Medicine's Failure to Treat the Whole Person

First of all, medicine ignores a fact that Royce clearly took for granted, namely, the significant role that the body plays in the concept of person. The body is that which realizes the person in the world; it is a primordial incarnation of personhood in the world. Body is that aspect of my person that is most "public" and "shareable" and thus it plays an important role in my self-identity and meaning, both socially and personally. If radical bodily change occurs—whether it be severe weight loss or gain, radical anatomical change such as a sex-change operation, or unusual facial or other physical appearance alteration—new persons emerge. Thus, in the case of the young man "Dax," who suffered severe disfigurement from burns, he was lead to conceive of himself as a new person with a new name. Radical change in neurophysiology can also alter persons, as in the cases of mind-altering substances, mind-altering diseases like Alzheimer's Disease, or accidental damaging of the brain, as with Press Secretary James Brady. Our behavior toward these persons alters considerably, for they are "different people."

And as the incarnation of personhood, the body also serves as a primary locus of our unique capacity to act in the world, to exercise our intentions, and to demonstrate our freedom. Thus, the ability to move is a manifestation of our freedom, demonstrated so well in our human fascination with the automobile, flight, and other means of transportation.[40] The automobile and flying are aspects of human freedom. Likewise, each of the human senses, in their own way, are tools of human action and freedom. Disability in movement or in sensory areas are deeply feared by humans. Loss of bodily functions represent loss of human freedom; loss of bodily control, as we have said, represents a serious blow to one's personhood, one's lifestyle and life projects. Persons cannot be treated merely as objects of biological, anatomical, and neurophysical scrutiny and manipulation. This scrutiny and manipulation impacts the whole person. Medicine, in ignoring body/person intimacy, fails to treat persons and to recognize the profound impact of bodily malfunction.

In focusing on body, separate from other aspects of the self, medicine fails the patient in a second way, namely, it doesn't allow the patient to benefit from potential healing resources available from an acknowledgment of mind-body interaction and unity. The field of psychoneuroimmunology is especially promising in this regard. Studies of stress and bereavement on immune functions, studies of various affective factors on resistance to diseases and disease manifestations, biofeedback research, and studies of the effects of positive attitudes and humor stimuli on immune enhancement all point to several important conclusions. First, the immunological, neurological, and psychological human systems are highly interactive. Second, all three systems are involved in defending and adapting, learning from experience and important information transfer.[41] Third, beliefs, positive emotions, attitudes, and values about mind/body can play a key role in "constructive living" and in "healing." Eastern medicine has been aware of all of this for centuries, and Western medicine has much to learn from a fruitful interaction between the two traditions.[42]

Further, in failing to give credence to complex mind/body interactions, medicine has failed to deal with an aspect of disease/illness about which it is expected to have singular expertise, namely, pain. There is evidence, for example, that physicians have underestimated "pain" in children, thus failing to take proper means to deal with it effectively. Recent neurophysiological evidence indicates that pain is a complex phenomenon, involving a number of neurophysiological mechanisms, but clearly also influenced by a number of psychological factors. Thus, for example, the same injury can produce different degrees of pain in a person, depending on the circumstances.[43] Then there is the puzzle of the "phantom limb" phenomenon, in which an amputated extremity continues to elicit pain.[44]

Pain, whatever its makeup, is crucial to human survival. It provides information: it warns, protects, and teaches us about harmful aspects of the world. But information involves interpretation and meaning, and, thus, a person's expectations and meaning systems will and do influence how pain is viewed and dealt with. All of us are aware, for example, of the way in which early childhood interactions might influence future handling of pain. A cry because of a scraped knee might elicit a communication from one's mother of the following sort: "You have an ouchy, let me put medicine and a band-aid on it and make it better." This conveys one manner of dealing with pain, namely, it acknowledges pain's legitimacy, it warrants sympathy and indirectly promotes a medical approach. Another communication may lead to a very different set of ideas about pain. For example, one can say "big boys don't cry," thus denying the validity of pain and promoting a kind of stoic resignation. A third kind of pain communication might counsel that hurting is part of life and healing and to be incorporated into a coping strategy.

Dr. Wilbur E. Fordyce, of the Multidisciplinary Pain Center at the University of Washington Medical School in Seattle, argues that for certain individuals "the rewards resulting from pain and illness out number the rewards of everyday life."[45] Fordyce and his associates begin by asking, "Why is the person suffering?" Often they discover that job and personal unhappiness are the best prediction of which patients develop various chronic pains.

"Persons more active and personally fulfilled are less likely to enter into a chronic pain cycle."[46] Importantly, Fordyce's group uses hypnosis, psychotherapy, biofeedback, and behavior modification techniques to teach patients to take responsibility for their own care, increase their activity, and reduce drug intake. A lesson for traditional medicine is that drug therapy is not the significant mode of treatment for pain; rather, a variety of methodologies are used which assume a more complex set of factors are involved in the pain, including the psychosocial.

To take this approach in no way denies the reality of the pain. Further, it does not locate it purely in the mind or *only* in body, but rather in a complex interactive mind/body system. Researchers who study pain now believe that it involves a complex set of neurophysiopsychological factors. There are definite subtle communications between the mind, the brain—particularly the thalamus and hypothalamus, the immune system, including bone marrow and lymph nodes, and the endocrine (hormonal) system.[47] Stress studies are among the areas of research that help confirm this understanding of the complex neuropsychophysiological phenomena underlying this condition, stress, which affects so many individuals today. These studies also raise further questions about medicine's inadequate view of mind/body in healing.

Dr. Marvin Stein and colleagues at Sinai School of Medicine in New York have studied the immune systems of husbands who grieve after their wives have died from advanced breast cancer. This bereavement, they discovered, is accompanied by intense depression and immunosuppression.[48] Dr. George Valliant of Harvard University, in a large study conducted over several decades, found that "poor mental health was associated with poor physical health, even when such variables as alcohol, tobacco abuse and obesity were statistically controlled."[49] Dr. Richard Bergland, author of *The Fabric of the Mind*, believes that many illnesses, particularly those related to stress, require an understanding of the hormonal signal system. He makes a most astounding statement about "mind" in this regard: "Central to this concept that mind is modulated by hormones is the recognition that the stuff of thought is not caged in the brain, but is scattered all over the body. . . ."[50]

Whatever mind/body theory one might hold, it should be clear that the Cartesian view of radical mind/body dichotomy, with its mechanistic view of body, and medicine's singular focus on body as physiological do a great disservice to the treatment of patients, who are much more complex and whose illnesses are multifactored. And certainly, a person's mental and social world and resources cannot be ignored in the healing process. Again, stress studies document both positive and negative influences of social support, as well as important roles for emotional stability and personality.[51] Further, health benefits, including decreased blood pressure and reduced anxiety, resulting from human-animal relationships and bonding have been reported for a variety of specific illnesses.[52]

Finally, mental attitudes and beliefs do play an important role in health and healing. Stress studies, for example, indicate that a key factor is the amount of control a person *believes* she or he has over stress.[53] Hypnosis as a method for relief seems to work because it allows a person to put pain outside one's circle of attention by focusing on other images or metaphors; it allows one to dissociate from the sensations felt.[54] Eastern medical practitioners have long been aware of the role of hypnosis in healing.[55]

There is evidence also of the role of positive emotions and feelings in facilitating the healing process. Norman Cousins, former editor-in-chief of the *Saturday Review*, highlighted this when he wrote about the beneficial effects of laughter on his own serious illness: "One of the common characteristics of serious illness is panic . . . the best way to deal with panic is to replace it with laughter."[56] Cousins also believed humor and laughter to have beneficial effects on pain and on the immune system.[57] It is ironic and interesting, in this regard, to read the words of a famous physician who practiced in the 1600s, Thomas Sydenham: "The arrival of a good clown exercises a more beneficial influence upon the health of a town than of twenty asses laden with drugs."[58]

Finally, of course, there are the various studies of placebo. Some would argue that the placebo effect may be the most powerful example of the power of mind and mental factors in healing. On average, about a third of patients given placebos will experience satisfying relief.[59] Yet, there is a fair amount of disagreement and interpretation about the placebo and why it works. Norman Cousins stimulated much controversy with his account of his recovery, which included moving out of a hospital into a hotel where he viewed old movies and video tapes which provided "belly-laughter."[60] He also was given vitamin C intravenously in doses far beyond any recorded prescribed amount. A number of articles critical of Cousins's account appeared.[61] Some believed that freedom from standard drugs that often overwhelm the body or create harmful effects was the answer in Cousins's case, as well as in that of other placebo effects.[62] Cousins placed his emphasis elsewhere. He wrote: "Is it possible that love, hope, faith, laughter, confidence and the will to live have therapeutic value."[63] He also was clear that laughter was not his single causal focus, as many assumed. Further, he was not arguing for complete substitution of mental for the physical. He writes: "Laughter was just the metaphor for the entire range of positive emotions. . . . I never regarded the positive emotions, however, as a substitute for scientific treatment, I saw them as providing an auspicious environment for medical care."[64]

Whatever we may decide about the causal and other aspects of the placebo, it does point to a significant need for medicine to pay attention to subtle mind/body interactions and to a patient's inner resources. Dr. Jon Levine, a neurobiologist at the University of California, San Francisco, for example, argues that the psychological intervention represented by the placebo helps patients to turn on their own pain relief mechanism, namely, the pain-control circuit involving the neurotransmitters called endorphins.[65] Again, Eastern medical practice has long drawn on various inner resources in healing, and a number of Western medical practitioners are exploring the notion of "healing from within."[66] Finally, there are also those who would link the placebo effect to physicians' behavior and attitudes or to the quality of the physician-patient relationship itself. Howard Spiro, for example, sees placebo as a symbol of the "therapeutic alliance" and discusses this alliance in terms of Royce's doctrine of loyalty.[67] We shall pursue this idea in our section on the physician-patient relationship.

It has been suggested that medicine with its Cartesian view of body and reductionist view of disease fails to heal and treat persons adequately. It fails in fully treating and understanding pain and stress, and it does not draw on the inner healing resources involved in the complex neuropsychophysiological and social processes underlying the complex phenomena of pain and stress. Further, medicine may even do harm by promoting patient alienation from body. Alienation is clearly evident not only in the Cartesian model but in patients' reports on their own illnesses. Thus, Cassell reports that patients' stories almost always include two characters—the person and the person's body to whom things happen.[68] But "alienation from body," if it is the case, might well be considered unhealthy. This certainly seems to be the case with illnesses such as bulimia or anorexia and those involving self-mutilation or self-induced paralysis. Body plays a significant role in a person feeling "at home in the world" and "at home with self," and in the illnesses cited this seems not to be the case.

Further, the eating disorders of bulimia or anorexia and the "hysteria" with self-induced paralysis studied by Freud in Victorian times point to another aspect of medicine's failure to deal with body as "embodiment" and "lived experience," namely the profound role of cultural pressures in certain disease phenomena. Like hysteria in the nineteenth century, the incidence of eating disorders is disproportionately high among females. Further, like hysteria, these disorders are situated in advanced industrial society. A number of feminists and other researchers have challenged the traditional medical account of these disorders as just another pathological condition to which culture and gender provide only a "modulation factor."[70] Rather, these studies argue that these so-called diseases are really profound cultural disorders.[71] While the medical model holds eating disorders to involve distorted perceptions of reality, even a visual-spatial problem resulting from impaired brain-function or inadequate infant development, the feminists point to a culture that equates slenderness with competence, self-control, and intelligence; large breasts with air-headedness.[72] The argument about these disorders continues with contributions from many areas of research. Although the issue is not settled, I believe it again suggests that medicine, if it clings to its traditional paradigm, does disservice to the patients it seeks to treat by ignoring the lived-experience aspects of body and the multi-faceted aspects of persons who are ill. Alienation from body does not serve persons.

There is an aspect of medicine other than through its concepts of body and disease, by which medicine exacerbates the alienation of person from body as well as the loss of a sense of familiarity with the world. This is the increased reliance of medicine on technology. Patients find themselves dealing with machines and technological reports they cannot fully understand, and yet these alien things will often dictate what will be done with their disease, with their bodies. Technology ignores the experience of the illness and even the body, for it seeks to get beyond or inside the body. Body even appears as a obstruction; the emphasis is on probing for the "real" causes of the disease. Technology and its use add to the way in which medicine turns persons into objects to be manipulated for study, even to be dissected and/or taken apart. Transformed into objects, persons lose their agency, their sense of acting and seeking certain goals. The loss of control is further emphasized by the dependence on the physician and on other health care providers that the ill person feels. These professionals are the technological experts. In seeking the help of the trained healer, the ill person enters into what is viewed as a disturbingly unequal situation. There is an assumed asymmetry of power in favor of the physician, who "professes to possess exactly what the patient lacks: the knowledge and power to heal."[73] The ill person is made to feel the passive object of the actions of others. She has entered into an alien experience in an alien world where her personal projects no longer seem to count.

There is a profound alienation of self in illness, but also a deep isolation. In the altered state of illness the sick person is unable to carry on usually routine and normal activities. Others, however, carry on their normal activities and remain in touch with the everyday world and the world of personal projects. The ill person is cut off, preoccupied with pain, sickness, incapacity, all of which remains on the periphery of the experiences of others, even of one's significant others. There is deep existential aloneness for the sick person. Robert Murphy describes it as follows: "Nothing is quite so isolating as the knowledge that when one hurts, nobody else feels the pain; that when one sickens, the malaise is a private affair; and that when one dies, the world continues with barely a ripple."[74]

Traditional medical practice by focusing on disease and its control, cure, elimination, fails to see that illness is a deep, fundamental threat to the whole person not just to the body. Further, this is so, even though the illness is medically perceived as less serious physically. Although trained to battle death and to fight for life, physicians often fail to see the forceful intrusion of death and finitude into illness, even these of seemingly non-life-threatening implication. In an experience of illness, persons must face the failure of a deeply held assumption, namely, that of personal indestructibility. "We take it for granted, Silberman says, "that life is predictable and we are immortal and that we can, therefore, control our fate. . . . Illness destroys this primordial sense of invulnerability, forcing us to acknowledge our impotence and our mortality."[75]

Medicine in practice, then, fails to see that illness involves a fundamental reassessment of one's personal project, a readjustment and a re-creation of the person's life story.

Another profound failure of medicine is to ignore the validity of the person's story and the relevance it has to the healing process. As Royce and others argue, the person is his or her story, his or her life-project, and to ignore this is to degrade the person and to trespass on individual autonomy. Respecting autonomy, in medicine, is more than just lip service to informed consent, although an expanded understanding of informed consent is also important to healing persons because it helps guarantee their right to make decisions. However, patients also want and need to have their stories told. The advocates of the patient-centered method recognize this and assert, "The task of the physician is twofold: to understand the patient and to understand the disease."[76] Sacks, in his work with victims of Parkinson's Disease and other debilitating neurological disorders, has done a wonderfully imaginative job of entering the experienced world of the patient and of conveying aspects of this to us in such classics as *Awakenings, A Leg to Stand On* and *The Man Who Mistook His Wife For a Hat and Other Clinical Tales.*[77] Even more important, those who have experienced illnesses are writing their own stories. Thus, Stephen Lishen and his doctor provide a fascinating and rich narrative account of a heart attack from the point of view of the person who suffered the attack and the doctor who treated him.[78] Other patients are providing their stories including physicians who have experienced illness.[79]

Unfortunately the traditional medical model, as we have seen, sees experiences as epiphenominal and only "facts" about the body-machine as real and of any significance to the healing process. Thus doctors focus on these elements of the illness. They listen only to those aspects of a patient's story considered important as medical history, the biomedical interpretation of the disease-state. This history contains facts such as "onset of symptoms, disease, etiology, pathophysiology, course of the disease, potential for and options for treatment."[80] What is needed in addition is another kind of narrative or history. This narrative would provide the story of the illness from the patient's point of view. Cassell has suggested that such a narrative should bring out the facts and events that brought the patient to the doctor and also should include the patient's explanations, interpretations, and understandings of such facts.[81] Sacks would add to this narrative the patient's account of feelings and experiences while ill.[82] Others would include a "values history," or a "values journal," or a "values preferences" developed in dialogue with other patients' stories.[83]

More importantly, these aspects of the patient's story should be seen as significant knowledge contributions to understanding the illness. Again, however, traditional medical education and practice has emphasized the medical history, the voice of medicine, the voice that represents the technical-scientific assumptions of medicine. In fact, it devalues the voice of the patient represented by the clinical narrative and considers it irrelevant and inconsequential. Elliott Mishler, in his analysis of medical interviews between physician and patient, reports that in standard interviews the voice of medicine predominates, controlling the form and content of the interview. The physician treats the voice of the lifeworld of the patient as non-medically relevant and therefore quickly suppresses this voice in the interview.[84] Further, operating from a scientific viewpoint, the physician abstracts from the individual patient's narrative a syndromic (etiological) case, basing it on his/her knowledge of other "cases" and of the physiological and pathological processes of the body.[85] Thus the patient becomes objectified and rationalized, and the person's lived experience and personal meaning of the illness is ignored.

It thus becomes clear that in addition to a better model of 'body' and 'disease', what is needed in medicine is a different view of the person as well as a new understanding of the health care practitioner's role as interpreter and mediator between the voice of medicine and the voice of the lifeworld, between the person and the alienated body.

Patient as Whole Person and Self as Narrative Process

Medicine, it has been argued, needs a new view of the human person if it is to adequately address many of the criticisms it is confronting. The Roycean perspective on person, mind/body, and self, I believe, would serve medicine well in its search for a new foundation. First, Royce's view is decidedly anti-Cartesian and in two significant respects: it is non-reductionistic, arguing for a multi-varied view of the human self/person as a complex phenomenon resulting from numerous interactive factors. Second, Royce emphatically denies a mind/body dichotomy and views self in terms of process and not in any manner as a thing or object. However, he also clearly accepts the self as naturally embedded and embodied and the human person as having essential neurophysiological, biological aspects. Third, Royce, long before Husserl, wrote about the "intentional nature" of self, and his view would encompass much of the valuable contributions of recent writings from the phenomenological perspective, including concepts of body and illness as "lived experiences," a view of time as "lived" and "temporal duration," and a view of suffering in terms of alienation within and from self.[86]

Finally, most important is Royce's understanding of the human self as narrative, interpretive process. This perspective will offer much for overcoming the rift between the worldviews of patient and physician and for allowing medicine to deal more adequately with illness as viewed by the patient.

In seeking to understand a patient as a person, Royce's view would urge us to see each individual as a "person in process" and personhood as involving process, achievement, growth, development, as well as the possibility of stagnation and loss. Patients as persons, from a Roycean perspective, should be seen in terms of the following broad set of concerns or focuses:

a. the idea of person as object of biological, anatomical, and neurophysiological understanding, but also as naturally embedded and embodied, a living, acting organism;

b. the idea of person as a social-behavioral object of understanding and interpretation, but also as a socially, culturally embedded acting being;

c. the idea of person as a psychological subject with mental attributes and behaviors, but also a subject of consciousness, and self-interpretation, a purposive being who experiences and acts with intentionality;

d. the idea of a person as the locus of moral attributes and as a source of value, but also a subject seeking to realize autonomous personhood.

For Royce, each of these viewpoints provides valuable information about self, and each aspect of self is a fundamental part of self. But *no one* can be seen as the *only* valid view. Each view interrelates with the others to provide a fuller, more adequate view of self. Thus, though valuable and valid in its own right, the scientific view *cannot* be seen as the whole story of the human being. Yet, medicine relies heavily on the scientific view, and physicians learn to look upon patients as a collection of diseases, of facts to be acted upon. Thus Spiro, himself a physician, describes resistance among physicians to any notion of placebo to be due in large part to the scientific fallacy that most physicians have accepted. This fallacy is delineated by Spiro as the belief that "(1) measurement and quantification are essential to knowledge and that (2) facts and observations are entirely objective."[87]

Royce views science, we will recall, as a social, communal process. Scientific knowledge is partially a social construct, and "natural fact" is social, shared, public fact. Science works with certain leading ideas that are molded by but not predetermined in their details by experience. Royce writes:

> We report facts, we let facts speak, but we, as we investigate,
> in the popular phrase, "talk back" to the facts. We interpret
> as well as report. Man is not merely made for science, but
> science is made for man. It expresses his deepest intellectu-
> al need; as well as his careful observations. It is an effort to
> bring internal meanings into harmony with external verifi-
> cations. It attempts to control, as well as submit, to con-
> ceive with rational unity, as well as to accept data. The
> theories of science are human as well as objective. . . .[88]

Science represents a human view of reality, one influenced by social/cultur-
al, historical context as well as human purposes. It also gives us a glimpse
into reality, for facts represent the "stubbornness" and "contribution of the
external." For Royce, "Neither God nor man faces any fact that has not
about it something of the immediacy of a sense datum."[89]

The scientific view of person Royce would acknowledge as an important
one for medicine, but one which must be seen in context with other perspectives. Also the neurophysiological facts must be seen as also interpreted
differently depending on social/cultural/historical content. Thus, Royce
would not find puzzling the view of feminists that culture strongly influences
the disease phenomenon of anorexia, nor would he reject views about the
role of attitudes, beliefs, emotions in healing, nor the strange fact of voodoo
operating in a particular psychological, social context. Rather, Royce would
urge a careful, sympathetic study of these interpretations in order to seek a
broader, more effective perspective on healing and disease. Likewise, a dialogue between the individual patient's perspective on the illness, as well as
that of significant others, and the scientific/medical view would be a must.

Further from the Roycean perspective, another kind of interaction
among the four focuses on person would also be important to highlight, particularly among the moral/value, the self-understanding, and the neuro-
physiological/embodiment arenas. A person for Royce, we recall, is a
life-plan, an intending, intentional subject seeking to embody certain freely
chosen values and to accomplish certain goals or ends. An individual patient,
then, may hold very strong value judgments about body and about organs
such as brain and heart. Physicians, from the medical-model point of view,
which looks upon body as a dead, inert machine, need to be more sensitive
and less arrogant about the scientific view as the *only* valid view of person as
biological organism. They need to confront and genuinely struggle with, and

ultimately, if possible, utilize other views in the healing process. Thus, for example, an individuals of Jehovah Witness persuasion will genuinely believe blood and soul to be entwined and thus will protect the sacredness of their blood. In the area of organ transplant "sacredness of body" and "body as the temple of the person" are views that need to be better understood and more adequately handled. Likewise, the close connection between brain and personhood needs to be much more carefully explored and interpreted. There are cultures, Japanese for instance, which do not accept the Western notion of brain death. And many Westerners have difficulty with the notion of cortical death and its implications for persons in a persistent vegetative state.

Indeed, mind/body assumptions embedded in various treatment modalities need to be made explicit and conscious and should be critically examined. Treatments such as drug therapy, psycho-surgery, and ECS, for example, suggest an equation between sick mind and sick brain. And clearly much recent scientific research, as well as the long history of Eastern medicine and various alternatives medicines suggest a need for a new mind/body paradigm, one which clearly acknowledges mind/body and various neurophysiological-psychological-social interactions.

In this regard, Royce's reflections on 'mind', particularly in his 1916 metaphysical speculations, offer a fruitful base for development of such a new mind/body paradigm. In these 1916 investigations of mind, Royce faulted both perceptual theories of mind, those advocating the view that mind can be perceived immediately, and conceptual theories, which advocate some kind of independent mind.[90] Indeed, in a typically pragmatic manner, Royce asks, "What difference would it make if mind were seen in any of these ways, e.g., as Aristotelian entelechy or 'Lebnizian monad?'"[91]

Royce, as an astute pragmatist, would be aware that unconscious notions about 'mind' in treatment modalities—for instance, that mind is an illusion and not an important variable—strongly influence the way treatment is perceived and implemented, that they focus, for instance, only on behavior in behavior modification theory. As for Royce's view, he sees mind as "essentially a being that manifests itself through signs" and as demanding "interpretations," which necessarily relate a mind to other minds, thus forming a community.[92] Royce writes:

> A world without at least three minds—one to be interpret-
> ed, one the interpreter and the third the one for whom or

to whom the first is interpreted—would be a world without any real mind in it at all.

... mind is an object to be known through interpretation, while its manifestations lie not merely in the fact that
it possesses or controls an organism, it expresses its purposes to other minds, so that it not merely has or is will, but
manifests or makes comprehensible its will, and not merely lives in and through itself, as a monad or a substance, but
is in essence a mode of self expression which progressively
makes itself known either to its fellows or to minds above
or below its own grade.[93]

We shall expand on this Roycean view of mind further when we discuss self
as interpretative, narrative process. As can be seen, this view would closely
connect two areas of self: that which views person as psychological, active
subject, and the view of person as a socially-culturally embedded subject,
fundamentally interrelated with other selves. In stressing self as self-expres-
sive of purposes and values, Royce's view also interrelates self seen as moral
subject with self viewed both as psychological subject and social-behavior, related subject.

Indeed, as indicated, Royce would advocate a holistic, integrative view of
self that encompasses all four perspectives. Such an integrative view of per-
son/patient needs to become part of medicine's worldview, as well as part of
the medical school curriculum. That would do much to restore the human
touch and respect for medical-care personnel. David Owen, a British physician, states the issue well when he suggests that holistic medicine, often called
alternative medicine, would help to strike a better balance in medical care:

The holistic approach is not a new fangled, trendy manifestation of quirky and way-out opinions. It is the reasser-
tion of the traditional medical values where a sensitivity to
the individuality of the person is a precious part of the practice of the healing profession. The practice of medicine involves the whole person.[94]

Another important fact of the four perspectives on self/person is that, in
Royce's view, they all should be seen as fundamentally involving growth, de-

velopment, and change, or the lack thereof. Thus, one's biological, anatomical, and neurophysiological aspects do develop as the human being matures, and they can certainly change, even quite radically, as well as experience stagnation, loss, even extinction. Medicine does not have too much difficulty encompassing this aspect of self in its worldview, for such change is usually at the center of disease, injury, illness. Medicine, however, does fail in at least *two* ways in handling the phenomenon of biological/neurological change and loss.

First, it fails to see this process of change, loss, stagnation as a fundamental fact of the human person as naturally embedded. Rather than understanding illness, healing, and particularly death as natural, in a fundamental way medicine seeks to battle and control natural processes through technological assault, and it often fails to draw on natural healing processes or to allow nature to take its course appropriately. Such an attitude, of course, helps alienate a patient from self as "naturally embedded and embodied" and it also exacerbates patients' feelings of uncertainty, finitude, and bodily failure. In addition, it promotes false expectations about what scientific and technological medicine can accomplish in healing and cure and in overcoming nature's limits.

Second, medicine fails to deal with self as process and loss in its understanding of chronic disease and old age. This is unfortunate given the dramatic increase in the numbers of old people who often suffer from chronic diseases as well as degenerative illnesses like Alzheimer's and vascular dementia. The models of the understanding of old age on which medicine relies are inadequate to real understanding of the elderly, who clearly are a heterogeneous group, characterized by a great variety of abilities and a plurality of personal orientations and understandings. Thus, for example, the "deficiency model," which sees old age as a process of ongoing deterioration of mental and physical abilities, would only fit *some* elderly persons. And obviously old age and chronic illness are much more than merely physiological phenomena. One of the most fruitful approaches to the phenomenon of old age and of chronic diseases and even of "handicaps" is that of narrative. The meaning of each of these can best be understood and evaluated against profound background knowledge of the person's biography or story. Further, it has been suggested that this needs to be correlated with various meta-stories or narratives of the person's family, culture, society, religious group, and so on. This is true "because life stories are connected in different ways at different levels, the question of the meaning of old age when accompanied by chronic illness and disorder cannot be answered from a personal standpoint alone, but must reflect the meaning of chronic illness in the network of interpersonal relationships."[95]

Royce's view of the relationship between human being and nature, as discussed in chapter 3, is also more fruitful in this regard. We recall that Royce believes there are four characteristics that nature and human conscious life share: (1) irreversibility, (2) communication, (3) formation of habits, and (4) evolutionary growth.[96] Such a view of the relation of human self and nature has a number of benefits for medical understanding and practice. First, the concept of irreversibility might allow medical practitioners as well as patients to view aging, disease process, and death in a different light. It would not necessarily counsel resignation, but rather could facilitate working to encourage natural processes to enhance development in various stages of the aging process as well as various natural healing systems. It could facilitate better understanding of bodily/organic limits as well as potentialities and could allow patients to be more "at home with their bodies" and more "forgiving of bodily breakdown and loss. It could lead to a reassessment and new evaluation of aging, of positive aspects of illness and disease, and of the dying process. Acceptance of death as a natural process, inevitable for all, could allow a reordering of life-attitudes, habits, and values. And such a view of the affinity of humans and nature could set the foundation for a more fruitful dialogue with Eastern medical practitioners, self-help and self-health groups, as well as the feminists who have rightly protested the medicalization of such natural feminine events as menstruation, birth, and "life-change."[97]

The Roycean stress on "communicative processes" in nature fits well with the new studies in neuroimmunology, stress, and biofeedback, which point to the complex interactions between neurophysiological, immunological, hormonal, and psychosocial systems. It fits well too with new views of the subject-object relationship in science and knowledge that actively draw on the commonality between mind and nature by stressing attunement and similarity between knower and known.[98] Royce's understanding of the affinity and continuity of human life with nature would also raise interesting questions about research with other organisms and the use of animals in treatment of humans, including animal organ use. Our focus in this regard might change considerably if the focus changed from the Cartesian notion of animals as machines to animals as embodied with varying levels of consciousness or feeling.

The notion of humans as "naturally embedded" could establish more clearly ideas about natural habits of body and listening to and being attuned to body. Likewise, again it could allow patients and doctors to understand body more fully as lived experience and as a crucial component of one's life-plan and narrative. Seeing body as natural, developmental process connected to a narrative process would also allow a more adequate understanding of persons whose development is arrested, stagnated, or reversed and lost, as with the neurophysiological retarded, the encephalic, the persistent-vegetative-state patient as well as those affected by diseases such as Parkinson's, Huntington's, MS, and Alzheimer's.

This brings us then to Royce's view of person/self as narrative process. Royce, we recall, saw the human person in terms of interpretation, both from one's own view and from the view of others. Human persons are self-interpreters; they weave a life-narrative. Royce's view is that "In brief, my idea of myself is an interpretation of my past linked to my hopes and intentions as to my future."[99] Likewise, each individual is interpreted by others and these interpretations can be ignored, incorporated to varying degrees in one's self-narrative or even conflict with that self-narrative. Charles Sanders Peirce best captured this aspect of the human person when he wrote, "Man is a sign."[100] To view human person in terms of a narrative, interpretive process is to identify certain key aspects of personhood. First, personhood is temporal, historical, contextual. Each person's narrative, whether from the view of the self or others, involves a temporal span of past, present, and future, however short or long. Indeed, although the individual self's narrative may be limited, even severely, by one's bodily limits or one's finitude, because the interpretive process itself, for Royce, is potentially infinite, the narrative of the self can be continued on indefinitely by the community of other selves, as have the stories of individuals like Plato, Jesus, Lincoln, even Elvis. This aspect of self as narrative might help us handle more effectively premature death and arrested or reversed human development. This individual self can have meaning in the lives of others, and the life-narrative can be constructed and carried on beyond the individual time span of the self.

The temporal nature of person as interpretive narrative has profound implications for understanding illness, particularly as experienced and understood by patients. Drawing on Husserl's work, Sartre's analysis of pain and illness, and her own experience as a sufferer from multiple sclerosis, S. Kay Toombs describes the temporality of illness viewed from four levels of experience.[101] Toombs brings to the fore Husserl's distinction between inner or "lived time" and objective or "outer time." Lived time, is probably best exemplified in our experience of music, an experience Royce also drew upon extensively in his analysis of human experiencing. One experiences music not in terms of distinct, atomistic notes but as a holistic melody extended in duration, as a "continuum of temporal phases which are inextricably interrelated."[102] In this type of inner time experience, past, present, and future form an inseparable unity.

Objective time, the time consciousness and concept of the scientific view, divides time equally, and time flows on in these equal periods, regardless of lived events, human purposes, and meanings. Alfred Shutz captures this notion of time when he writes:

> The hand of our watch runs equally over half the dial,
> whether we wait before the door of a surgeon operating on
> a person dear to us or whether we are having a good time
> in congenial company.[103]

Royce, for example, spoke of a "spacious present," observing that one can hold in one present, without conscious use of memory, "a succession of three or four beats of a pulse, or of ticks in a watch."[104] In this regard, Husserl distinguishes the retentive memory of time-consciousness which he called "primary memory," from "secondary memory," or "recollected memory."[105] The importance of these time-consciousness distinctions for medicine is that the patient's primary experience of illness is via "internal time consciousness," and thus illness is viewed essentially as a time-phenomenon. The physician, on the other hand, whose view is primarily scientific, sees the illness via objective time and in terms of distinct "states." Thus, as Toombs rightly concludes, "Illness represents [for patient and physician] in effect two distinct realities—the meaning of one being distinctly and qualitatively different from the meaning of the other."[106]

To grasp the radical difference in view between patient and physicians, we will consider Toombs's analysis via the view of Jean Paul Sartre and his explication of pain and illness. Sartre identifies four distinct levels of experience of pain and illness: (i) pre-reflective sensory experiencing, (ii) "suffered illness"; (iii) disease; and (iv) the "disease state."[107] The first level of experience of illness is that of the "felt experience of some alien body sensation."[108] Further, at this level of experience there is no consciousness/body distinction; rather, pain *is* the stomach at this moment. The pain is "lived pain."[109]

The next level of experience involves reflection on the pain, and pain is seen in terms of psychic object, as in "pain in the stomach." This stage is "suffered illness," yet, importantly, it is experienced in terms of inner-time consciousness as a temporal duration. Sartre notes that at this level, one does not conceive of illness as cause of pain, but rather, "Each concrete pain is like a note in a melody; it is at once the whole melody and a 'moment' in the melody."[110] Further, the illness is apprehended in and through each pain, and yet, like a melody, "it transcends them all, for it is the synthetic totality of all the pains, the theme which is developed by them and through them."[111] This is "suffered illness."

It is only at the next two levels of experience that the notion of disease that prevails in medicine comes to the fore. For a patient, who normally does not experience body as a neurophysiological organism, illness as objective disease, as a stomach ulcer, for instance, represents an abstract and reflective level of experience, indeed, primarily as an external experience of others. A patient is able to see her body as an object, "a being for others," only by drawing on bits of knowledge acquired from others.[112] To name the immediate, painfully-lived experience of the stomach "gastralgia" is to see one's body as from outside, as alien and abstract. The physician's conceptualization of the patient's illness constitutes a fourth, even more abstract level of experience. The illness is identified with pathoanatomical or pathophysiological specificity, as "a question of bacteria or of lesions in tissue."[113]

In the latter two levels of experience, the illness and the body have become objectified, and "objective time sequence" and "causal chain" now become paramount. Patient now sees body and illness as external object, and physician views the patient as object, and the disease as fact and not as lived-experience illness and pain. But unfortunately for medicine, the lived experience cannot be readily ignored if the whole person is to be treated and healed. Further, there is a radical communication/meaning gap between physician and patient. Edward Scarry captures this communication gulf vividly when he describes the "unsharability" of pain in the following way:

... when one speaks about "one's own physical pain," and about 'another person's physical pain,' one might almost appear to be speaking about two wholly distinct orders of events. For the person whose pain it is, it is "effortlessly" grasped (that is, even with the most heroic effort it cannot *not* be grasped); while for the person outside the sufferer's body, what is "effortless" is *not* grasping it (it is easy to remain wholly unaware of its existence; even with effort, one may remain in doubt about its existence or may retain the astonishing freedom of denying its existence; and, finally, if with the best effort of sustained attention one successfully apprehends it, the aversiveness of "it" one apprehends will only be a shadowy fraction of the actual "it."[114]

This Husserlian/Sartrean analysis of time and the experience of pain and illness portrays a sense of profound alienation between patient and body and a disturbing perpetual disparity between physician and patient. If healing, in the sense of restoring some harmony and wholeness is to take place, medicine needs not only a new view of person, but a related new approach. Such an approach is to be found, we believe, in Royce's doctrine of interpretation.

Before turning to this, however, we would like to approach the alienation and disparity from a different point of view, namely, that of the patient as intentional subject, as a person with values and goals and as a plan of action. This, for Royce, is the essential aspect of person, as he makes clear in the following two statements: "I am a will, a will which is not there for the sake of something else, but which exists solely because it deserves to exist";[115] and, *"By the meaning of my life-plan, by this possession of an ideal . . . by this, and not by possession of any Soul-Substance, I am defined and created a Self."*[116] In this regard, one needs to see pain, illness, and suffering not only in terms of experience and time, but in the context of the purposive activity of human subjects. Freud, in his book, *Civilization and Its Discontent,* suggests that a person may "suffer" in three different ways: via body, via relations with others, and via the "powers of the self."[117] In each of these areas, conflict and frustration of the subject's will, goal, and plans may occur. Royce, as we know from previous chapters, also saw the self as conflictual within and without. Royce would have added a fourth manner in which conflict for self can occur, and that is in terms of one's relationship to the whole, namely, to the universe and its purpose. One might call this "spiritual conflict."

In a provocative analysis of the concept of suffering, Mary Rawlinson identifies these four arenas of possible conflict as "the realm of embodied action," "the theatre of intersubjective life," the "arena of will," and the "realm of universal harmony."[118] She sees these also, and rightfully in my judgment, as "four orders of meaning," or "horizons of value." In each of these areas, frustration and disruption of a subject's values and purposes can occur. Thus, in the realm of embodied action, where body represents our "system of access to the world" and the background and means for gestures, words, mobility and behavioral actions,[119] there can be disruption between our embodied capacities and our possibilities of action.[120] This kind of disruption and frustration clearly occurs in disease, illness, aging, and accident, including inherited physical disability, where our body fails us and prevents us from doing what we normally might do.

In the "theatre of intersubjective life" the rupture occurs between, on the one hand, roles with which the self has identified and which play a key function in self-identity and, on the other hand, roles into which a person is cast.[121] As previous chapters indicate, Royce saw role-playing and role-modeling to be a crucial part of the creation of self. Further, he would agree with those interpretations which see social/culture intersubjective life very much in terms of various roles one takes on: for instance, those of colleague, friend, parent, lawyer, lover. And most importantly, Royce would find acceptable the understanding of illness in terms of a deep disruption of one's normal roles and relationships. Because these are so crucial to self, illness is a profound disruption for self. Further, in illness, the subject-actor has to take on a role alien to free intentionality, namely, the "sick role" which involves passivity and dependency. *To heal* would be to overcome this disruption in the theater of intersubjective life by restoring, as much as possible, the capacity for social life.

The "arena of will," manifests itself in three ways in a person's life. First, it does so in the life-plan, the life-narrative, through which the self weaves a life history, tying together past, present, future, promises, obligations, values, desires, and goals. The second manifestation of will is in work and mastery, the ability of self to make things, to have achievements, etc. The final area of will is that of the moral self, the self who has principles and through those principles has integrity. One has consistency of action and lives in accord with one's principles. Suffering occurs when there is disruption in any of their three areas of will, and illness can cause such disruptions. Illness can be such a crisis for self, as with the paraplegic, that it becomes extremely difficult to incorporate one's present dysfunctional state within one's life history. And certainly disease or accident, for instance, can prevent one from making, working and accomplishing. Indeed, this is the tragedy of early loss of life. Finally, being a patient with limited freedom and perceived as passive, makes one especially vulnerable to a rupture between the ability to act and the recognition of the moral principles one finds binding.

A final arena of suffering is the spiritual, where rupture occurs between the patient's present condition as ill or dying and his image of the whole. A crisis of faith often occurs in dealing with severe illness or a crippling accident. In all four areas of disruption, healing calls for some kind of reconciliation, some kind of harmony. However, medicine is ill-equipped to deal with any of these alienations. Indeed, it assumes them unimportant and ignores them.

A different view of medicine as "mediating practice" and of physician as "interpreted healer" might well, however, help make for a different story.

Medicine as Mediating Practice, Physician as Interpreter

It has been argued that medicine, as presently practiced and conceived, fosters conflict and alienation. Operating with a Cartesian view of body and of the mind-body relation, medicine promotes the alienation of patients from their bodies, from their life-plans, from their intersubjective relations and everyday life, and even from their value and spiritual systems. Further, because medicine, in practice, operates from the objective/scientific/technological point of view, it sets the stage for conflicts of interests, understandings, and actions between the physician and the patient, whose primary perspective is that of personal and everyday praxis. If medicine is conflictual and adversarial, it fails its primary mission of healing, namely, to bring about harmony and functionality. Medicine, then, needs to reconceptualize its view and reorder its values. A new view of self has already been suggested, and now also imperative is a re-conceptualization of medical practice that provides more adequate healing of the "whole person."

Such a way, I believe, is provided via Royce's doctrine of interpretation and his discussion of the notion of mediation.[122] Royce, we recall, had a lifelong concern for the "harmony of will," believing that ultimately the self could not escape willing to live in harmony with all conflictive wills.[123] His goal, always, was to urge the building of community within self and between selves. To this end, he developed the doctrine of interpretation, the philosophy of loyalty and combined them into a theory of mediation, not of the forensic (adversarial) type, but designed "to prevent disputes from arising."[124]

Medicine, I want to argue, must become a "mediating practice," along with law, politics, and theology. These practices have an obligation to integrate and intersect various levels of human meaning and *praxis* in order to promote the harmony of individuals and communities. Each of these mediating practices have a healing function: to overcome disruption and dysfunction in each of the arenas of meaning for purposive subject/action, namely, the arena of embodied action; the theater of intersubjective life; the arena of will, and the spiritual universal arena. And, although each of the mediating practices focuses its attention to *one* arena of meaning—for instance, law and politics in the theater of intersubjective relations and theology in the spiritual arena—they each must also give attention to all four orders of meaning if they are to heal whole persons.

Practitioners of mediating practices should be seen as having special relationships with those whom they seek to heal, namely relationships built on trust and loyalty founded on their healing and interpretive roles and at both the individual and communal level. These relationships call for certain moral attitudes and virtues, i.e., certain character traits or behaviors, which, for Royce, are founded on the principle of loyalty to loyalty, namely, the principle of fostering loyalty and broadening the scope of community. Indeed, the disruptions in the various arenas of meaning may be seen as disruptions of loyalty and community. In the arena of body there is disloyalty to the body and disruption of the community of self and body. In the theater of intersubjective relations, there is disloyalty to others and disruption of the community of self and others. In the arena of will there is disloyalty to self-chosen goals and principles and disruption of the community of self. Finally, in the spiritual realm, there is disloyalty to one's ultimate concern and disruption of the beloved and universal community. Viewing these disruptions as disturbances in loyalty makes good sense from a Roycean perspective. Further, it is also in partial agreement with the view of the sociologist Talcott Parsons, who authored the model of the "sick role," and who placed illness along with crime, sin, and treason under the broader category of "disturbances of obligations."[125]

Turning to medicine as a mediating practice, its primary focus, of course, is on the healing of disruptions, of disloyalties and loss of community in the patient's arena of embodied action. However, because it seeks to heal the whole person and because illness, as made clear earlier, disrupts the lived experience of the patient, medicine cannot ignore disruptions in the other areas of meaning. Illness impacts significantly on a patient's normal intersubjective relations, on her ability to work and be productive, on her lifeplan and narrative. And, depending on the nature and severity of the illness and the types of decisions required for its management and treatment, illness can cause major disruption of one's moral and spiritual understanding. Thus, the physician and other health-care providers, whose main healing task is to reestablish some harmony between embodied capacities and the patients' given and chosen possibilities, must also be cognizant of the other types of disruptions and be prepared to deal with them themselves or with the help of other professionals. Indeed, physicians, whose main goal is healing of disruptions in patients' various arenas of meaning, should see their task as done in conjunction with other healing practitioners. A community of healers and of healing makes sense for a person viewed as a complex of meanings, rather than as merely a biological organism. To operate in a team mode or as a member of a community of healers, however, will require a reconceptualization of the physician's role in health care.

The mediating and interpretive task for the medical practitioner, then, requires utilization not only of scientific knowledge, which highlights the neurophysiological, anatomical, and biological capacities of the person, but also the resources of the behavioral/social sciences, which bring perspective on the intersubjective social/cultural context of the person and of embodied action, together with the insights of the humanities, which illuminate the volitional capacities of the person as well as the capacity for narrative construction. This, of course, argues for changes in medical education, which, by and large, has focused on heavy doses of the various natural sciences, with neglect of other views of the person and of meaning. Medical practitioners need a good background in the social sciences and the humanities. This should be true for physicians as well as for other health-care providers, especially as the team or communal approach to healing is developed. Nurses traditionally have some of this background, but all who work in health care should have a broad-based education in the humanities and social sciences as well as the natural sciences. Because of the many science requirements, these other areas of study are often ignored.

Advocates of broadening the educational base for medical practitioners have made their argument for some time. Our perspective adds another basis for such claims. Thus, several prominent physician scholars, namely, Eric Cassell and Edmundo Pellegrino, have long argued for a prominent place for the humanities in medicine and in medical education.[126] Pellegrino, throughout his career in medicine and medical education, has expressed his commitment to a close association of medical learning with humanistic learning. This commitment is found in his often-quoted statement of 1970 that "medicine is the most humane of sciences, the most empiric of arts and the most scientific of the humanities."[127]

In a recent article on the place of humanities in medicine, Cassell argues that the humanities can help put the "living person back into medicine."[128] Literature, for example, offers the opportunity to see the interplay of illness and the individual, to share the perception of doctors by lay people, and to heighten sensitivities to the human reality of pain, loss, and death.[129] History would help medicine overcome its cohort egocentricity, its "belief that what we do today is the best that has ever been done, . . . that what we lack is just around the corner."[130] History would also help medicine to understand that illness is a temporal process.[131] Language study would allow the doctor to see that "the spoken language is the most important tool in medicine."[132] Philosophy would provide skills to reason carefully, to formulate a clinical problem, and to utilize appropriately both analytic and valuational modes of thought.[133] From a Roycean perspective, of course, all these aspects of humanistic study are essential to personal narrative construction, to community building and to the art of interpretation.

Another area needing study for medical practitioners concerns the ethnic and gender context of patients. Although women and children comprise the majority of the patient population, they often do not receive equal treatment in health care or in medical research. Over-medical, radical approaches such as radical mastectomy, unnecessary surgeries such as hysterectomies and cesarean sections have been part of the history of medical care for women. Further, women perceive that they are often treated by medical practitioners as incapable of understanding and participating in medical care decisions.

Recent technological advances in reproductive medicine have brought forth many questions about conception, abortion, pregnancy, and childbirth, all crucial issues for women and children. New technologies have also raised fundamental questions about the care of human offspring including prenatal and other genetic testing, fetal therapy, and the care of critically ill infants. Yet the fields of medicine and even bioethics are dominated by male voices and perspectives; health-care research has focused on male populations. Little attention has been given to the perspectives and interests of women and children as well as to the meaning and role of family in health care. Further, women's health problems are often seen only in terms of the reproductive function, and these functions are seen as over-medicalized. Fortunately, a number of feminists and female bioethicists have recently addressed all of these concerns and more. Three fine examples of this effort are: *No Longer Patient,* by Susan Sherwin; *Women and Children in Health Care,* by Mary Briody Mahowald; and *Feminist Perspectives in Medical Ethics,* edited by Helen Bequaert Holmes and Laura M. Purdy.[134] This material should be incorporated into medical-school and nursing-school curricula, as well as into the educational materials for other health-care practitioners.

A noteworthy example of such an effort is the Medical College of Pennsylvania, which, in 1993, initiated an interdisciplinary Women's Health Education program for first- and second-year medical students and their faculty facilitators. The approach is to integrate women's health issues completely into all aspects of the curriculum, including basic and cultural sciences and the teaching of psychosocial issues.[135]

In addition to gender issues, medicine and medical education need also to incorporate and address issues of race and class. The African-American population as well as other ethnic groups have received unequal and less than satisfactory health care due to at least three factors: institutional racism, economic inequality, and attitudinal barriers to access.[136] In order to provide healing to patients, attention must be given to cultural and societal aspects of health care. An excellent introduction to these issues, especially as concerns African-Americans, can be found in *"It Just Ain't Fair": The Ethics of Health Care for African Americans,* edited by Annette Dula and Sara Goering.[137] A medical education project that seeks to address this has been initiated at Pennsylvania State University, sponsored by the Foundation for the Improvement of Postsecondary Education (FIPSE) funding. The project provides "Human Diversity Training" for medical students through curricular material, case studies, case conferences, and actual clinical experiences with diverse populations.[138]

The broader education of health care professionals, particularly physicians, is crucial to providing healing to persons seen as complex and in process. However, several other complementary approaches would change medical practice and help move toward a more holistic healing approach. One of these approaches has already been mentioned, namely, working in health care teams and as a community of health. Rather than expect one physician or health-care provider to be able to deal with all arenas of meaning for the patient—including gender, racial, and ethnic arenas—expertise can be provided by other members of the team, including nurses, social workers, clergy, and psychiatrists. In addition, these teams can include physicians, nurses, and other health-care providers from minority groups and/or providers who are bilingual or specially trained in cultural, racial, ethnic, and/or gender sensitivity.

One of the interesting developments in health care in the United States is the effort of various HMO's to sign up minority populations, to recruit ethnic physicians, and to train doctors and staff to provide culturally sensitive care. They are also hiring bilingual support staff and are translating materials such as enrollment forms, benefit summaries, and physician directories. Some are also changing their ways of delivering health care. A clinic in Phoenix, for example, schedules female doctors one morning a week to perform gynecological exams on Hispanic and other women who might be reluctant to see a male doctor.[139] Other groups are relaxing policies on visits to patients in hospitals, even intensive care units, to allow groups whose cultures are oriented toward "extended families" to have family members stay with patients.[140]

Many patients who come from a different cultural and language background prefer doctors and health-care providers who share their background. Thus, HMO groups are negotiating contracts with groups of Hispanic and Asian doctors such as the Chinese American Medical Society. This can help medicine deal with the broader aspects of the patient's life and thus promote better healing. For example, George Liu, an internist in New York, who belongs to the Chinese network of an HMO, sees many Chinese patients who have irregular heartbeats caused by taking certain herbal medicines. He, unlike a non-Chinese doctor, can more likely recognize the cause of this condition and be able to persuade a Chinese patient to abandon a traditional remedy.[141] This is the case because he understands the patient's arena of meaning that embodies traditional Chinese medicine.

Of course in promoting the team approach to medicine, and a notion of a "community of healing," the traditional understanding of the doctor-patient relationship needs to be reassessed and reconceptualized.

Much of the discussions of the role of the humanities in medicine focuses on the centrality of the doctor-patient relationship in the healing process. Again, Edmund Pellegrino helps capture this centrality when he speaks of medicine as an art and describes this art as "the ability to acquire and integrate subjective and objective information to make decisions in the best interest of the patient, and to strengthen and utilize the relationships between patient and doctor for therapeutic ends."[142] We shall discuss this idea shortly. However, we first need to know that there have been numerous analyses of the doctor-patient relationship—what it has been, is, and should be. A good overview of these is provided by James T. Childress and Mark Siegler in their article "Metaphors and Models of Doctor-Patient Relationships: Their Implications for Autonomy."[143] As this article makes clear, each model of the relationship implies a different conception of the moral principles of autonomy and beneficence and which of these principles should have moral priority in medicine.

Several models focus primarily on benevolence and are paternalistic, that is, they envision the relationship on the prototype either of the *parent-infant* or *parent-adolescent* relationship. The physician is active guide and actor in such models; while the patient is passive and cooperative and obedient. These models assign moral authority to the physician and assume that "good health" is a shared value with the patient and one commonly defined. In sum, these models "tend to concentrate on care rather than respect, patients' needs rather than their rights and physicians' discretion rather than patient's autonomy or self determination."[144] From a Roycean perspective, these models would be judged defective, for they are antithetical to his view of person and of genuine relationships. Many contemporary scholars also find paternalism morally defective, particularly those who hold for the moral priority of the principle of autonomy in medical relationships.[145]

There are two varieties of models that stress autonomy: those emphasizing the contractual nature of the physician-patient relationship and those emphasizing partnership or covenant.[146] Eric Cassell advocates both the centrality of autonomy and a partnership model: "Autonomy for the sick patient cannot exist outside of a good and properly functioning doctor-patient relation. And the relation between them is inherently a partnership."[147] Cassell stresses collegiality, collaboration and association, as well as the pursuit of the shared value of health. More importantly, the stress is on equality of contribution and respect for the autonomy of all participants involved. Cassell, however, does not deny a division of competence and responsibility in the relationship. Thomas Szasz and Marc Hollender describe this model as an adult-adult relationship. In this model the presuppositions are that "the participants (1) have approximately equal power, (2) are mutually interdependent (i.e., need each other), and (3) engage in an activity that will be in some ways satisfying to both."[148] Another key aspect of this model is that it acknowledges that the patient's own experiences furnish indispensable information.[149] As we develop our own Roycean perspective on the doctor-patient relationship, we shall see many affinities between that view and the partnership model.

The contractual model is advocated by Robert Veatch, its strongest proponent, and others as a necessary compromise between the *ideal* of partnership and "the *reality* of medicine, where mutual trust cannot be presupposed."[150] Contracts, argues Veatch, protect the autonomy and integrity of both parties in health care. Such a view of the doctor-patient relationship, I believe, is inadequate for many reasons. It fails to fit health care because such care is rarely perceived and should not be viewed as another consumer good to be bought and sold. The contractual model also harms the notion of medicine as a professional practice with a moral base and a goal of service. In addition, it exacerbates medicine's present tendency to treat patients as objects. Finally, the contractual model tends to see the doctor-patient relationship as an economic pay-off arrangement and certainly not as therapeutic. Even the more economically oriented managed-care environment does not see the doctor-patient relationship as contractual. Rather, the view, as we shall see, is one of joint stewardship of health care resources.

Turning to our view of medicine as a mediating practice and the health care provider as interpreter and community enhancer, what does this imply for the doctor-patient relationship? Interpretation, for Royce, we recall, was a key part of building one's self-narrative and life-plan, as well as for building genuine community. It was also an important, third form of knowledge. Interpretation is a form of mediation that brings together two minds, ideas, hopes, and persons. Its goal is to take selves outside of themselves to create new unities or harmonies, that is, some commonly shared ideas, goals, and values. In achieving this new view—this new union of ideas or values—a contribution to knowledge, to the stock of ideas, has been made. In the case of medicine, interpretation would seek to bridge the gap between the perspective of the health care practitioner and that of the patient. Some commonalties of goals, values, feelings would be sought. We have already seen that these two perspectives on illness are very different. Further, in a very pluralistic society with a multitude of cultural/ethnic social groups and related values and views, some common base for the healing process needs to be sought. As Childress and Siegler note, "The assumption that the physician and patient have common values about health may be mistaken."[151] Childress and Siegler, as well as others who propose models for the physician-patient relationship, assume *differences* in meaning and values as a given around which the relationships must operate. The Roycean focus on interpretation, however, argues for an *active* role, if possible, on the part of the physician, the patient, and others to overcome some of these differences, to seek to build *some* community of meaning. And, indeed *both* patient and physician can and should function as interpreters, as well as others crucially involved in the situation.

To see that this is the case, we need to recall some crucial elements of Royce's view of interpretation. The first element is respect and regard for each self and idea involved. Like the partnership model, it would be assumed that patients' experiences and perspectives are valid contributions to understanding the nature of the illness, its impact, and meaning. Likewise patient's priorities, views of health, and life-plan are to be considered important components of treatment plans, etc. Physician and patient, as well as other health care providers and the patient's significant others, can act and should act as interpreters, so that the most adequate view of the patient's overall situation may be attained. In order to allow the interpreter role to become a crucial part of health-care delivery, however, the physician and the patient, as well as other health-care providers, will need to reconceptualize their roles, their conceptions of medicine, and even their views of health care ethics, especially as it concerns the principles of autonomy and beneficence and their proper role in health-care decision making. Indeed there are elements in the contemporary health-care scene already forcing reconceptualizations.

Before we address these reconceptualizations of provider roles and of medical practice, however, it is necessary to remember several important points about traditional medical practice. First, professional autonomy for the physician used to be a strong operating assumption. With a monopoly on medical knowledge and science, the physician had uncontested independence in treatment decisions. This included control over admission of patients to hospitals and specialist care. Further, because of self-regulation of the profession, physicians controlled entry into medical education and into the profession; they successfully prevented competing practitioners, such as chiropractors, out of the mainstream of medicine. The medical practitioner was truly autonomous, both individually and as a professional.

Second, patient autonomy is a relatively new concept in medicine. The notion of "beneficent paternalism," of the physician operating for the best interests of the patient and often deciding for the patient, was, and perhaps still is, a dominant notion in medical practice. Patient autonomy, which includes access to information and freedom of action in treatment decision making only became operationalized legally in 1957 in the doctrine of informed consent.[152] The concept of patient's rights is also new and was imported into the medical context from an extrinsic, social agenda, namely, the Civil Rights Movement of the 1960s. The movement to establish the patient's right to refuse treatment has, in fact, been an uphill battle.[153] This is most evident today in the controversy over the right to die. Many patients fear that medicine will rob them of control in the situation of terminal illness and that they will die alone, in pain, surrounded only by machines.

Thirdly, even physician advocacy for the patient is a relatively new idea in medical practice, originating probably in the 1980s. This notion encompasses a mix of ideas including always acting in the best interest of the patient; a commitment to continual care (that is, not abandoning the patient); a norm of doing good for the patient, that is, benevolence and effacement of the physician's self-interest in favor of the patient.[154] The physician had a duty to faithfully ascertain patients' interests and desires and to advocate for them. Professional advocacy is seen in the context of an indissolubly individual relation between physician and patient.[155] These traditional notions of physician autonomy and advocacy are now being challenged by changes in health-care delivery in the United States under the pressures of a drive to contain escalating health-care costs. The movement is toward a situation in which managed-care arrangements are dominant. "Managed care" is a term referring to a variety of alternative health delivery plans, including health maintenance organizations (PPO). Such plans seek in some degree to combine financial and medical decisions—for instance, case management and hospital preadmission certification—and often involve third-party payers.

It is being claimed that physicians who operate in these delivery systems, and this is an increasing number of practitioners, will find new challenges to professional autonomy and the traditional understanding of the patient-physician relationship. Some argue that even the traditional medical ethic is being challenged. The first challenge to professional autonomy concerns treatment decisions. Independence in treatment decisions is being restricted in managed care situations because many of these will have to be justified to a third party who controls payment, and these decisions are subject to their approval. Further, physicians will be directly subject to financial risk because of costly treatment decisions and will be recipients of monetary incentives if decisions are made for more cost-effective treatment plans. This will significantly affect the ability of physicians to advocate for idiosyncratic patient needs. The physician will have the role of gatekeeper to medical services, a role they have played in the past but with a crucial difference. The new emphasis is on keeping costs down. Physicians will be redirected to focus on primary and outpatient care and to avoid hospitalization and high-cost treatment. Service for patients will be standardized. In these types of managed care situations, it is being argued that the principles of autonomy and beneficence will take on different meaning. Thus, the physician will now have a dual obligation of "fidelity to individual patient" and "stewardship of society's resources."[156] Further, physicians are urged to adopt the following principle: *"As a clinician I believe it is ethically mandatory to recommend the least costly treatment unless I have substantial evidence that a more costly intervention is likely to yield a superior outcome."*[157]

Indeed, a new and significant emphasis in health care delivery is to focus on outcomes and more particularly on the notion of quality health care defined in terms of contribution to the patient's health and well being. Traditionally, quality of health care was judged according to three main parameters: (1) process (whether medicine was competently and properly practiced); (2) structure (the settings in which care took place); and (3) outcome (the effect of care on patients' health and satisfaction).[158] However, the assessment of quality primarily concerned process, especially how well science and technology were applied to diagnosis and treatment, and little concrete data on this was actually collected. The assessment of the structural component primarily concerned the number of beds and qualified personnel available, as well as availability of standard and specialized equipment. Little attention was given to outcomes for patients and especially to patient perspectives on and satisfaction with the care given.

The new quality-assurance movement in health care, like that in education, emphasizes provider performance in terms of outcomes for patient well being and health. As in education, the emphasis is likely to be on peer review of performance, but peer review of performance based on standards of acceptable care. Further, these standards probably will not be determined solely by practitioners, as in the past. Rather, the standards will have to gain the confidence of *both* those judged by them as well as those to whom the standards apply, namely, the patients.[159] The emphasis will be upon patient satisfaction and patient decision making. Thus, patient education will become an important task for the medical field and for health care providers. Individual patients and the public will be educated about effective and ineffective health services, in order to improve patients' ability to choose the care they want to receive.[160]

The new health care reforms seem, then, to be projecting new roles for physicians and for patients. For the patient, emphasis seems to be on autonomy in the sense of "consumer sovereignty," that is, making informed choices about health-care providers and services. Indeed, the direction that the quality assurance movement in health care seems to be heading is toward a "*patient accountability paradigm*," which "guides physicians and providers and subjects them to patient control. It enlists the participation of patients and consumers to evaluate and change the medical care system and to promote the rights and choices of patients and consumers."[161]

Such as paradigm holds that there must be new mechanisms to hold doctors and other medical providers accountable to patients. One mechanism suggested the use of *voice*: for instance, the voicing of complaints and grievances and the promotion, through association and other mechanisms, of specialized interests. Two excellent examples of this are the women's health movement and the disability rights movement.

One aspect of the women's health movement, for example, is the formation of self-help groups such as the Women's Health Book Collective of Boston and the Los Angeles Feminist Women's Health Center. These groups perform many functions, including sharing and emotional support, providing advocates and advocacy, and even providing information on competing services and institutions. Another important function is providing information about women's health in such books as the Boston Collective's *Our Bod-*

ies, Ourselves. These groups have also helped train medical personnel to be more sensitive to women's needs and interests in providing medical care.[162]

Likewise, the disability rights movement has formed self-help groups, but also has promoted the concept of independent living. The latter activity challenges the dependency of the disabled on professional experts to make decisions concerning services that disabled people need as well as the best way to provide them. Rather, independent-living advocates argue for the ability and necessity of the disabled to make their own decisions and to assess their own risks relative to functioning in the real world.[163]

Another focus of the "patient accountability paradigm" is the concept of 'exit'. This notion concerns patients "exiting" from health-care-providers relationships and seeking medical services elsewhere. This concept relates most clearly to the movement known as medical consumerism. This movement perceives medical care as a service and patients as consumers who can and should choose both service providers and the kinds of services given. The emphasis is on increasing the amount of information to the public about health care providers and the services they give. The advocates of medical consumerism contend that the medical care delivery system will respond to patient demand, and they believe that commercialization and entrepreneurial activity in medicine will ultimately increase the quality of health care and benefit patients.[164]

The contemporary health care scene, then, is one of uncertainty and of change. Physicians' roles and obligations are being redefined as are those of the patient. The physician is being held accountable to society for stewardship of health care resources and to the patient for health care which meets better their needs. The real question in this regard is whether this dual obligation can be met and whether, in fact, they might be contradictory obligations. As indicated, the demands for cost-cutting tend to lead to standardization of health care services rather than meeting patients' needs. This problem may be partially addressed in the reconceptualization of the patient role, namely, in the emphasis on educated choice—finding and using services that meet individual needs, including gender, ethnic, and racial concerns. The major question is whether the demand for an educated, informed patient is realistic in all cases and whether such a demand does not, in fact, discriminate against the poor and the more vulnerable.

I believe the Roycean perspective that emphasizes interpretation and loyalty can provide helpful guidance in these issues. The delivery of health care must be refocused around the notion of a community of healing that must include various health-care providers, third-party payers, and patients as "members" whose perspectives, contributions, needs, and interests are respected and taken into account in significant and relevant ways. Each of these groups must perform the role of interpreter, as appropriate, and all must be seen as loyal to a common goal, the goal of healing—seeking the adequate functioning of the patient in terms of the four arenas of meaning. The relationships involved must be conceptualized in terms of this loyalty so that the traditional dyadic, individualized relationship between physician and patient is overcome, and triadic relationships become important.

With the focus on loyalty and community comes the principle of loyalty to loyalty, which includes a commitment to the broadening of the community of healing. This, in turn, would carry with it a concern for the access of all to the resources of healing and for the stewardship of healing or health-care resources. For health-care providers this would mean a commitment to outcomes and to performance that produces proper and fitting care for patients. It would become an ethical duty to assess, in concert with the patient and other health-care providers, what constitutes the most efficacious and economic treatment for this individual whose goal is to function with his or her context of meaning. This may well require various forms of interpretation, mediation, and advocacy in order to provide a harmony of interests. For patients this would require a refocusing on their life-plan and context of meaning, as well as a more careful consideration of costs to community as well as to self. Patients will also need to reassess the role of technology in providing healing and to begin to deal with the concepts of limits to the use of health-care resources. Patients, too, must become stewards and accountable for their medical-care decision making. Financial incentives in this regard might well be appropriate. However, medical consumerism and the emphasis on economics is dangerous in promoting the increasing reduction of humans to economic self-interested individuals and of health care to just another commodity. The better concept is stewardship.

'Voice' and 'exit' are also important concepts. Indeed, these concepts were developed in the context of loyalty.[165] As Royce makes clear in his discussion of loyalty and community, the voices of each member of a community is important to the overall well-being and proper functioning of the community. 'Exit' should only occur after repeated efforts to voice one's concerns have failed. This is essential, for example, for whistleblowing, which is considered morally justified. 'Exit' also, from the view of a community, should be perceived as a "tragic failure." Genuine communities develop mechanisms for the expression of all its members' voices. The mechanisms adopted by the women's health movement and by the disability rights movement, such as self-help groups, advocacy, and education, are correct and should be promoted, for they represent those "enlightened provinces" discussed earlier. Small enlightened provinces—for instance, of nurses, physicians, clergy, social workers, and ethnic groups—within the "healing community" would be beneficial to the overall community. These groups and individuals can educate and interpret and thus help build a harmony of interests and goals.

This brings us back to physician and patient and to ethics and virtues. In order to help develop a community of healing, however, the physician who has the social power and the authority of expertise must have the will to interpret as well as the courage to facilitate interpretation by others. The physician must, in fact, seek to embody a group of virtues, courage among them, because the process of interpretation for Royce has a strong moral base. It requires the virtues of *humility, compassion, patience, hope, prudence, courage,* as well as a deep commitment to the principle of loyalty to loyalty. Indeed, as we shall see, this principle unifies and transcends the principles of autonomy and benevolence.

The will to interpret involves *humility,* as a recognition of one's own and others' partial perspectives and meaning. It involves *hope* that some harmony may be possible, that a fuller meaning and view will be obtained. It involves *courage,* for one must be willing to reach out to others and to open oneself to communication. One must be able to risk having one's ideas tested and compared against the ideas of others. *Compassion* is another virtue involved in the will to interpret because one needs to try to understand, experience, even sympathize with what is significant to the other. One needs also *patience* and *tolerance* to be able to confront, understand, and seek some common ground with values and views quite foreign to one's own. Finally, interpretation involves commitment to the principle of loyalty to loyalty, the desire to harmonize conflicting loyalties and values so that broader truth and value can be realized. This principle demands that one seek to foster loyalty and community and to overcome conflict and betrayal.

As a healing, mediating practice, it seems most appropriate that medicine should have loyalty to loyalty as a central moral principle. In fact, such an idea has already been proposed by Howard Spiro, a practicing physician:

"Loyalty could provide a useful guiding principle for the relationship of professional to client, loyalty to what physician *and* patient *agree* to be the patient's best interests."[166] Although Spiro draws on Royce's philosophy in making this proposal, he does make an assumption that tends to prevail in much of the discussion of medicine and of the physician-patient relationship, namely, that the moral burden, even the moral superiority, belongs only to the physician. Thus, McCullough and Chervenak, in their otherwise illuminating discussion of patient-physician relationships, exemplify this tendency when they write: ". . . the creation of the moral relationship between physician and patients is asymmetrical."[167] It is not moral asymmetry that is involved, but rather a power-asymmetry. Physicians, in our present patriarchal social structure and in the traditional medical model, are looked upon as both moral and technical experts. However, physicians are only experts in medicine and should not presume their moral vision to be superior to that of patients or other health care providers. Indeed, physicians must have the courage to use their power to enhance the ability of patients to make decisions and to deal adequately with their illnesses. They need to act as interpreters as well as to facilitate the interpretations of patients and others who might contribute to the healing process.

Further, physicians must have the courage to question the present social structures of medicine, particularly the corporatization tendencies in health care, but also the patriarchal-discriminatory practices that do exist. Spiro states the issues very well when he writes:

> Loyalty to the patient means many things. It raises questions about corporate practice of medicine, now so popular. It brings in to focus the conflicting obligations of salaried physician to those who hire him and to those whom he treats. It even raises questions about who should enlist patients in controlled clinical trials. Such trials are essential for the assessment of clinical prospects, but I must wonder whether the physician who is 'in charge' of the patient can put knowledge to be gained ahead of his patient's welfare unless he is convinced that the treatments to be compared are equal and that to trust to chance is not harmful. Loyalty to the patient will not permit the extra diagnostic test for a fee or the ordering of a study for defensive

medicine. Thoroughgoing loyalty puts the patient's interest above all others, requires a second opinion in uncertainty, puts the patient's case above the physician's.[168]

Spiro, unfortunately, writes in the spirit of the traditional dyadic physician-patient relationship. This, we have argued, must be transcended and become a triadic relationship with the focus on healing as mutually perceived and on stewardship as also part of loyalty to the broader community. Again, patients must become educated to their roles, responsibilities, and powers. Patients, too, need virtues. Karen Lebacz has, in fact, provided us with a very nice piece on "the virtuous patient."[169] She argues, I believe correctly, that virtue is not simply character traits but appropriate responses to situations.[170] This fits well the argument for the centrality to medicine of the Roycean principle of loyalty to loyalty, for, as Oppenheim argues, Royce pioneered in creating "an ethics of the fitting."[171] We shall return to this point, shortly

Lebacz, in this context, sees "being a patient" as a role and virtues of a patient as having to do with "excellence in the role as well as responses to pain and personal change."[172] One essential value for the patient, in Lebacz's view, is fortitude, which she partially interprets as follows: "To accept limitation, to endure in the face of the unchangeable, to quiet the heart. . . ."[173] However, as part of fortitude, she also includes the ability to "reassert autonomy" and to seek control.[174] I would add to this the courage to interpret and to demand interpretation. The other two virtues identified by Lebacz are those we also highlighted as part of the will to interpret, namely, *prudence* and *hope*.[175] Hope involves "perfecting the will to trust in the attainment of the end," and to believe that meaning will "emerge out of the chaos, pain and sense of injustice."[176] Prudence is "the ability to perceive the reality of the situation, to discern what is required as a fitting response, as well as the willingness to act on what one perceives."[177]

These virtues are those of an interpreter and thus would be required of anyone who takes on that role, whether patient or physician or another. Indeed, an "ethics of the fitting" seems imperative to a reconceptualized health care system which seeks to balance autonomy, beneficence, and justice in a context of loyalty to healing and stewardship. Cost-cutting must not do harm or inappropriately override autonomy and human dignity, and stewardship of health care resources must not be achieved at the expense of the poor and the vulnerable.

Pellegrino has written extensively on the "virtuous physician" and he too stresses the virtue of prudence. Pellegrino's analysis focuses on virtue as "defined in terms of the ends of medicine." Further, he argues that the patient's good is the end of medicine. This concept Pellegrino describes in terms of four basic components, namely: "(1) clinical or biomedical good; (2) the good as perceived by the patient; (3) the good of the patient as human person; and (4) the good or ultimate good."[178] Each of these components of the patient's good must be served, and thus prudence is the essential virtue for medicine, because, writes Pellegrino, "Medicine is itself ultimately an exercise of practical wisdom—a right way of acting in difficult and uncertain circumstances for a specific end, i.e., the good of a particular person who is ill."[179] Pellegrino's analysis is illuminating and is in partial agreement with my own. The four types of 'good' he identifies are roughly parallel to our four areas of meaning. However, an important point about Pellegrino's analysis, and one which weakens its value, is that it is basically a paternalistic view, emphasizing the principle of benevolence over that of autonomy, although it obviously does not ignore autonomy. Indeed, Pellegrino develops an extensive philosophy of medicine based on the principle of "enlightened beneficence."[180] It is our view that neither the principle of benevolence nor the principle of autonomy is alone able to understand an adequate physician-patient relationship. Pellegrino and others have acknowledged that there is a difficult tension in medicine between autonomy and benevolence and that there is a need to maintain a balance between the two. Pellegrino writes: ". . . the vulnerability of the sick person confronts the power and authority of the physician exposing the subtle ambiguities that may attend the operations of autonomy principle . . . the doctor's concern for doing 'good' may conflict with the patient's definitions of what is 'good.' The whole is further complicated by the pathophysiological impediments illness may place in the way of fully autonomous decisions by those who are ill."[181]

A view of medicine as mediating practice and Royce's doctrine of interpretation, I believe, help confront and hopefully overcome this difficult tension between the principles of autonomy and benevolence. This is the case because loyalty, as a principle, integrates the three principle ideas of ethics. Royce proclaims this interpretive power of loyalty when he writes, "Loyalty, as you remember, is an effort to bring into union; into a sort of synthesis and cooperation, the three leading ethical ideas, the idea of independence, the idea of the good and the idea of duty."[182] The interpreter, committed to the principle of loyalty to loyalty, is committed to treating all persons respect-fully, to enhancing autonomy, and to the common good. Most importantly, however, the interpreter has the primary duty of building a genuine com-munity, which enhances all individuals while also seeking to find the right interpretation and right set of choices fitting to the situation, allowing re-spect, healing, and a common good to be achieved.

Much more needs to be said about creating a genuine community in medical practices and about healing in all areas of human meaning and dys-function. Obviously the task of mediating and interpretation is one that all those involved in health care need to undertake—patient, physician, nurse, ethicist, hospital administrator, social worker, priest. It is truly a communi-ty effort. Further, education is a key task, not just medical education but education in a broader sense, in the art of loyalty, which Royce describes as follows:

> Three principles of the Art of Loyalty have been set before you. First, the principle: Steadfastly train yourself to the re-solve that your various causes shall be harmonized. Second-ly, the principle: In case of the appearance of conflict, look beneath the superficial conflict to find if possible the deep-er common loyalty, and act in the light of that common loyalty. Thirdly, the principle: If conflict cannot otherwise be resolved, act in consistency with your prior loyalty, re-membering that, if a change of flag may indeed be some-times required by some transformation of your insight, fickleness is never a part of loyalty. Your cause, once chosen, is your larger self. Fickleness, if deep and deliberate, is moral suicide.[183]

Or, more succinctly, the art of loyalty discerns what fits one's unique self as devoted to one's particular community(ies) and the universal community.[184] There is much in these ideas for medicine and medical practice and for all who wish that the healing of whole persons will occur. I certainly intend to explore the concept of loyalty in the Roycean sense as the foundational value for medicine, and for other professional practices. I hope others will be stim-ulated to that task also.

Groundwork for the Future

A T THE BEGINNING of this book, we posed two major questions: Why a book on public philosophy, and why one founded on the thought of Josiah Royce? Both questions I believe have been satisfactorily answered. Public philosophy is desperately needed today in the United States because there are many public issues that are matters of great concern to many diverse communities and that have profound effects on those groups of people. Almost every aspect of life common to all our people struggles with crisis, confusion, conflict, and, even more fundamentally, a basic questioning of ultimate meaning and worth.

This is true of the family, sexual relations, education, work, politics, the law, the press, and the church. For example, in the area of family, the meaning of parenthood is being radically altered by the new genetic and reproductive technologies, while, at the same time, the traditional authority of the parent is being severely challenged, even ripped asunder in the courts. Familial worth and relations are being sorely tested by various forms of violence and abuse afflicted on spouse, parent, child. The acts of violence on children; surrogate parent technologies, black markets in baby selling, and procuring children for sex, as well as the precarious lifestyles of street children and latchkey children lead many to believe that children are no longer valued as persons. Further, with the spectres of AIDS, the threatening clouds of sexual harassment, the increasing rates of divorce and remarriage, and the questioning of the assumed validity of heterosexual relationships as the primary human relationship, many find the whole area of sexual relationship confusing, disappointing, or even terrifying. Yet many also search desperately for satisfactory human companionship.

Education, as made clear in chapter 6, has been under a continual barrage of criticism. Public education in the United States is considered by many to be a failure, and a number of parents seek alternative forms of education. Violence and despair afflict many public schools in this country and not just in the inner city. Too many "quiet," small communities have recently witnessed school shootings or inexplicable teen suicides. Many of the younger generation are being lost to drugs and violence, and even the very young are becoming vicious killers.

The workplace is rapidly changing as technology takes hold in more and more areas of productive work. Downsizing in the corporate community has left many persons dazed, confused, unemployed after years of loyalty and service to a company. Employee dissatisfaction has led to increased white-collar crime and even murderous violence against bosses and fellow employees. For too many persons, work is drudgery, something that merely has to be done but that has little or no meaning or ultimate worth. Areas of business and investment once thought to be solidly reliable have been brutally tested by savings-and-loan and bank failure, by stock market scandal, by collapse or insecurity of insurance and pension funds, and even more recently by the financial bankruptcy of the reputed wealthy and stable government of Orange County, California.

The area of politics is one of great disenchantment for most Americans. It seems to be dominated by inefficiency, nasty and dirty campaigning, greed, and scandal. More people than ever before agree with the phrase, "The less government the better." Yet many also depend on government funding for health, for sustenance, for education, for work, and many who have no other recourse seek government funding. Gridlock, lack of progress, and petty squabbling seem endemic to the political system. The electorate votes to overturn legislation and to oust current office holders. Self-interest groups of all sorts hold sway and compete for power and influence, and there is no real sense of public good or pubic interest. The media, which traditionally has protected the public interest seems more interested in money, influence, sensationalism, and entertainment. Those with powerful media influence often represent the most of limited self-interest or revel in blatant negativity.

The legal profession is perceived by many to be dominated by greed and self-interest. Lawyers are blamed for exacerbating the already litigious, adversarial nature of U.S. society. They are faulted, in this regard, for helping to raise the costs of medical care as well as the costs of environmental protection. Many believe too many sensitive issues are being fought out bitterly and adversarially in court, rather than settled quietly and with more compassion in private. The fairness quotient of the criminal justice system for minorities and for women, especially in areas of spousal abuse and rape, has long been an issue. As crime rates seem to soar, the public rallies to more and more punitive, expensive, and not necessarily successful measures. Prison expenses and population increase more rapidly than funds for education and health. Finally, even the high court is tainted by scandal, in the movies, in fiction, and in real life via the Anita Hill case.

Certainly, many issues pose important problems and greatly stimulate a variety of concerns among the public in the United States. Yet, it is doubtful whether there is much public philosophy, at least, as defined by Sullivan in his book *Reconstructing a Public Philosophy*.[1] Sullivan identifies two key aspects of a public philosophy: (1) a "public life"; and (2) a "public understanding." "Public life" he defines as a condition "when a society realizes that reciprocity and mutual aid are worthy of cultivation both as a good in themselves and as providing the basis of the individual self."[2] Public understanding Sullivan believes, is captured in shared traditional beliefs about being a responsible member of community, both of one's particular communities and of those that transcend and yet are "of common concern to many diverse communities."[3]

These two aspects of "public philosophy," I believe, have a difficult time developing or flourishing in the atmosphere of self-interested individualism that pervades so much of life, both individually and communally in the United States. The notions of freedom and autonomy have been key components of the our American psyche, seemingly from the beginning of our existence. These closely related concepts found abiding ideological homes within American popular, legal, and political culture and are expressed in our celebration, in numerous ways, of the individual. They are also manifested through our anger at infringement by others of our rights, particularly those of property and taxation without representation. Our constitutional protections of personal liberty are sacred and have meant much in our historical, political, and social development as a country.

Closely connected with these aspects of autonomy and freedom is our American belief in the validity of the concept of the "rational economic man" and our faith in *lassiz faire* economics. There is a strong conviction in this country that markets are the fairest and most efficient means of distributing social goods, and for many the business contract has become the supreme model of a sound moral relationship.[4] Further, even giving and benevolence are individually based, each person choosing his or her own charity or cause, thus providing those tiny pinpoints of light, identified by President Bush. Religion, which might normally temper egoism and teach love and community, in this country is itself deeply infected by rugged individualism, often in very subtle ways.[5] Individual salvation and individual choice in religious belief or nonbelief have been exalted, often leading to a deep intolerance of the beliefs of others or ironically falling into a ironclad collectivism. Indeed, one wonders if rugged self-interested individualism is a good breeding ground for both intolerance and mob-rule collectivism. Royce's experiences in the mining communities of California would lend support to such a supposition.

None of these comments should imply that 'autonomy', 'freedom', and 'individualism' are not vital, important concepts. At the center of all philosophical and legal discussion about morality is the assumption that human beings possess free will, choice between options. It is here that human responsibility resides. The sense of our own autonomy, the potential to control our destiny, is clearly one of our essential attributes as human persons. I have, on other occasions, argued for the necessity of a concept of autonomy and free 'will' against the reductionist materialistic behaviorism that pervades the social sciences.[6] However, the meanings of *autonomy* and of *freedom* have been distorted by overemphasis, by lack of attention to the limitations of these concepts, and by ignoring the need to balance carefully and integrate these ideas with others of equal importance, namely, love, loyalty, compassion, community.

Both John Stuart Mill and Immanuel Kant, the two philosophers key to providing the moral and political philosophical foundations for our doctrines of moral autonomy and political freedom, did place limits on these concepts, and it is well, at this point, to reconsider those limits, as well as the deeper aspects of the concepts themselves. First, both Kant and Mill were clear that 'free choice' was intrinsically valuable, that is, valuable in itself and not because of the goods that it might lead to or because of any other factors. Autonomy, that is, free will, was, for Kant, that which distinguished the human being from all other species. He writes:

> Man in the system of nature is a being of slight importance . . . but man regarded as a person—that is, as the subject of a morally practical reason, is exalted above any price. . . . Autonomy then is the basis of [human] dignity."[7]

However, although autonomy, i.e. the exercise of free will is essential to human nature, the ultimate good, for Kant, is "good will." He proclaims, "It is impossible to conceive anything at all in the world, or even out of it, which can be taken as good without qualification, except a *good* will."[8] It is not *free will* alone that is good but free action for the good of self and others. Kant's notion of good will, of course, has received much discussion, but it seems reasonable to assume that he intended the exercise of free will to be tempered by "sympathy and concern" for others and to be set in a context of community. Willard Gayland, for example, argues that conscience is the equivalent of a good will.[9] Further, Gayland relates conscience to the emotions, particularly those of guilt, shame, and pride, but also to those "vital to the development of the most refined and elegant qualities of human potential-generosity, service, self-sacrifice, unselfishness, love and duty."[10] Indeed, with Martin Buber, Gayland believes that guilt and conscience are also essential to that which is specifically human nature.[11]

Kant's own concern for community, for others, for the "kingdom of ends" is expressed, I believe, quite clearly in his statements of the categorical imperative, that is, the supreme moral principle. The first version of that imperative is "Act only on that maxim which you can at the same time will to be universal law." Although there are problems in interpreting this rule, one aspect of it seems basically non-controversial, namely, that it intends moral action to have a perspective that takes into account others and communal life together and that rules out a single-minded, self-interested perspective in the sense of being advantageous to oneself. Thus, the willingness to universalize one's maxim is a willingness to see one's rule—for example, the rule that it is okay to break one's promises if it suits one's purposes—acted on by everyone in a situation of a similar kind, even if he himself turns out to be on the receiving end of a broken promise. Kant calls upon us to reflect upon the *kind* of communal life we would establish by our actions and their implied values and principles. A promise-breaking society would not, for example, be a pleasant society in which to live.

The second statement of Kant's categorical imperative exalts "autonomous personhood" as a key moral value but places limits on the exercise of that autonomy by each individual in terms of others and in terms of the individual's autonomy and life-plans. Kant states this imperative as follows: "Act in such a way that you always treat humanity whether in your own person or in the person of any other, never simply as a means but always at the same time as an end." Autonomy, for Kant, has its fullest meaning and expression in the context of others, the community, the "kingdom of ends," I would say, in the context of Royce's notion of the "beloved and universal community," and guided by the principle of loyalty to loyalty.

Turning to John Stuart Mill, the other philosopher of 'freedom' and 'autonomy', we find again both exaltation of autonomy and the exercise of individual free will, but also a clear statement of limits to this capacity. Mill believed that the development of individuality is essential for human well-being and that this individuality is best seen in terms of 'liberty', that is, "framing the plan of our life to suit our character, or doing as we like, subject to such consequences as may follow . . . even though they [our fellow creatures] should think our conduct foolish, perverse or wrong."[12] Gerald Dworkin asserts that Mill's argument for free choice of the individual was in no way consequential. Its value did not rely on goods that free choice might bring, but rather Mill's emphasis is on the "absolute value of choice itself."[13] Only individuals, believed Mill, will be most interested in their own well being and most knowledgeable about what that might be.[14]

However, for Mill, as for Kant, free choice as self-regarding behavior has its social communal context and its limits. The liberty of an individual should be, argues Mill, exercised "without impediments from our fellow creatures," but within a very important constraint, namely, "so long as we do not harm others."[15] Indeed, Mill went on to argue that even the sanction of law and public opinion could be brought to bear on an individual who ignored obligations to others—for example, a legitimate third party, a child perhaps, needing blood. Mill writes that "when a person is led to violate a distinct and assignable obligation to any other person or persons, the case is taken out of the self-regarding class."[16] We recall from Willard Gaylin's argument about conscience and good will that Mill also wrote extensively on the concept of 'natural sympathy for others', as well as on the role of emotions in human behavior.

We are brought back, then, to the tension between individual and community and to that between the moral principles of autonomy and benevolence, as well as to the demands of justice. Public life and public understanding, the key components, at least according to Sullivan, of public philosophy, face a difficult challenge in the milieu and ethos of the United States. This is so, I believe, because individualism and autonomy have been overstressed and distorted by separation from the social and communal context. These notions have also gained exaltation through the distortions of community into mass collectivism and benevolence into blatant paternalism. The whole moral story has not been told. Further, as human beings we are too easily enticed by the simplicity of black-and-white thinking, by clear either/ors. We seem to fear the ambiguities and tragedies of real life. As Thomas Murray rightly speculates, the "near-exclusive emphasis on autonomy is attractive in part because it permits us to avoid many unpleasant and complex realities."[17] It is not easy to live in communities where others stubbornly and unreasonably, from our point of view, hold beliefs and engage in practices we find foolish, perverse, or wrong. Family life, parenthood, even intimate relationships, though promising to be deeply satisfying, are troublesome, difficult, frustrating to sustain and develop over time. Caring without sacrificing self is not easy. Further, many of us find it difficult, confusing, even embarrassing to face the often ugly particulars of the human psyche, whether it be our own or that of another. The trouble with a conscience, as Pinocchio discovered, is that it can be a damn nuisance. The psychopath, the extreme conscience-free individual, of course, has no such difficulties.

Sin and guilt are things none of us wish to feel. Indeed, it is so much easier to share it with anonymous others. Collective guilt seems easier to swallow, although it, too, pales because we do not believe in communal will, mind, or action. It is difficult for those of us raised on a philosophy of rugged individualism, laissez faire, and the American Dream to think about limits. We find them inimical to our notion of free action. Individual initiative, especially without over-interference from others, we believe will gain us wealth and happiness. This perhaps is why illness and death are seen as such grave evils: they seriously, even finally, frustrate our goals and plans. Raised with the myth of conquering the frontier and believing in the great power of human initiative and creativity, as expressed in technological progress and advance, we, as participants in the American ethos, are not creatures who like limits or boundaries. Like the starship *Enterprise* we hope to transcend them and unendingly find new and better worlds.

Yet, there is no doubt that we also long for community. We search desperately for human companionship, even if of a self-defeating and limiting kind, like a gang or an abusive marriage. We seek happiness and peace, trying every means from drugs to New Age philosophy. We seek communion with nature, even if in our technological cocoons, our campers. And many of us, though often deeply cynical, believe in human goodness, in sympathy, in service, in acts that are not self-interested. Many of us engage in such acts, consciously or by accident. Human goodness does often get press time, though it seems far overshadowed by the evils, the flaws, or even the foolish trivialities of human action.

What is needed is a framework, a grounding for our better tendencies, our communal, concerned, loving tendencies; but for us it must be a framework that also acknowledges the great value of those three things we hold so dear—our autonomy, our freedom, and our individuality. This framework, I argue, is one based on the thought of Josiah Royce. A public philosophy, with this base and center, would, I believe, go a long way toward helping us address in a critical and adequate way the major issues we, as a multicultured, multiethnic society, face. This book, I believe, has done much to establish such an argument and position.

In the chapters on genuine community, genuine individualism, and on loyalty as a major mechanism for building community in a very individualistic world, I believe I have explicated the crucial aspects of Royce's thought that would allow us to create a viable and fruitful public philosophy. There we pursued Royce's belief that worthwhile individuality can only arise out of a communal context, but a communal context that is supportive of true individuality and that fosters the building of broader and broader senses of supportive community. We examined the many ways in which community can foster genuine, moral, responsible individuals with a life-plan and narrative uniquely their own. Likewise, I explicated the Roycean conditions for a genuine community, many of these also identified by the popular writings of M. Scott Peck.[18] Among these conditions was the individual's need and power to extend self temporally, perceptively, emotionally, cognitively, behaviorally. As finite and limited, the individual needs others.

An important process for individual and community development is the Roycean process of interpretation, a process that mediates between past, present, and future, between the various ideas, actions, feelings of self and those of different individuals and communities. Its goal is some common unity, some harmony. The process of interpretation for Royce, however, rests on the individual will to interpret that requires such moral attitudes and behaviors as those of humility, tolerance, courage, integrity. Community building requires intentional human action and cannot depend merely on formalized democratic processes and rules.

Further, Royce, with Peck, recognizes the great difficulty of building genuine community and that it involves deep commitment and love. Also involved is the ability to deal with the depth of human sin, the possibility of grave betrayal, and a profound guilt. As indicated, both present-day communitarians and the great advocate of democratic community, John Dewey, fail to deal adequately with these aspects of human nature and community.

What is needed for the building of a public life and understanding are free individuals with good will, enlightened individuals. In chapter 3, we dealt extensively with Royce's fruitful views of the human self and of the conditions necessary for genuine selfhood and personhood. Royce's writings on psychology and on moral and social development present a holistic, full-blooded picture of the human self as fully a psychological, biological, natural being but also equally a social-behavioral relational being, a self-conscious intentional acting subject, a locus of moral attributes, a source of value, a being to whom moral and legal responsibility can be clearly be attributed. We discovered Royce's views on self to be remarkably contemporary, sharing with present-day psychologists a recognition of the importance of mutual interaction and recognition to self-development, of the importance of habit, of play and imagination, of sensory stimulation and enrichment, of emotional enrichment and expression to adequate human individual development. Underlying all of this is the subtle interplay and balancing of individualism and community, autonomy and social concern, captured in Royce's affirmation of two essential motives of human "conscience" and moral actions: be humane, self-sacrificing, devoted to a will beyond one's own, and be reasonable, autonomous with a consistent, self-chosen life-plan.[19]

In chapter 4, we continued to pursue in more depth Royce's development of a viewpoint that is person/individual and autonomy centered yet that also stresses community and community building. The key is Royce's understanding of the concept of loyalty and advocacy of the principle of loyalty to loyalty, a principle which he claims unites the three moral principles of freedom, the good, and duty. This principle, argues Royce overcomes the human sin of "mere self-interest" and the communal sin of "arrogant exclusivity." Unlike communitarianism, Royce also addressed head-on the issues of "wicked loyalties," "wicked communities," "blind allegiances" and "dangerous partriotisms." The notion of enlightened provincialism is a subtle balancing of self-interest and communal good, of particular group good and broader public, universal goods. It is also a call to building community from the ground up. Further, Royce provides us with a number of fruitful insights about training for loyalty, the need for ritual and myth-making in building community, and the connection between religion, seen as communal and as "beloved, transcending, universal community," and loyalty.

Having explicated the many fruitful insights of Royce's thought, section two of the book is devoted to testing these thoughts in three areas, three "forms of life," of common concern to many diverse communities. The three, although all too briefly explored, were family, education, and medicine. Royce saw family as the original community, that is, as that "formative crucible" where genuine individuals could develop and where the first of the genuine communities, the "enlighted provinces," could be built and experienced. After surveying some destructive models of family, we considered suggestions, based on Roycean concepts, for a different view or model of family, for some conditions for building supportive, caring families. Family storytelling was seen as one important mechanism in this regard, along with a "family-interpretive methodology." Family, as enlightened province, as an interpretative, mediating structure between individual selves and the larger community, was also discussed.

Turning to education, we argued for the overcoming of the old dominant paradigm of self as passive, cognitive knower, teaching as transmission of knowledge and teacher as lecture/discipline expert. Education, as presently conceived, I argued, betrays the self by neglect of the imaginative, emotional, bodily, relational, and evaluative aspects of the human person. Education today, I asserted, causes undue harm by splitting the academic from the communal and from the professional. Using Roycean concepts, we considered a new paradigm based on a view of self as life-plan/life-narrative, a view of knowing and learning as communal, cooperative processes, which, though always fallible, seek to overcome limited perspectives and to teach tolerance. The classroom must be seen, it seems to me, as a genuine community of learning with the teacher acting as symphony director, facilitator, and enhancer. Teacher/scholars are also learners in such a view.

A similar approach was taken in dealing with the field of medicine, namely, to critique the traditional paradigm, that of the Cartesian, mechanical, determined, isolated body. Drawing on various resources, including phenomenological and existential analysis, I faulted medicine for failing the concept of the fully embodied self and for ignoring the fact that illness attacks the total self. Illness was seen in terms of alienation, disruption in four areas of human meaning: embodied action, the theater of intersubjective activity, the arena of will and the realm of universal meaning. Drawing on Royce's view of self and his doctrine of interpretation, we developed a notion of medicine as a mediating practice and physician as interpreter: facilitating interpretation, common meaning, and healing.

In testing Roycean concepts in the three areas of family, education, and medicine, I fully recognize that we have only made a beginning in these areas in developing the implications of a Roycean-based public philosophy. What has been established is that such a public philosophy is full of potential for a more adequate discussion of the issues in these areas and hopefully some resolution of those issues. I intend to engage in fuller exploration in these arenas; I believe it is imperative to bring philosophical insights to these important human forms of life. It is my hope that others will be stimulated to engage in such explorations as well as to dialogue, critique, and interact with Royce and with my interpretations and applications of Roycean concepts.

Other important areas of human activity should also be explored from the perspective of a Roycean-based public philosophy. Two such areas, which I will pursue in another context, are the areas of technology and the law. I have briefly explored religion and may also return to that area because I believe that Royce's *The Problem of Christianity* is a neglected classic analysis of religious thought and life. Thus, as a I draw this work to a close, I offer it, not as a full-blown public philosophy but as a sketch, laying a fruitful, provocative groundwork for much needed exploration of grave issues facing the people of the United States, their national community.

NOTES

BIBLIOGRAPHY

INDEX

NOTES

INTRODUCTION

1. Walter Lippmann, *The Phantom Public* (New York: Harcourt, Brace & Co., 1925). See also John Dewey, "Practical Democracy," review of *The Phantom Public* by Walter Lippmann, *New Republic* 45, no.2 (December 1925): 52–54, reprinted in John Dewey, *Later Works, 1925–1953,* vol. 2, ed. JoAnn Boydston (Carbondale: Southern Illinois University, 1984), hereafter cited as *L.W.*

2. Richard Sennet, *The Fall of Public Man* (New York: W. W. Norton, 1974).

3. Christopher Lasch, *The Culture of Narcissism* (New York: W. W. Norton, 1979).

4. Morris Dickstein, *Double Agent: The Critic and Society.* (New York: Oxford, 1992).

5. Russell Jacoby, *The Last Intellectuals: American Culture in the Age of Academe* (New York: Basic Books, 1987), ix.

6. Ibid., 5.

7. Ibid.

8. Charles J. Sykes, *Prof Scam* (Washington, D.C.: Regnery Gateway, 1988), 6

9. Jacoby, 151

10. John E. Smith, *The Spirit of American Philosophy* (Albany: State University of New York Press, 1983), 221–22.

11. Walter Lippmann, *The Essential Lippmann: A Political Philosophy for Liberal Democracy,* ed. Clinton Rossiter and James Lane (New York: Random House, 1963), 90.

12. Ibid., 91

13. Lippmann, *Phantom Public,* 192.

14. Dewey, *L. W.,* 2: 293.

15. *L.W.* 2: 309, 319.

16. See Fred Hirsch, *Social Limits to Growth* (Cambridge, Mass.: Harvard University Press, 1976), and Robert Heilbroner, *Business Civilization in Decline* (New York: W. W. Norton, 1976).

17. William M. Sullivan, *Reconstructing Public Philosophy* (Berkeley: University of California Press, 1982), 9.

18. Ibid.

19. Ibid., 11.

20. Ibid., 10.

21. H. L. Mencken, *Prejudices: A Selection,* ed. James T. Farrell (New York: Vintage Books, 1958), 149.

22. John Dewey, "Challenge to Liberal Thought, *Fortune* 30 (August 1944): 155–57, reprinted in *L.W.,* 15: 261.

23. William Ernest Hocking, *The Coming World Civilization* (London: George Allen, Unwin, 1958), 16.

24. Paul Tillich, *The Courage to Be* (New Haven: Yale University Press, 1952), 46.

25. Bruce Kuklick, *The Rise of American Philosophy: Cambridge, Massachusetts 1800–1930* (New Haven: Yale University Press, 1977), 314.

26. Ibid., 311.

27. Jacoby, 146.

28. See John Rawls, *The Theory of Justice* (Cambridge: Harvard University Press, 1971); Robert Nozick, *Anarchy, State and Utopia* (New York: Basic Books, 1968); John Locke, *Two Treatises of Government,* ed. Peter Laslett, 2d ed., 2 vols. (London: Cambridge University Press, 1967); John Stuart Mill, *On Liberty* (Indianapolis: Bobbs-Merrill, 1956); Adam Smith, *An Inquiry Into the Nature and Causes of the Wealth of Nations* (New York: Modern Library, Random House, 1985).

29. Sullivan, 1982, x.

30. John Dewey, *Liberalism and Social Action* (New York: Columbia University Press, 1935); John Dewey, "Challenge to Liberal Thought," in *L.W.* 15: 261–75.

31. Kuklick, 312.

32. Josiah Royce, *The World and the Individual* (Gifford Lectures), 2 vols. (New York: Macmillan, 1899 and 1901; reprint, New York: Dover, 1959); *The Problem of Christianity,* 2 vols. (New York: Macmillan, 1918; reprint, Chicago: Henry Regnery, 1968). References will be to the reprints.

33. Josiah Royce, *The Hope of the Great Community* (New York: Macmillan, 1916).

34. See Royce, *The World and the Individual,* vol. 1, Lecture 3, "The Independent Beings, 91–138, and vol 2, Lecture 4, "Physical and Social Reality," 155–204.

35. See Josiah Royce, "Mind," in *Encyclopedia of Religion and Ethics*, ed. James Hastings (New York: Charles Scribner & Sons, 1916), 8: 649–57, reprinted in Josiah Royce, *Logical Essays,* ed. Daniel Robinson (Dubuque, Iowa: W. C. Brown, 1951), 146–78.

36. Frank M. Oppenheim, *Royce's Mature Ethics* (Notre Dame, Ind.: University of Notre Dame Press, 1993), 85–116.

37. See Kuklick, 313, and Josiah Royce, *The Philosophy of Loyalty* (New York: Macmillan, 1908).

38. See Royce, *The Problem of Christianity.*

39. Stanley J. Scott, *Frontiers of Consciousness* (New York: Fordham University Press, 1991), 31.

40. Royce, *The World and the Individual,* 2: 165–66.

41. Royce, *The Problem of Christianity,* 2: 418.

42. Robert V. Hine, *Josiah Royce: From Grass Valley to Harvard* (Norman, Oklahoma: University of Oklahoma Press, 1992), 160.

43. Kuklick, 313.

44. John Clendenning, *The Life and Thought of Josiah Royce* (Madison: University of Wisconsin Press, 1985).

45. Josiah Royce, *The Spirit of Modern Philosophy* (Boston: Houghton, Mifflin, 1892), 10.

46. Josiah Royce, *California From the Conquest in 1846 to the Second Vigilance Committee in San Francisco (1856): A Study of American Character,* American Commonwealth Series (Boston: Houghton, Mifflin, 1886), republished with an introduction by Robert Glass Cleland (New York: Knopf, 1948); Josiah Royce, *The Feud of Oakfield Creek: A Novel of California Life* (Boston: Houghton, Mifflin, 1887). See also Clendenning, chapter 4.

47. Clendenning, 132.

48. Vines, 192.

49. Ibid., 198.

50. Ibid., 200.

51. Quoted in Vines, 1992, 187.

52. Vines, 1992, 203.

53. See Josiah Royce, "Recent Discussions of Class Feeling," *Berkeleyan* 1 (January 1874): 7; "The Problem of Class Feeling," *Berkeleyan* 1 (February 1874): 5; "The Modern Novel as a Mode of Conveying Instruction and Accomplishing Reform," *Berkeleyan* 1 (April 1874): 10–11; "The Literary Artist and the Work of Literary Art," *Berkeleyan* 2 (January 1875): 3–5; "Truth in Art," *Berkeleyan* 2 (April 1875): 3–4.

54. See Scott, 15.

55. Kuklick, 291.

56. Josiah Royce, "Present Ideals of American University Life," *Scribner's Magazine* 10 (1891): 376–88; "Is There a Science of Education," *Educational Review* 1 (1891): 15–25, 121–32.

57. Alexis de Tocqueville, *Democracy in America,* trans. Henry Reeve (New York: Abelaid & Saunders, 1838), 2: 508; 4: 93.

58. Alasdair MacIntyre, *Is Patriotism A Virtue?* (Lawrence: University of Kansas Press, 1984).

59. George P. Fletcher, *Loyalty: An Essay on the Morality of Relationships* (New York: Oxford University Press, 1993).

60. John Cottingham, "Partiality, Favouritism and Morality," *The Philosophical Quarterly* 36, no. 44 (1987): 357.

61. Ibid., 359

62. Lawrence Blum, "Iris Murdoch and the Domain of Morality," *Philosophical Studies* 50 (1986): 343.

63. Iris Murdoch, *The Sovereignty of Good* (London: Routledge & Kegan Paul, 1971), 36

64. Ibid., 38.

65. Royce, *The World and the Individual,* 1: 460.

66. Josiah Royce, *The Problem of Christianity,* 1: 88.

67. Carol Gilligan and Grant Wiggins in *The Emergence of Morality in Young Children,* ed. Jerome Kegan and Sharon Lamb (Chicago: University of Chicago Press, 1987), 282.

68. Lawrence Blum, "Gilligan and Kolhberg: Implications for Moral Theory." *Ethics* 98 (April 1988): 474.

69. Jacquelyn Ann K. Kegley, "Josiah Royce: A Source of New Insight for Religion Today," *Religious Studies* 18 (1979): 221–24; "Josiah Royce on Self and Community," *Rice University Studies* 66 (Fall 1980): 33–53.

70. Amitai Etzioni, *The Spirit of Community: Rights, Responsibilities and the Communitarian Agenda* (New York: Crown, 1993).

71. Ibid., 2.

72. *The Chronicle of Higher Education,* 21 April 1993, A7.

73. Ibid., A13.

74. See Etzioni.

75. John Dewey, "The Challenge of Democracy to Education," *Progressive Education* 14 (February 1937): 79–85. In *L. W.* 2: 188.

76. Dewey, *Liberalism and Social Action,* 3.

77. Royce, *The Problem of Christianity* (1968), 1: 14.

78. Paul Nagy, "The Beloved Community of Jonathan Edwards," *Transactions of the Charles S. Pierce Society* 7 (Spring 1971): 94.

79. John McDermott, Introduction, in John Dewey, *L.W.*, 2: xxxii.

80. Sullivan, 189.

CHAPTER 2

1. A historian, Jackson Wilson, has developed this theme of quest for community in examining the social philosophy of C. S. Peirce, James M. Baldwin, Edward Alsworth Ross, Granville Stanley Hall, and Josiah Royce. See Jackson Wilson, *In Quest for Community: Social Philosophy in the United States 1860-1920* (New York: John Wiley & Sons, 1968).

2. William F. May, "Adversarialism in America and the Professions," in *The Longing for Community*, ed. Charles H. Reynolds and Ray W. Norman (Berkeley: University of California Press, 1988).

3. Jules Henry, *Culture Against Man* (New York: Knopf, 1963), 322.

4. Christopher Lasch, "The Narcisstic Personality of Our Time," in *Our Selves/Our Past, Psychological Approaches to American History*, ed. R. J. Bogger (Baltimore: John Hopkins University Press, 1981), 401.

5. Michael Maccoby, *The Gamesman: The New Corporate Leaders* (New York: Simon & Schuster, 1976).

6. Eugene Emerson Jennings, *Routes to the Executive Suite* (New York: McGraw Hill, 1971).

7. Gail Sheehy, author of a leading personal growth book, writes, "The current ideology is a mix of personal survivalism, revialism and cynicism." *Damages: Predictable Crises of Adult Life* (New York: Dutton, 1976), 20.

8. Lasch, 1981, 401.

9. Ibid.

10. Jeffrey C. Goldfarb, *The Cynical Society: The Culture of Politics and the Politics of Culture in American Life* (Chicago: University of Chicago Press, 1991), 14.

11. Goldfarb, 16.

12. John Adams, Letter to Thomas Jefferson, 21 December 1819 in *The Adams-Jefferson Letters*, ed. Lester J. Cappon (New York: Simon & Shuster, 1971), 551.

13. Henry David Thoreau, *Walden: One Life in the Woods* (New York: Library of America, 1985), 107, 172–73.

14. Alexis de Tocqueville, *Democracy in America*, trans. Henry Reeve (1835–1840; reprint, New York: Gryphon Editions, 1988).

15. Thoreau, 173.

16. Goldfarb, 14, 22.

17. Ibid., 181–82.

18. Tocqueville, 290.

19. George Santayana, *Character and Opinion in the United States* (New York: Norton Library, 1967), 18.

20. John Patrick Diggins, *The Lost Soul of Politics: Virtue, Self-Interest and the Foundations of Liberalism* (New York: Basic Books, 1984), 7.

21. Ibid., 71.

22. Ibid.

23. Alexander Hamilton, *The Federalist*, no. 17.

24. John Winthrop, "A Model of Christian Charity," in *Winthrop Papers* (Boston: Massachusetts Historical Society), 2: 284.

25. See Paul Nagy, "The Beloved Community of Jonathan Edwards," *Transactions of the Charles S. Peirce Society* 7 (Spring 1971): 93–104.

26. Abraham Lincoln, *The Collected Works of Abraham Lincoln*, ed. Roy P. Basler (New Brunswick, N.J.: Rutgers University, 1953), 2: 424.

27. See Diggins, 60–170, for an extensive discussion of these individuals and their thought and work.

28. Robert N. Bellah et al. *Habits of the Heart: Individualism and Commitment in American Life* (New York: Harper & Row, 1985); *The Good Society* (New York: Vintage Books, Random House, 1992).

29. Bellah et al., *Habits of the Heart*, vii.

30. Robert N. Bellah et al., eds., *Individualism and Commitment in American Life: Readings on the Theories of Habits of the Heart* (New York: Harper & Row, 1987).

31. Robert N. Bellah et al., *Good Society*.

32. Amitai Etzioni, *The Spirit of Community* (New York: Crown, 1993).

33. Ibid., 2.

34. Ibid., 15.

35. Ibid., 31, 44. The Italics are in the Text.

36. Scott Peck, M.D., *The Different Dream* (New York: Simon & Schuster, 1987), 17.

37. Ibid., 59.

38. Bernard Yack raises the issue of competing forms of human community in an article entitled

"Liberalism and Communitarian Critics: Does Liberal Practice 'Live Down to Liberal Theory'?" in *The Longing for Community,* ed. Charles H. Reynolds and Ralph W. Norman. He argues that communitarians cannot just argue against Liberalism the thesis that the individuals and their rationality are socially constituted; afterall individualistic individuals are also socially constituted. The real question, then, argues Yack, is over choices between different brands of communities and socially constituted individuals (see p. 158).

39. Josiah Royce, "The External World and the Social Consciousness," *The Philosophical Review* 3, no. 5 (September 1884): 519.

40. The outer world is "the world whose presence can only be indicated to you by your definable communicable experience." Ibid., 520.

41. Josiah Royce, *The World and the Individual* (New York: Dover Publications, 1959), 2: 179.

42. Ibid. See D. W. Winnicott, *Playing and Reality* (New York: Basic Books, 1971).

43. D. W. Winnicott, "Ego Distortion in Terms of the True and False Self," in *The Child and the Family,* ed. Janet Hardenburg (New York: Penguin Books, 1964). In the area of metaphysics, although Royce believed realism inadequate as a conception of Being, he, like Peirce with his "Firstness," emphasized the brute stubborness of independent reality, including the uniqueness of another individual mind. In his *Last Lectures on Metaphysics* he makes this clear when he writes, "The whole intention with which we can approach idealism is the intention *to be as realistic as we can*" (quoted in Frank M. Oppenheim, *Royce's Mature Ethics* (Notre Dame, Ind.: University of Notre Dame Press, 1993), 109. For a discussion of Royce's criticisms of realism and his own view see Oppenheim, 104–10. See also: Gabriel Marcel. *Royce's Metaphysics* (Greenwood Press, 1956), 3–11.

44. Jessica Benjamin, *The Bonds of Love* (New York: Pantheon, 1988), 16, 26.

45. Ibid., 27.

46. Ibid.

47. Royce, Josiah Royce, *The Problem of Christianity* (Chicago: Henry Regnery Company, 1968), 2: 125.

48. Royce, *The World and the Individual,* 2: 165–66.

49. Ibid., 171–72. Italics are Royce's.

50. Peck, 57.

51. Ibid.

52. Ibid., 58.

53. Ibid.

54. Royce, *The Problem of Christianity,* 2: 60-61.

55. Peck, 65.

56. William James, *Pragmatism* (Cleveland: World, 1955), 50–51.

57. Peck, 83.

58. This aspect of communication makes puzzling, if not silly, the admonition by a judge to ignore remarks in court to which there has been objection. Perhaps this is related to over-emphasis on forms and rules of communication and evidence, with too little attention given to the substance of communication.

59. Genuine communication surely involves both care and caution. If we genuinely want to communicate, we want to mean what we say, not to distort words and meaning. We also would want to be concerned about the impact of our words on others.

60. William James, "On a Certain Blindness in Moral Beings," in *The Works of William James.* James was concerned in this essay with intolerance and ignorance that involved insensitivity to what makes life significant for others. He argued that it is our task to make it significant to ourselves, however different we may be from him or her.

61. This summary of Peirce's view is provided by John E. Smith in "Community and Reality," in *Perspectives on Peirce,* ed. Richard J. Bernstein (New Haven: Yale University Press, 1965), 110.

62. Royce, *The Problem of Christianity,* 2: 64.

63. Ibid., 67.

64. Frank M. Oppenheim, "A Roycean Road to Community," *International Philosophical Quarterly* 10 (September 1970): 363.

65. Peck, 41, 45.

66. Ibid., 62.

67. Ibid., 125.

68. Josiah Royce, *The Sources of Religious Insight* (The Bross Lectures, Lake Forest College, 1911) (New York: Charles Scribner's Sons, 1912).

69. Royce, *The Problem of Christianity,* 1: 302.

70. Ibid., 307.

71. Ibid., 307–8. Italics are in the text. In thinking about betrayal and atonement one might contemplate the way in which former enemies are restored to the world community.

72. Ibid., 2: 85.

73. John J. McDermott, Introduction, *John Dewey: The Later Works 1925-1953*, vol. 2 (Carbondale and Edwardsville: Southern Illinois University, 1987).

74. Quoted in Oppenheim, *Royce's Mature Ethics*, 116. For an extensive discussion of Royce's thoughts on freedom and the problem of evil, see Marcel, 60–85.

75. John Dewey, "Liberalism and Social Action: Studies in the History of Philosophy," in *The Later Works* 3:6.

76. Michael Sandel, *Liberalism and the Limits of Justice* (Cambridge: Cambridge University Press, 1982), 17.

77. MacIntyre, *After Virtue* (Notre Dame, Ind.: University of Notre Dame Press), 207.

78. Quoted in Alessandro Ferrarce, "Universalism: Procedural, Contextual and Prudential," in *Universalism vs. Communitarianism: Contemporary Debates in Ethics*, ed. David Rasmussen (Cambridge, Mass.: MIT Press, 1990), 26.

79. John Dewey, "Liberalism and Civil Liberties," *Social Frontier*, February 2, 1936. Reprinted in *The Later Works,* 2: 375.

80. See Ferrarce, 29–30.

81. See Alasdair MacIntyre, *Whose Justice? Which Rationality?* (Notre Dame: University of Notre Dame Press, 1988).

82. Peck, 70–71.

83. Ibid., 68.

CHAPTER 3

1. See Alasdair MacIntyre, *After Virtue* (Duckworth: London, 1981); *Whose Justice? Which Rationality?* (Notre Dame: Notre Dame University Press, 1988); Richard Rorty, 1979. *Philosophy and the Mirror of Nature* (Princeton, N.J.: Princeton University Press, 1979); and Bernard Williams, *Ethics and the Limits of Philosophy* (Cambridge, Mass: Harvard University Press, 1985).

2. See C. B. MacPherson, *The Political Theory of Positive Individualism* (London: Oxford University Press, 1962); "Rawls's Models of Man and Society," *Philosophy of the Social Sciences* 3 (December 1973): 341–47 ; Terry Pinkard, "Models of the Person," *Canadian Journal of Philosophy* 10 (December 1980): 623–35.

3. See Thomas C. Heller, and David Wellby, ed. *Reconstructing Individualism* (Stanford: Stan-

ford University Press, 1984).

4. Amartya Sen and Bernard Williams, *Utilitarianism and Beyond* (Cambridge: Cambridge University Press, 1982). Also see as alternatives to John Rawls: Michael Sandel, *Liberalism and the Limits of Justice* (Cambridge: Cambridge University Press, 1982) and Michael Walzer, *Spheres of Justice: A Defense of Pluralism and Equality* (New York: Basic Books, 1983).

5. See Alan Donagan, *The Theory of Morality* (Chicago: University of Chicago Press, 1977); Alan Gewirth, "The Justification of Morality," *Philosophical Studies* 53 (1988): 245–62; Charles Larmore, *Patterns of Moral Complexity* (Cambridge: Cambridge University Press, 1987); Michael Slote, "The Schizophrenia of Modern Ethical Theory," *Journal of Philosophy* 73, no. 4 (August 1977): 453–62; and Michael Slote, "Morality and Self-Other Assymmetry," *The Journal of Philosophy* 31, no. 4 (April 1984), 179–92.

6. Christopher Lasch, *The Culture of Narcissism* (New York: W. W. Norton, 1979); Philip Rieff, *The Triumphs of the Therapeutic* (Chicago: University of Chicago Press, 1968); and *Freud: The Mind of the Moralist* (Chicago: University of Chicago Press, 1979).

7. Robert N. Bellah et al., *Habits of the Heart: Individualism and Commitment in American Life* (New York: Harper & Row, 1985), 99–102.

8. Erik Erikson, *Insight and Responsibility* (New York: W. W. Norton, 1964); Lawrence Kohlberg, *Essays in Moral Development*, vols 1 and 2 (New York: Harper & Row, 1981 and 1984).

9. Jerome Kagan, *The Nature of The Child* (New York: Basic Books, 1989); and D. Steon, *The Interpersonal World of the Infant* (New York: Basic Books, 1985).

10. Jessica Benjamin, *The Bonds of Love* (New York: Pantheon, 1988); Lawrence A. Blum, "Gilligan and Kohlberg: Implications for Moral Theory," *Ethics* 98 (April 1988), 472–91; Carol Gilligan, *In A Different Voice, Psychological Theory and Women's Development* (Cambridge, Mass: Harvard University Press, 1982); Carol Gilligan and Grant Wiggins, "The Origins of Morality in Early Childhood," in Jerome Kagan and Sharon Lamb, *The Emergence of Morality in Young Children* (Chicago: University of Chicago Press, 1987), 277–305; and Margaret Mahler et al., *The Psychological Birth of the Human Infant* (New York: Basic Books, 1988).

11. Josiah Royce, "On Certain Psychological Aspects of Moral Training," *International Journal of Ethics* 3 (1893): 413–36; "Self-Consciousness,Social Consciousness,and Nature," *Philosophical Review*, 4 (1895): 465–85, 577–602; "Some Observations on the Anomalies of Self-Consciousness," *Psychological Review* 2 (1895): 433–57, 574–84; "Preliminary Report on Imitation," *Psychological Review*, 2 (1895): 217–35; "Outlines of Psychology, or a Study of the Human Mind," in *In Sickness and in Health,* ed. James W. Roosevelt (New York: Appleton, 1896), 171–233; "The Social Basis of Conscience," in *Addresses and Proceedings of the National Educational Association,* 1898, 196–204; *Outlines of Psychology* (New York: Macmillan, 1903); "Some Psychological Problems Emphasized by Pragmatism," *Popular Science Monthly* 83 (1913): 394–411.

12. Royce, "On Certain Psychological Aspects of Moral Training," 425.

13. Ibid., 419.

14. Ibid., 426.

15. Josiah Royce, *The World and the Individual* (New York: Dover, 1959), 2: 268.

16. Josiah Royce, *Outlines of Psychology: An Elementary Treatise with Some Practical Applications* (New York: The Macmillan Company, 1911), 9–10.

17. Ibid., 13.

18. Ibid., 12.

19. Ibid., 12–13. Royce writes about the method of introspection as follows: "If carried on alone, without constant reference to the physical conditions of the mental life observed, and without a frequent comparing of notes with one's fellows, introspection can accomplish little of service for psychology." *Outlines,* 17.

20. Ibid., 334.

21. Ibid.

22. Ibid., 337.

23. Ibid., 336.

24. Ibid., 305. For a discussion of contemporary evidence that experience drives and individuates brain growth, see, Robert Ornstein and Richard F. Thompson, *The Amazing Brain* (Boston: Houghton Mifflin, 1984), 165–71.

25. Ibid., *Outlines,* 158.

26. Ibid., 128.

27. Ibid., 160. Royce's sensitivity to this issue may have been due in part to his own puritanical upbringing: avoiding dance, theater, and other

supposedly immoral activities were part of his religious experience, but it was rich in musical expression. See R. V. Hine, *Josiah Royce: From Grass Valley to Harvard* (Norman: University of Oklahoma Press, 1992), chapters 2 and 3.

28. Ibid., 161.

29. Ibid., 66. Italics are in the text.

30. Ibid., 322–23. Italics are in the text.

31. Ibid., 326–27. Italics are in the text. "Restlessness" was a key part of Royce's own life. His family, especially his father, often moved on to new places and tasks. They were true pioneers. Royce himself was always seeking contrast and disputation of his own ideas.

32. Ibid., 254.

33. Royce, *The World and the Individual,* 2: 219–24.

34. Ibid., 224.

35. Ibid., 225.

36. Evelyn Fox Keller, *Reflections on Gender and Science* (New Haven: Yale University Press, 1985). See also her *A Feeling for the Organism: The Life and Work of Barbara McClintock* (New York: W. H. Freeman, 1983).

37. Royce, *The World and the Individual,* 2: 256.

38. Ibid., 257.

39. Ibid.

40. Ibid.

41. Josiah Royce, *The Religious Aspect of Philosophy* (Boston: Houghton, Mifflin, 1885), 314.

42. Royce, *The World and the Individual,* 2: 261–62.

43. Ibid., Italics are in the text.

44. Royce, *Outlines of Psychology,* 326. Italics are in the text.

45. See *Outlines,* 248ff.

46. Jessica Benjamin, *Bonds of Love: Psychoanalysis, Feminism and the Problem of Domination* (New York: Pantheon, 1988), 12.

47. Ibid., 21.

48. Ibid., 16.

49. Ibid., 24.

50. Ibid., 23.

51. Ibid., 12.

52. Josiah Royce, *The Problem of Christianity* (Chicago: Henry Regnery, 1968), 1: 152.

53. Benjamin, 39.

54. Ibid., 39–40.

55. Royce, *The World and the Individual,* 2: 166.

56. Josiah Royce, "The External World and the Social Consciousness," *The Philosophical Review* 3, no. 5 (September 1904): 520.

57. Ibid., 519.

58. Royce, *The World and the Individual*, 2: 179.

59. Royce, *Outlines of Psychology*, 355–63.

60. D. W. Winnicott, *Playing and Reality* (New York: Basic Books, 1971), 38.; "Ego Distortion in Terms of True and False Self," in *The Child and the Family* (New York: Penguin Books, 1964), 19.

61. Royce, *Outlines of Psychology*, 362–63.

62. Benjamin, 28.

63. Ibid., 29.

64. Richard Sennett, *The Fall of Public Man* (New York: W. W. Norton, 1974 and 1976), 320–22.

65. Ibid., 267.

66. Ludwig Wittgenstein, *Philosophical Investigations*, trans, G. E. M. Anscombe (New York: Macmillan, 1953), paras. 243, 258–59, 295.

67. Royce, *Outlines of Psychology*, 282, 281.

68. Ibid., 283. Italics are in the text.

69. Ibid., 284. Italics are in the text.

70. Charles S. Peirce, *Collected Papers of Charles Sanders Peirce* (Cambridge, Mass.: Belknap Press of Harvard University Press, 1960), 6: 157.

71. Royce, *The Problem of Christianity*, 2: 42.

72. See also Wiggins.

73. Peirce, *Collected Papers*, 615.

74. Joseph Margolis, *Texts Without Reference* (London and New York: Basil Blackwell, 1989), 289.

75. Royce, *Outlines of Psychology*, 14–15.

76. Royce, *The World and the Individual*, 2: 276. Italics are in the text.

77. Josiah Royce, *Urbana Lectures,* part 2, in the *Journal of the History of Philosophy* 5 (1967): 273.

78. Jonathan A. Jacobs, *Virtue and Self-Knowledge* (Englewood Cliffs, N.J.: Prentice-Hall, 1989), 47.

79. Alasdair MacIntyre, *After Virtue: A Study in Moral Theory* (Notre Dame, Ind.: University of Notre Dame Press, 1981).

80. Josiah Royce, *The Conception of God*, The Supplementary Essay (New York: Macmillan, 1898), 291.

81. Josiah Royce, *The Spirit of Modern Philoso-phy* (Boston: Houghton, Mifflin, 1896), 253.

82. Ibid.

83. Ibid.

84. Blum, 472–74.

85. Michael Slote, "The Schizophrenia of Modern Ethical Theories," 453.

86. Ibid., 454.

87. Bernard Williams, "A Critique of Utilitarianism," in *Utilitarianism: For or Against*, ed. J. J. C. Smart and B. Williams (Cambridge: Cambridge University Press, 1973). See also Barbara Harmon, "Integrity and Impartiality," *The Monist* 66, no. 2 (1983): 233–50, for a discussion of and response to Williams's criticisms.

88. Slote, "Morality and Self-Other Asymmetry," 179–80.

89. Blum, 475.

90. Erikson, 222.

91. Lawrence Kohlberg and Carol Gilligan, "The Adolescent as a Philosopher: The Discovery of the Self in a Post-Conventional World," *Daedalus* (Fall 1971): 1066–67.

92. Gilligan and Wiggins, 285, 281.

93. Blum, 476.

94. Royce, " On Certain Psychological Aspects of Moral Training," 413–36.

95. Ibid., 418.

96. Ibid., 419.

97. Ibid., 423.

98. Ibid., 423–24.

99. Ibid., 425. Royce also writes: "It [the dual conscience] is in one sense innate; for had not one inherited a socially suggestible and a practically reasonable temperament, you could never teach him a single moral truth, however keen his lower wits might be," 425.

100. Ibid.

101. Martin L. Hoffman, "Empathy, Role Taking, Guilt, and Development of Altruistic Motives," in *Moral Development and Behavior*, ed. Thomas Lickona (New York: Holt, Rinehardt and Winston, 1976), 124.

102. Ibid.

103. Ibid., 129–30.

104. Ibid.

105. See Edward Mueller, "Alternative Approaches to Moral Socialization," in *The Emergence of Morality in Young Children*, ed. Jerome Kagan and Sharon Lamb (Chicago: University of Chicago Press, 1987), 151–54.

106. Lawrence Blum, "Particularity and

Responsiveness," in *The Emergence of Morality in Young Children*, ed. Jerome Kagan and Sharon Lamb (Chicago: University of Chicago Press, 1987), 311.

107. Royce, "On Certain Psychological Aspects of Moral Training," 428–29.

108. Ibid., 426–36.

109. Gilligan and Wiggins, 299–300.

110. Ibid., 301.

111. Royce, "On Certain Psychological Aspects of Moral Training," 415.

112. Ibid., 418–19.

113. Royce, *The Problem of Christianity,* 1: 88.

114. Ibid., 95.

CHAPTER 4

1. Bryan S. Turner, Preface to *Citizenship and Social Theory*, ed. Bryan S. Turner (London: Sage, 1993), 11.

2. Robert N. Bellah et al., *Habits of the Heart: Individualism and Commitment in American Life* (New York: Harper & Row, 1987), 106.

3. Amitai Etizoni, *The Spirit of Community* (New York: Crown, 1993), 44. Italics are in text.

4. Carol Kinsey Goman, *The Loyalty Factor: Building Trust in Today's Workplace* (New York: Master Media, 1990).

5. Josiah Royce, *The Philosophy of Loyalty* (1908; reprint, New York: Hafner, 1971); and *The Problem of Christianity*, 2 vols. (Chicago: Henry Regnery, 1968).

6. Alasdair MacIntyre addresses the dangers of patriotism in his book *Is Patriotism a Virtue?* in (Lawrence: University of Kansas Press, 1984).

7. Richard J. Bishirjian, *A Public Philosophy Reader* (New Rochelle, N.Y.: Arlington House, 1978).

8. See Peter L. Berger and Richard John Neuhaus, *To Empower People: The Role of Mediating Structures in Public Policy* (Washington, D.C.: American Enterprise Institute for Public Policy Research, 1977); and *Democracy and Mediating Structures: A Theological Inquiry*, ed. Michael Novak (Washington, D.C.: American Enterprise Institute for Public Policy, 1980).

9. Royce, *Philosophy of Loyalty*, 15.

10. George P. Fletcher, *Loyalty: An Essay on the Morality of Relationships* (New York: Oxford Press, 1993), 5.

11. Royce, *Philosophy of Loyalty*, 16–17. Italics are in the text.

12. Ibid., 17.

13. See Lecture VI, "Training for Loyalty," in *Philosophy of Loyalty*, 254–67.

14. Andrew Oldenquist, "Loyalties," *The Journal of Philosophy* 79 (April 1982): 175.

15. Royce, *Philosophy of Loyalty*, 25, 27.

16. Fletcher, 25.

17. Ibid., 8.

18. Oldenquist, 176.

19. Royce, *Philosophy of Loyalty*, 19.

20. Ibid., 20.

21. Fletcher, 15.

22. Ibid.

23. See R. N. Allen, "When Loyalty No Harm Meant," *Review of Metaphysics* 43 (December 1989): 281–94. Allen reads Royce as "allowing any sort of cause to be an object of loyalty," 286.

24. Royce, *Philosophy of Loyalty*, 130.

25. Fletcher, 10.

26. Goman, 4. Italics are in the text.

27. Ibid., 8.

28. Royce, *Philosophy of Loyalty*, 54–55, 114.

29. Ibid., 57.

30. Josiah Royce, "Urbana Lectures," Royce Papers, Harvard University Archives, folio 76, no. 3, 2–3.

31. Royce, *Philosophy of Loyalty*, 171.

32. Ibid., 177.

33. Ibid., 175

34. Fletcher, 21.

35. Ibid., 20, 16.

36. Royce, *Philosophy of Loyalty*, 121.

37. Josiah Royce, *The World and the Individual* (New York: Dover Publications, 1959), 2: 59. Italics are in the text.

38. Paul Ramsey, "The Idealistic View of Moral Evil," *Philosophy and Phenomenological Research* 6 (June 1946): 577.

39. Royce, *Philosophy of Loyalty*, 77.

40. Josiah Royce, "Urbana Lectures." Royce Papers, Harvard University Archives, folio 69, no. 3, 4–5.

41. Josiah Royce, *The Sources of Religious Insight* (The Bross Lectures, Lake Forest College, 1911) (New York: Charles Scribner's Sons, 1912), 1: 48–49.

42. Ibid., 55.

43. Royce, *Sources of Religious Insight*, 1: 66.

44. Royce, *Philosophy of Loyalty*, 224.

45. Josiah Royce, *The Problem of Christianity* (Chicago: Henry Regnery, 1968), 1: 308.

46. Royce, *Philosophy of Loyalty*, 108.

47. Ibid., 12–13.

48. Leo Tolstoy, *Writings on Civil Disobedience and Non-Violence* (New York: New American Library, 1968), 104.

49. Royce, *Philosophy of Loyalty*, 214.

50. William James, "The Moral Equivalent of War" (first published in *McClure Magazine,* August 1910 and *Popular Science Monthly,* October 1910), in *William James: The Essential Writings,* ed. Bruce W. Wilshire (New York: Harper & Row, 1971), 349–61.

51. Royce, *Philosophy of Loyalty*, 185.

52. William James, *The Will to Believe* (New York: Dover Publications, 1956).

53. Royce, *Philosophy of Loyalty*, 189. Italics are in the text.

54. Josiah Royce, "The Urbana Lectures," Royce Papers, Harvard University Archives, folio 76; and *Philosophy of Loyalty*, 104–7.

55. Royce, *Philosophy of Loyalty*, 104–5.

56. Ibid., 104, 105.

57. Ibid., 105.

58. Ibid., 259–60.

59. Ibid., 262–3.

60. Ibid., 266.

61. Michael Novak, *The Joy of Sports: End Zones, Bases, Baskets, Balls and the Consecration of the American Spirit* (New York: Basic Books, 1976).

62. Royce, *Philosophy of Loyalty*, 275–76.

63. Goman, 63ff.

64. Royce, *Philosophy of Loyalty*, 284–85.

65. Josiah Royce, *The Religious Aspects of Philosophy* (1885; reprint, Boston: Houghton Mifflin, 1985); *The Sources of Religious Insight* (New York: Charles Scribner's Sons, 1912); *The Problem of Christianity* (Chicago: Henry Regnery Company, 1968), vols. 1 and 2.

66. Jacquelyn Ann Kegley, "Josiah Royce, a Source of New Insight for Religion Today," *Religious Studies* 18 (1984): 211–24.

67. Royce, *Sources of Religious Insight*, 8–9.

68. Ibid., 28–29.

69. Royce, *Problem of Christianity*, 1: 105.

70. Ibid., 430. Italics are in the text.

71. Fletcher, 95.

72. Ibid., 99.

73. Ibid.

74. Ibid., 100.

75. See Berger and Neuhaus.

76. Ibid., 2. Italics are in the text.

77. Ibid., 3.

78. Berger and Neuhaus, 3–4.

79. Michael Novak, ed., *Democracy and Mediating Structures: A Theological Inquiry* (Washington, D.C.: Enterprise Institute for Public Policy, 1980).

80. James Luther Adams, in *Democracy and Mediating Structures: A Theological Inquiry,* ed. Michael Novak (Washington, D.C.: Enterprise Institute for Public Policy, 1980), 1.

81. Royce, *The Philosophy of Loyalty*, 239–40.

82. Ibid., 245. Italics are in the text.

83. Josiah Royce, "Provincialism," in *Race Questions, Provincialism and Other American Problems* (New York: Macmillan, 1908), 57–108; reprinted in John J. McDermott, *The Basic Writings of Josiah Royce* (Chicago: University of Chicago Press, 1969), 2: 1067–88. Citations will be to the McDermott volume.

84. Ibid., 1069.

85. Edmund Burke, *Selected Writintgs of Edmund Burke,* ed. W. J. Bate (New York: Modern Library, 1960), 174.

86. Josiah Royce, *War and Insurance* (New York: Macmillan, 1914).

CHAPTER 5

1. William Sullivan, *Reconstructing a Public Philosophy* (Berkeley: University of California Press, 1982).

2. These three descriptors of "family" are identified by Frank M. Oppenheim, *Royce's Mature Ethics* (Notre Dame, Ind.: University of Notre Dame Press, 1993), 163.

3. David Cooper, *The Death of the Family* (New York: Vintage Press, 1970), 8.

4. See Lasch, *The Culture of Narcissism* (New York: W. W. Norton, 1979), 4.

5. *Chidren's Defense Fund*, in *Hastings Center Report* (July–August 1994): 3

6. Robert Nisbett, *The Twilight of Authority* (Oxford: Oxford University Press, 1975).

7. Jean Bethke Elshtain presents this view as "the strong case for democratic authority and the family," in her "The Family in Political Thought, Democratic Politics and the Philosophy of Authority," in *Fashioning Family Theory*, ed. Jetse Sprey (Newbury Park, Calif.: Sage, 1990), 59–61.

8. Ibid., 62

9. *Children's Defense Fund*, 3.

10. Dorothy Dinnerstein, *The Mermaid and the Minotaur* (New York: Harper & Row, 1976).

11. Nancy Friday, *My Mother/My Self* (New York: Delacorte, 1977); Judith Arcana, *Our Mothers' Daughters* (Berkeley: Shameless Hussy, 1979).

12. Shulamith Firestone, *The Dialectic of Sex* (New York: Morrow, 1970).

13. Ned L. Gaylin, in *Family Strengths: Positive Models for Family Life*, ed. Nick Stennett et al. (Lincoln: University of Nebraska Press, 1980), 6.

14. Ibid., 7.

15. Mary Jo Bane, *Here to Stay: American Families in the Twentieth Century* (New York: Basic Books, 1976). Ned Gaylin also cites evidence of the remarriage phenomenon, Gaylin, 61.

16. *Ibid.*; Gaylin, 8. See also Brigitte Berger, "The Family as Mediating Structure," in *To Empower People: The Role of Mediating Structures in Public Policy*, ed. Peter L. Berger and Richard John Neuhaus (Washington, D.C.: American Enterprise Institute for Public Policy Research, 1977), 156–58.

17. See Kath Weston, *Families We Chose: Lesbians, Gays, Kinship* (New York: Columbia University, 1991).

18. Barrie Thorne, "Feminism and the Family: Two Decades of Thought," in *Rethinking the Family: Some Feminist Questions*, ed. Barrie Thorne and Marilyn Yalom (Boston: Northeastern University Press, 1992), 5.

19. Ibid.

20. Judith Stacey, "Backward Toward the Postmodern Family: Reflections on Gender, Kinship and Class in the Silicon Valley," in *Rethinking the Family: Some Feminist Questions*, ed. Barrie Thorne and Marilyn Yalom (Boston: Northeastern University Press, 1992), 91–118.

21. Ibid., 92–93.

22. Ibid., 102–3. See also Coleen Leafy Johnson, *Ex-Families: Grandparents, Parents and Children Adjust to Divorce* (New Brunswick, N.J.: Rutgers University Press, 1988).

23. Stacey, 103.

24. Patricia Hill Collins, "Black Women and Motherhood," in *Rethinking the Family: Some Feminist Questions*, ed. Barrie Thorne and Marilyn Yalom (Boston: Northeastern University Press, 1992), 216.

25. Ibid., 215.

26. Ibid., 218.

27. Ibid., 219. See also Rosalie Riegle Troester, "Turbulence and Tenderness: Mothers, Daughters and Other Mothers," in Paule Marshall, *Brown Girl Brownstones* (New York: Sage, 1984), 13–16; and Herbert Gutman, *The Black Family in Slavery and Freedom*, 1950–1925 (New York: Random House, 1976).

28. Quoted from Gloria Wade-Gayles, "She Who is Black and Mother: On Sociology and Fiction, 1940–70," in La Frances Rodgers-Rose, *The Black Woman* (Beverly Hills: Sage, 1980), 92.

29. Collins, 1992, 226.

30. Ibid., 233.

31. Ibid., 234–38.

32. Thorne, 1992, 6.

33. Janet Farrell Smith, "Parenting as Property," in Joyce Trebilcot, *Mothering Essays in Feminist Theory* (Towata, N.J.: Rowman and Allenhe, 1983), 199–212.

34. Kath Weston, *Families We Choose;* and her "The Politics of Gay Families," in *Rethinking the Family: Some Feminist Questions*, ed. Barrie Thorne and Marilyn Yalom (Boston: Northeastern University Press, 1992).

35. Weston, 121, 120.

36. Elshtain, 55.

37. Weston, 126, 137.

38. Thorne, "Feminism and the Family," 5.

39. Nancy Chodorow and Susan Contralto, "The Fantasy of the Perfect Mother," in *Rethinking the Family: Some Feminist Questions*, ed. Barrie Thorne and Marilyn Yalom (Boston: Northeastern University Press, 1992), 121–13.

40. Ibid., 191.

41. Ibid.

42. Chodorow and Contralto, 1992, 201–2.

43. Ibid., 198–99. See Jean Lazarre, *The Mother Knot* (New York: Dell, 1976); and Kate Millett, *The Basement: Meditations on a Human Sacrifice* (New York: Simon & Shuster, 1979).

44. Ruth H. Bloch, "American Feminine Ideals in Transition: The Rise of the Moral Mother 1785–1815," in *Feminist Studies* 2 (June 1978): 100–125.

45. See Christopher Lasch, *Haven in a Heartless World: The Family Beseiged* (New York: Basic Books, 1977).

46. Selma Fraiberg, *Every Child's Birthright: In Defense of Mothering* (New York: Basic Books, 1977).

47. Benjamin Spock, *The Pocket Book of Baby*

and Child Care (New York: Pocket Books, 1968).

48. Sarah Ruddick, "Thinking About Father," in *Rethinking the Family: Some Feminist Questions*, ed. Barrie Thorne and Marilyn Yalom (Boston: Northeastern University Press, 1992), 176–90.

49. Ibid., 177.

50. Ibid.

51. Ibid., 179–81.

52. Ibid., 185.

53. Ibid., 187.

54. Ibid., 187.

55. Ibid., 188.

56. Thomas W. Laquer, "The Facts of Fatherhood," in *Rethinking the Family: Some Feminist Questions*, ed. Barrie Thorne and Marilyn Yalom (Boston: Northeastern University Press, 1992), 172.

57. David Morgan, "Issues of Critical Sociological Theory: Men in Families," in *Fashioning Family Theory*, ed. Jetse Sprey (Newbury Park, Calif.: Sage, 1990), 69.

58. See Linda Gordon, *Heroes of Their Own: Politics and History of Family Violence* (New York: Vintage, 1988); and "Family Violence and Social Control," in *Rethinking the Family: Some Feminist Questions*, ed. Barrie Thorne and Marilyn Yalom (Boston: Northeastern University Press, 1992), 262–86.

59. Linda Gordon, *The American Family in the Age of Uncertainty* (New York: Basic Books, 1991), 3.

60. Philip S. Curtis, "Court Widens Family Definition," *New York Times*, 7 July 1989, A13.

61. Ibid.

62. Ruddick, 189.

63. Loren E. Lomasky, *Persons, Rights and the Moral Community* (New York: Oxford University Press, 1987), 26.

64. Ibid., 167.

65. Ibid., 168.

66. Jessica Benjamin, *Bonds of Love: Psychoanalysis, Feminism and The Problem of Domination* (New York: Pantheon, 1988), 24.

67. Gaylin, 8.

68. Ibid.

69. Douglas Gunn, "Family Identity Creation: A Family Strength-Building Role Activity," in *Family Strengths: Positive Models for Family Life*, ed. Nick Stennett et al. (Lincoln: University of Nebraska Press, 1980), 17–38.

70. Ibid., 20–21.

71. Ibid., 24–25.

72. Ibid., 25.

73. Ibid., 26–29. See also J. H. S. Bossard, *Ritualism in Family Living* (Philadelphia: University of Pennsylvania Press, 1950).

74. Micaela DiLeonard, "The Female World of Cards and Holidays: Women, Families and The Work of Kinship," in *Rethinking the Family: Some Feminist Questions*, ed. Barrie Thorne and Marilyn Yalom (Boston: Northeastern University Press, 1992), 246–61.

75. Ibid., 251, 247.

76. Gunn, 30.

77. Josiah Royce, *Feud of Oakfield Creek: A Novel of California Life* (Boston: Houghton, Mifflin, 1887).

78. There is a box of "Letters to Family" in the newly discovered Crystal Falls Collection of Royce materials (Harvard Archives: Royce Papers, 1989 Crystal Falls Collection, Box A, "Josiah Royce's Letters to Family"). See also John Clendenning, . *The Letters of Josiah Royce* (Chicago: University of Chicago Press, 1970).

79. Royce, *The Problem of Christianity*; *The Religious Aspects of Philosophy* (1885; reprint, Boston: Houghton Mifflin, 1985); Josiah Royce, *The Sources of Religious Insight* (New York: Charles Scribner's Sons, 1912).

80. Carlfried B. Broderick, "Family Process Therapy," in *Fashioning Family Theory*, ed. Jetse Sprey (Newbury Park, Calif.: Sage, 1990), 171, 178, 179.

81. Debra Renee Kaufman, "Engendering Family Therapy," in *Fashioning Family Theory*, ed. Jetse Sprey (Newbury Park, Calif.: Sage, 1990), 108, 112.

82. Charles A. Smith, "Parents as People Teachers: The Presocial Environment of Children," in *Family Strengths: Positive Models for Family Life*, ed. Nick Stennett et al. (Lincoln: University of Nebraska Press, 1980), 185.

83. Ibid.

84. Ibid., 186–96.

85. Broderick, "Family Process Therapy," 179–80.

86. Ibid., 180–81.

87. Josiah Royce, *War and Insurance* (New York: Macmillan, 1914), 29.

88. Ibid., 30.

89. Ibid., 35.

90. Ibid., 36.

91. Ibid., 51–54.

92. Ibid., 54. Italics are in the text.

93. Ibid.

94. Josiah Royce, *The Problem of Christianity*, 2: 365–72.

95. I am deeply indebted for this discussion to Frank Oppenheim's treatment of this in his *Royce's Mature Ethics* (Notre Dame, Ind.: Notre Dame University Press, 1993), 170–71. See also Josiah Royce Extension Course on Ethics, 1915–1916: Harvard University Archives, Royce Papers, fol. 94, nos. 1–2, and fol. 95, no. 1.

96. Oppenheim, 171.

97. Ibid.

98. For an excellent discussion of love as mutuality, see Charles W. Kegley, "The Concept of Mutuality," Linfield College Lectures published posthumously by The Charles W. Kegley Lecture Committee (Bakersfield, Calif.: California State University Foundation, 1989).

99. John Dewey, in John Dewey and James H. Tufts, *Ethics* (New York: Henry Holt, 1908), 580–81.

100. Oppenheim, 171.

101. Patricia Hill Collins, "Black Women and Motherhood," in *Rethinking the Family: Some Feminist Questions*, ed. Barrie Thorne and Marilyn Yalom (Boston: Northeastern University Press, 1992), 215–45.

102. For one interesting study of mediation and negotiation between family and the wider community, see Gordon, 262–86.

103. Oppenheim, 133–42.

104. Ibid., Appendix B and 141–42.

105. Ibid., 139.

106. Ibid.

107. Arlene Skolnick, *Embattled Paradise* (New York: Basic Books, 1991), 212.

108. Judith Stacey, *Brave New Families* (New York: Basic Books, 1990), 258.

CHAPTER 6

1. See John Dewey, *Democracy and Education* (New York: Macmillan, 1916); *Freedom and Culture* (New York: G. P. Putnam's Sons); Educational Policies Commission, National Education Association of the United States, and the American Association of School Administrators, *The Purposes of Education in American Democracy* (Washington, D.C.: Educational Policies Commission, 1938); Robert Maynard Hutchins, *Edu-*

cation for Freedom (Baton Rouge: Louisiana State University Press, 1943); *The Republic and the School: The Education of Free Men*, ed. Lawrence A. Cremin (New York: Teachers College, Columbia University, 1957); and Benjamin R. Barber, *An Aristocracy for Everyone: The Politics of Education and the Future of America* (New York: Ballantine, 1992).

2. See Theodore William Schultz, *The Economic Value of Education* (New York: Columbia University Press, 1963); and Task Force on Education for Economic Growth, Education Commission of the States, *Action for Excellence: A Comprehensive Plan to Improve Our Nation's Schools* (Denver: Task Force on Education and Economic Growth, 1983)

3. See Upton Sinclair, *The Goose-Step: A Study of American Education* (Los Angeles: West Branch, 1923.); American Council on Education, *Emotion and the Educative Process* (Washington, D.C.: American Council on Education, 19380; Harvard University Committee on the Objectives of General Education in a Free Society, *General Education in a Free Society* (Cambridge, Mass.: Harvard University Press, 1945); Educational Policies Commission, *Education for All American Youth* (Washington, D.C.: Department of Education, 1952); *National Policies for Education, Health, and Social Services*, ed. James Earl Russell (New York: Russell & Russell, 1961); *Models for Educational Change*, ed. Alvin Lee Bertrand (Austin, Texas: Southwest Educational Development Laboratory, 1968); Scott Nearing, *The New Education* (New York: Arno, 1969); Harold O. Rugg, *The Child-Centered School* (New York: Arno, 1969); Ivan Illich, *Deschooling Society* (New York: Harper & Row, 1971); Saylor, J. Julen, *The School of the Future* (Washington, D.C.: Association for Supervision and Curriculum Development, 1972); Richard J. Kraft, *Education Issues for the 70's* (New York: MSS Information Corporation, 1974); *The Third Century: Twenty Six Prominent Americans Speculate on the Educational Future* (New Rochelle, N.Y.: Change Magazine Press, 1977); Carnegie Foundation, *Common Learning* (Washington, D.C.: Carnegie Foundation on Common Learning, 1981); National Commission on Excellence in Education, *A Nation at Risk: The Imperative for Educational Reform* (Washington, D.C.: The Commission, 1983); Diane Ravitch, *The Schools We Deserve*

(New York: Basic Books, 1985); National Governors Association Center for Policy Research, *Time for Results* (Washington, D.C.: The Association, 1986); Lamar Alexander, *The Nation's Report Card* (Cambridge, Mass.: National Academy of Education, 1987); *Education Reform in the 90's*, ed. Chester E. Finn (New York: Maxwell Macmillan International, 1992); Terry A. Astuto, *Roots of Reform: Challenging the Assumptions That Control Education Reform* (Bloomington, Ind.: Phi Delta Kappa Educational Foundation, 1994).

4. Ivan Illich, *Deschooling Society* (New York: Harper & Row, 1971).

5. National Commission on Excellence in Education, *A Nation at Risk: The Imperative for Educational Reform* (Washington, D.C., 1983)

6. Tom Wicker, "America and Its College: End of an Affair." *Change* 26, no. 3 (May/June 1994): 21–29.

7. Benjamin R. Barber, *An Aristocracy for Everyone: The Politics of Education and the Future of America* (New York: Ballantine, 1992), 4.

8. Ibid., 5 & 19.

9. See Natalie S. Glance and Bernardo A. Huberman, "The Dynamics of Social Dilemmas," *Scientific American* 270, no. 3: 76–82.

10. These were identified by Ned L. Gaylin in *Family Strengths: Positive Models for Family Life* (Lincoln: University of Nebraska Press, 1980), 8.

11. (New York: W. W. Norton, 1954).

12. See Thomas Kuhn, *The Structure of Scientific Revolutions*, 1st and 2d editions (Chicago: University of Chicago Press, 1961 and 1970); Evelyn F. Keller, *Reflections on Gender and Science* (New Haven: Yale University Press, 1985); K. D. Knorr-Cetina, *The Manufacture of Knowledge* (Elmsford, N.Y.: Pergammon Press, 1981).

13. Gaylin, in *Family Strengths*, 8.

14. Stephen Steinberg, "Travels on the Net," *Technology Review* 97, no. 4 (1994): 20–31.

15. See, for example, *Changing College Classrooms: New Teaching and Learning Strategies for an Increasingly Complex World,* ed. Diane Halpern (San Francisco: Jossey-Bass Publishers, 1994).

16. Betty Edwards, *Drawing on the Right Side of the Brain* (Los Angeles: Jeremy R. Tarcher, 1989).

17. Michael Novak, *The Joy of Sports: End Zones, Bases, Baskets and Balls and the Consecration of the American Spirit* (New York: Basic Books, 1976).

18. Bruce Jennings, James Lindemann, and Erik Parens, "Values on Campus: Ethics and Value Programs in the Undergraduate Program" (Briarcliff Manor, N.Y.: Hastings Center, 1994).

19. Michael Moffatt, *Coming of Age in New Jersey: College and American Culture* (New Brunswick, N.J.: Rutgers University Press, 1981).

20. Barber, 201–5.

21. Ibid., 206.

22. See Alan Donagan, *The Theory of Morality* (Chicago: University of Chicago Press, 1977); Michael Slote, "The Schizophrenia of Modern Ethical Theory," *Journal of Philosophy* 33, no. 4 (August 1976): 423–62; and Michael Slote, "Morality and Other-Self Asymmetry," *Journal of Philosophy* 73 no. 4 (April 1994): 192–97.

23. Jennings et al., 2.

24. Wingspread Group on Higher Education, *An American Imperative: Higher Expectations for Higher Education* (Racine, Wis.: Johnson Foundation, 1993).

25. See D. W. Johnson et al., "Effects of Cooperative, Competitive and Individualistic Goal Structures on Achievement: A Meta-Analysis," *Psychological Bulletin* 89 (1981): 47–62; and R. E. Slavin, "When Does Cooperative Learning Increase Student Achievement?" *Psychological Bulletin* 94, no.3 (1983): 429–45.

26. Daniel Coleman, *Emotional Intelligence* (New York: Bantam Books, 1995).

27. A number of community service programs are being sponsored by the Fund for the Improvement of Postsecondary Education (FIPSE) of the U.S. Department of Education. See Program Book 1994, 192–218.

28. The Albany Law School, for example, has a Mediation Assistance Program that teachs Alternative Dispute Resolution, e.g., reaching solutions through the use of mediation. For further information contact Albany Law School, 80 New Scotland Avenue, Albany, New York 12208.

29. Josiah Royce, *War and Insurance* (New York: Macmillan Company, 1914). See also *The Doctrine of Interpretation: Building Community Out of Conflict*, ed. Jacquelyn Ann K. Kegley (Hayward, Calif.: California State University, Hayward Press).

30. *The California School-to-Career Plan*, 23 February 1995 (Sacramento, Calif.: School-to-Career Interagency Staff), 8, 43.

31. See Jennings et al.; and Marie I. George,

"Two Suggestions for Teaching the Virtues," *Newsletter on Teaching Philosophy*, 93, no. 1 (Spring 1994): 127–28.

32. Josiah Royce, *The Problem of Christianity* (1918; reprint, University of Chicago Press, 1968), 2: 42.

33. James L. Cooper, Pamela Robinson, and Molly McKinney, "Cooperative Learning in the Classroom," in *Changing College Classrooms: New Teaching and Learning Strategies for an Increasingly Complex World,* ed. Diane Halpern (San Francisco: Jossey-Bass Publishers, 1994), 74.

34. Ibid., 74–76.

35. Ibid., 78.

36. Alexander W. Astin, *What Matters in College? Four Critical Years* (San Francisco: Jossey-Bass, 1992).

37. Craig Bloom, "Using the Internet for Teaching, Learning and Research," in *Changing College Classrooms: New Teaching and Learning Strategies for an Increasingly Complex World,* ed. Diane Halpern (San Francisco: Jossey-Bass Publishers, 1994), 191–212; James M. Hassett, Charles M. Spuches, and Sarah P. Webster, "Using Electronic Mail for Teaching and Learning," in *To Improve the Academy* ed. Ed Neal and Laurie Richlin (Stillwater, Okla.: New Forums, 1995), 221–38. This is a publication of the Professional and Organizational Developmental Network in Higher Education.

38. Susan G. Nummedal, "How Classroom Assessment Can Improve Teaching and Learning," in *Changing College Classrooms: New Teaching and Learning Strategies for an Increasingly Complex World,* ed. Diane Halpern (San Francisco: Jossey-Bass Publishers, 1994), 292.

39. T. A. Anglo, "Ten Easy Pieces: Assessing Higher Learning in Four Dimensions," in *Classroom Research: Early Lessons From Success,* ed. T. A. Anglo (San Francisco: Jossey-Bass, 1991).

40. Novak, "Rooting, Aqnon," in *Joy of Sports,* 279.

41. Ibid., 283.

42. Ibid., 282.

43. Ibid., 281.

44. Ibid., 282.

45. Ibid., 280.

46. Josiah Royce, *The Philosophy of Loyalty* (1908; reprint, New York: Hafner, 1971)), 266.

47. Ibid., 267.

48. Josiah Royce, *Outlines of Psychology: An Elementary Treatise with Some Practical Applications* (New York: Macmillan, 1911), 322–33. Italics are in the text.

49. Ibid., 326–27.

50. Richard Sennett, *The Fall of Public Man* (New York: W. W. Norton, 1976), 320.

51. Ibid., 321.

52. Barber, 21.

53. Ibid., 22.

54. Ibid., 34, 36.

55. Ibid., 41.

56. The Johnson Foundation, *An American Imperative: Higher Expectations for Higher Education, Report of the Wingspread Group on Higher Education* (Racine, Wis.: Johnson Foundation), 2.

57. See Alexander W. Astin, *Minorities in Higher Education: Recent Trends, Current Prospects, and Recommendations* (San Francisco: Jossey-Bass, 1982); T. J. Brown, *Teaching Minorities More Effectively: A Model for Educators* (Lanham, Md.: University Press of America, 1986); John C. Condon and Fathi S. Yousef, *An Introduction to Intercultural Communications* (New York: Macmillan, 1988); Lois Weis, *Between Two Worlds: Black Students and An Urban Community College* (Boston: Routledge & Kegan Paul, 1985).

58. See Condon and Yousel, and Gary M. Phillips and Eric C. Ericksen, *Interpersonal Dynamics in the Small Group* (New York: Random House, 1970).

59. See J. A. Anderson, "Cognitive Styles and Multicultural Populations," *Journal of Teacher Education* 39, no. 1 (1988): 2–9; T. L. Good, "Teacher Expectations and Student Perceptions: A Decade of Research," *Educational Leadership* 38 (1980): 415–22; Jay Teachman, Family Background, Educational Resources, and Educational Attainment, *American Sociological Review* 52 (1987): 548–57.

60. See R. B. Kaplan, "Cultural Thought Patterns in Intercultural Education," *Language Learning,* 16 1990: 1–20; Carol A. Jenkins and Deborah L. Bainer, "Common Instructional Problems in the Multicultural Classroom," *Journal on Excellence in College Teaching* 2 (1991): 77–88.

61. See R. Scollon, *Teacher's Questions about Alaska Native Education* (Fairbanks: University of Alaska Center for Cross Cultural Studies).

62. See G. G. Barber, *Planning and Organizing for Multicultural Education* (Reading, Mass.:

Addison-Wesley, 1983); J. A. Banks, *Multiethnic Education: Theory and Practice* (Boston: Allyn & Bacon, 1981); D. M. Gollnik and P. Chinn, *Multicultural Education*, 2d edition (Columbus, Ohio: Charles E. Merrill, 1986).

63. *Multicultural Nonsexist Education: A Human Relations Approach*, ed. Nicholas Colangelo, Cecelia H. Foxley, and Dick Dustin (Dubuque: Kendall/Hunt, 1979).

64. See M. B. Balenky, B. M. Clinchy, N. R. Goldberg, and J. M. Tarule, *Women's Ways of Knowing* (New York: Basic Books, 1986); and Blythe McVicher Clinchy, "Issues of Gender in Teaching and Learning," *Journal on Excellence in College Teaching* 19 (1990): 52–67.

65. See, for example, Ron Takaki, *Strangers From A Different Shore* (Boston: Little Brown, 1989); Gary Nash, *Red, White and Black: The Peoples of Colonial America* (Englewood Cliffs, N.J.: Prentice-Hall, 1982); Rudolfo Acuna, *Occupied America: A History of Chicanos* (New York: Harper & Row, 1988); Louise Erdrich, *Love Medicine* (New York: Holt, Rinehart & Winston, 1984); Carl Degler, *At Odds: Women and the Family in American History* (New York: Oxford University Press, 1980); Mirra Komarovsky, *Women in the Modern World* (New York: Basic Books, 1953).

66. Josiah Royce, *California From the Conquest in 1846 to the Second Vigilance Committee in San Francisco (1856): A Study of American Character* (Boston: Houghton, Mifflin, 1886).

67. Josiah Royce, *Race Questions, Provincialism, and Other American Problems* (New York: Macmillan, 1908).

68. Carlos E. Cortes, "*Pluribus* and *Unum*: The Quest for Community and Diversity," *Change* 23 (September/October 1991): 10.

69. Royce, *The Problem of Christianity*, ed. John E. Smith, 60–68.

70. Ibid., 62.

71. John A. Kouwenhoven, *The Beer Can by the Highway* (New York: Doubleday, 1961), 53.

72. Royce, "Provincialism" (1892), in *The Basic Writings of Josiah Royce*, ed. John McDermott (Chicago: University of Chicago Press), 2: 1069–1070, 1074–76.

73. Ibid., 1070.

74. Ibid., 1074.

75. Josiah Royce, *The Problem of Christianity*, 2: 67.

76. See Marilyn Edelstein, "Ethics, Education, and Political Correctness," *Issues in Ethics* 5, no. 2 (Summer 1992): 1, 8; and Lee A. Daniels, "Diversity, Correctness and Campus Life" *Change*. 22 (September/October 1990): 16–20.

77. Bobbi Hansen, "Questioning Techniques for an Active Classroom," in *Changing College Classrooms: New Teaching and Learning Strategies for an Increasingly Complex World,* ed. Diane Halpern (San Francisco: Jossey-Bass Publishers, 1994), 93–108.

78. See Betsey Newell Decyk, "Using Examples to Teach Concepts," in *Changing College Classrooms: New Teaching and Learning Strategies for an Increasingly Complex World,* ed. Diane Halpern (San Francisco: Jossey-Bass Publishers, 1994), 39–63.

79. See E. Aronson, *The Jigsaw Classroom* (Newbury Park, Calif.: Sage, 1978).

80. See Cris E. Guenter, "Fostering Creativity Through Problem Solving," in *Changing College Classrooms: New Teaching and Learning Strategies for an Increasingly Complex World,* ed. Diane Halpern (San Francisco: Jossey-Bass Publishers, 1994), 64–73.

81. See G. Shirts, *Ba Fa' Ba Fa': A Cross-Cultural Simulation* (Del Mar, Calif.: Simulation Training Assistance, 1977).

82. Ellen N. Junn, "Experiential Approaches to Enhancing Cultural Awareness," in *Changing College Classrooms: New Teaching and Learning Strategies for an Increasingly Complex World,* ed. Diane Halpern (San Francisco: Jossey-Bass Publishers, 1994), 128–64.

83. Lee S. Shulman, "Teaching as Community Property: Putting An End to Pedagogical Solitude," *Change* 25, no. 6 (1993): 6.

84. Kate Kinsella, "Peer Coaching Taching: Colleagues Supporting Professional Growth Across Disciplines," in *To Improve the Academy* ed. Ed Neal and Laurie Richlin (Stillwater, Okla.: New Forums, 1995), 111.

85. Ibid.

86. See Roy Killen, "Improving Teaching through Reflective Partnerships," in *To Improve the Academy* ed. Ed Neal and Laurie Richlin (Stillwater, Okla.: New Forums, 1995), 125–37.

87. See D. J. Cole, "Developing Reflection In Educational Course Work Via The Professional Portfolio," *Gateways to Teacher Education* 4, no.1 (1991): 1–12; P. Seldin, *The Teaching Portfolio: A Practical Guide to Improved Performance and Pro-*

motion/Tenure Decisions (Bolton, Mass.: Anker, 1991); N. G. Vall and J. M. Tennison, "International Student Teaching: Stimulus for Developing Reflective Teachers," *Action in Teacher Education* 13, no. 4 (1992): 31–36, and R. Killen, and A. Killen, "Faculty Development through Reflective Teaching," *The Journal of Staff, Progam and Organizational Development* 10, no. 2 (1992); 69–74.

88. Zeichner, "Preparing Reflective Teachers," *International Journal of Teacher Education* 34, no. 3 (1987): 3–9.

89. See Pat Hutchins, "Windows on Practice," *Change* 25, no. 6 (December 1993): 14–21; Using Cases to Improve College Teaching: A Guide to More Reflective Practice, American Association of Higher Education, 1993.

CHAPTER 7

1. See, for example, *Competitive Approaches to Health Care Reform*, ed. Richard J. Arnold, Robert F. Rich and William D. White (Washington, D.C.: Urban Institute Press, 1993); Keith J. Mueller *Health Care Policy in the United States* (Lincoln: University of Nebraska Press, 1993); *Why the United States Does Not Have a National Health Program*, ed. Vincent Navarro (Amityville, N.Y.: Baywood Publishing, 1993).

2. See "The Clinton Reform Plan,"Special Section, *Journal of Health Politics, Policy and Law* 19, no. 1 (Spring 1994): 191–264; Arthur L. Caplan and Reinhard Priester, "For Better or Worse? The Moral Lessons of Minnesota's Health Right Legislation," *Kennedy Institute of Ethics Journal* 2, no. 3 (September 1992): 201–16.

3. *The Body in Medical Thought and Practice*, ed. Drew Leder (Boston: Kluwer Academic Publishers, 1992), 8.

4. Kenneth R. Pelletier and Denise L. Herzing, "Psychoneuroimmunology: Toward a Mind-Body Model," in *Eastern and Western Approaches to Healing*, ed. Anees A. Sheikh and Katharina A. Sheikh (New York: John Wiley & Sons, 1989), 344–94, esp. 368, 379.

5. Larry Dossey, "The Importance of Modern Physics for Modern Medicine," in *Eastern and Western Approaches to Healing*, ed. Anees A. Sheikh and Katharina A. Sheikh (New York: John Wiley & Sons, 1989), 395–423, esp. 420.

6. David Jennings, M.D., "The Confusion between Disease and Illness in Clinical Medicine," *Canadian Medical Journal* 135 (15 October 1986): 865–70.

7. Anthony L. Suchman, M.D., and Dale A. Matthews, M.D, "What Makes the Patient-Doctor Relationship Therapeutic? Exploring the Connexional Dimension of Medical Care," *Annals of Internal Medicine* 108 (1988): 125–30.

8. Joseph H. Levenstein et al., "The Patient-Centered Clinical Method, A Model for the Doctor Patient Interaction in Family Medicine," *Family Practice* 3, no. 1 (1986): cine.

9. See J. H. Buchanan, *Patient Encounters: The Experience of Disease* (Charlottesville, Va.: University of Virginia Press, 1989); and "*While I'm Here, Doctor,*" in *A Study of Change in the Doctor-Patient Relationship*, ed. A. Elder and O. Samuel (New York: Tavistock Publications, 1987).

10. George Ritzer and David Walczak, "Rationalization and the Deprofessionalization of Physicians," *Special Forces* 12, no. 2 (September 1988): 1–22.

11. Ibid.

12. Leder, in *The Body in Medical Thought and Practice*, ed. Drew Leder (Boston: Kluwer Academic Publishers, 1992), 1–2.

13. Carole Spitzack, "Foucault's Political Body in Medicine," in *The Body in Medical Thought and Practice*, ed. Drew Leder (Boston: Kluwer Academic Publishers, 1992), 58; See also Michael Foucault, *The Birth of the Clinic: An Archaeology of Medical Perception*, trans. A. M. Sheridan Smith (New York: Vintage Books, 1975).

14. Susan Sherwin, *No Longer Patient* (Philadelphia: Temple University Press, 1994), 6

15. Ibid, 183.

16. Ibid, 137–58.

17. Ibid, 222, 232.

18. See George L. Engel, "The Need For a New Medical Model: A Challenge for Biomedicine," *Science* 196 (1977): 129–36; E. Pellegrino and D. C. Thomasma, *A Philosophical Basis for Medical Practice toward a Philosophy and Ethics of the Healing Professions* (Oxford: Oxford University Press, 1981); and R. M. Zaner, *The Problems of Embodiment: Some Contributions to a Phenomenology of the Body* (The Hague: Martinus-Nijhoff, 1964).

19. Lawrence B. McCullough and Frank A. Chervenak, *Ethics in Obstetrics and Gynecology* (New York: Oxford University Press, 1994).

20. Drew Leder, "A Tale of Two Bodies: The Cartesian Corpse and 'Lived Body,'" in *The Body*

in Medical Thought and Practice, ed. Drew Leder (Boston: Kluwer Academic Publishers, 1992), 17–35, esp. 17–21.

21. Ibid., 21, as discussed by Leder from Foucault, *The Birth of the Clinic*.

22. Ibid., 23. Italics are in the text.

23. See Howard M. Spiro, M.D., *Doctors, Patients and Placebos* (New Haven: Yale University Press, 1986).

24. See Maurice Merleau-Ponty, *Phenomenology of Perception*, trans. C. Smith (London: Routledge & Kegan Paul, 1962); *The Humanity of the Ill*, ed. Victor Kestenbaum (Knoxville, Tenn.: University of Tennessee Press, 1982); and Richard M. Zaner, *The Problem of Embodiment: Some Contributions to a Philosophical Discipline* (The Hague: Martinus Nishoff, 1964).

25. See Jacquelyn Ann K. Kegley, "Royce and Husserl: Some Parallels and Food for Thought," *Transactions of the Charles S. Peirce Society* 14, no. 3 (Summer 1978): 184–99.

26. Leder, "A Tale of Two Bodies," 27.

27. Eric J. Cassell, "The Nature of Suffering and the Goals of Medicine," *The New England Journal of Medicine* 306 (1982): 640.

28. Robert F. Murphy, *The Body Silent* (New York: Henry Holt, 1987), 63.

29. Robert M. Veatch, "The Medical Model: Its Nature and Problems," *Hastings Center Studies* 1 (1973): 59–76, reprinted in *Psychiatry and Ethics*, ed. Rem B. Edwards (Buffalo, New York: Prometheus Books, 1982), 88–108. Page references will be from the reprint.

30. Ibid., 93.

31. Ibid., 94.

32. Ibid., 96.

33. Ibid., 89 ff.

34. Ibid., 97.

35. Ibid., 98.

36. See, for example, W. Miller Brown, "On Defining Disease," *The Journal of Medicine and Philosophy* 10 (1985): 311–28.

37. See C. Boorse, "Health as a Theoretical Concept," *Philosophy of Science* 44 (1977): 542–73; "On the Distinction between Disease and Illness," in *Concept of Health and Disease: Interdisciplinary Perspectives*, ed. A. L. Caplan, H. T. Englehardt, Jr., and J. J. McCarthy (Reading, Mass: Addison-Wesley.), 545–660; Carol Whitbeck, "Causation in Medicine: The Disease Entity Model," *Philosophy of Science*, 44: (1977):

619–37; C. Whitbeck, "A Theory of Health," in *Concept of Health and Disease: Interdisciplinary Perspectives*, ed. A. L. Caplan, H. T. Englehardt, Jr., and J. J. McCarthy (Reading, Mass: Addison-Wesley.), 611–26; and George J. Agich, "Disease and Value: A Rejection of the Value-Neutrality Thesis," *Theoretical Medicine* 4 (1983): 27–41.

38. See, for example, Dorian Apple, "How Laymen Define Illness," *Journal of Health and Human Behavior* 1 (1960): 219–25; John H. Marry, "Lay Concepts of Etiology," *Journal of Chronic Disease* 17 (1964) :371–86; Charles E. Sefferman, "From the Patient's Bed," *Health Management Quarterly* 13 (1991): 12–15.

39. Gordon Waddell, Martin Bircher, David Finlayson, and Chris J. Mann, "Symptoms and Signs: Physical Disease or Illness Behavior?" *British Medical Journal* (Clinical Research Edition), 289 (1984): 739–41.

40. See Douglas Browning, "The Meaning of Automobiles," in *Technology and Human Affairs*, ed. Larry Hickman and Azizah al-Hibrii (St. Louis: C. V. Mosby, 1981), 13–17.

41. Pelletier and Herzing, 368–70.

42. See *Eastern and Western Approaches to Healing*.

43. Richard M. Restak, M.D., "Pain and Healing," in *The Mind* (Toronto: Bantam Books, 1988), 138.

44. Ibid.

45. Ibid., 145.

46. Ibid.

47. Ibid., 145–51.

48. Ibid., 152.

49. Ibid.

50. Quoted by Restak, Ibid., 151.

51. Pelletier and Herzing, 364–67. See, for example, M. Pilisuk and S. H. Parks, *The Healing Web: Social Networks and Human Survival* (Hanover, N.H.: University Press of New England, 1986); L. Tomoshok, B. H. Fox, "Coping Styles and Other Psychosocial Factors Related to Medical Status and to Prognosis in Cutaneous Malignant Melanoma," in *Impact of Psychoendocrine Systems in Cancer and Immunity*, ed. B. H. Fox and B. H. Newberry (New York: Hogrefe, 1984).

52. Ibid., 367–68. See, for example, B. Fogle, *Interrelations Between People and Pets* (Springfield, Illinois: Thomas, 1981); J. Arehart-Treichel,

"Pets: The Health Benefits," *Science News* 121 (1982): 220–24; M. M. Baun et al., "Effects of Bonding Vs. Non-Bonding on the Physiological Effects of Petting," *Proceedings of the Conference on the Human-Animal Bond* (University of Minnesota, June 13–14, 1983, and University of California, June 17–18, 1983).

53. Restak, 153.

54. Ibid., 156.

55. See Anees A. Sheikh, Robert G. Kunzendorf, and Katharina S. Sheikh, "Healing Images: From Ancient Wisdom to Modern Science," in *Eastern and Western Approaches to Healing*, ed. Anees A. Sheikh and Katharina A. Sheikh (New York: John Wiley & Sons, 1989), 470–515; and Lorne D. Bertrand and Nicholas P. Spanos, "Hypnosis: Historical and Social Psychological Aspects," in *Eastern and Western Approaches to Healing*, ed. Anees A. Sheikh and Katharina A. Sheikh (New York: John Wiley & Sons, 1989), 237–63.

56. Norman Cousins, *Anatomy of an Illness as Perceived by the Patient* (New York: Bantam, 1981), 32.

57. Ibid.

58. Quoted in Restak, 159.

59. Restak, 160. See E. Weiss and O. S. English, *Psychosomatic Medicine* (Philadelphia: Saunders, 1943); and Howard M. Spiro, *Doctors, Patients and Placebos* (New Haven: Yale University Press, 1986).

60. Norman Cousins, "Anatomy of an Illness (as Perceived by the Patient)," *New England Journal of Medicine* 295 (1976): 1458–63. See also Norman Cousins, *The Healing Heart* (New York: Norton, 1983)

61. Herman Kahn, "The Anatomy of Norman Cousins' Illness," . *Mt. Sinai Journal of Medicine* 48, 9 (1981): 305–14.

62. F. A. Ruterman, "A placebo for the doctor," *Commentary* 69 (May 1980): 54–60.

63. Cousins, "Anatomy of an Illness," 1460.

64. Cousins, *The Healing Heart*, 50.

65. Restak, 161–62.

66. See Dennis T. Jaffee, *Healing From Within* (New York: Knopf, 1980); and Stephen Locke, M.D., and Douglas Colligan, *The Healer Within: The New Medicine of Mind and Body* (New York: Hutton, 1986).

67. Spiro, 225, 233ff.

68. Eric Cassell, *Clinical Technique* (Cambridge, Mass: MIT Press, 1985), 15.

69. Susan Bordo, "Eating Disorders: The Feminist Challenge to the Concept of Pathology," in *The Body in Medical Thought and Practice*, ed. Drew Leder (Boston: Kluwer Academic Publishers, 1992), 197.

70. Ibid.

71. See *Gender Body/Knowledge: Feminist Reconstructions of Being and Knowing*, ed. A. Jaggar and S. Bordo (New Brunswick, N.J.: Rutgers University Press, 1989); M. Boskind-White, Rand W. White, "Bulimarexia: A Historical-Sociocultural Perspective," in *Handbook of Eating Disorders*, ed. K. Brownell and J. Foreyt (New York: Basic Books, 1986), 353–66; K. Chernin, *The Hungry Self: Women, Eating and Identity* (New York: Harper, 1985); P. Garfinkel and D. Garner, *Anorexia Nervosa: A Multidimensional Perspective* (New York: Warner, 1982); and E. Szekey, *Never Too Thin* (Toronto: Women's Press, 1988).

72. Vanderheyden, et al., "Critical Variables Associated with Bingeing and Bulimia in a University Population: A Factor Analysis Study," *International Journal of Eating Disorders* 7 (1988): 321–29; and B. Silverstein, et al., "Possible Causes of the Thin Standard of Bodily Attractiveness for Women," *International Journal of Eating Disorders* 5 (1986): 907–16.

73. Pellegrino, 1982, "Being ill and being healed: some reflections on the grounding of medical morality," in *The Humanity of the Ill*, ed. Victor Kestenbaum (Knoxville, Tenn.: University of Tennessee Press, 1982), 159.

74. Murphy, 64.

75. Robert Silberman, *Crisis in American Medicine* (New York: Panthion Books, 1994), 67.

76. Joseph H. Levenstein, et al., "The Patient-Centered Method: A Model for the Doctor-Patient Relationship," *Family Practice* 3 (1986): 1, 24.

77. Oliver W. Sacks, *Awakenings* (New York: E.P. Dutton, 1983); *A Leg to Stand On* (New York: Summit Books, 1984); and *The Man Who Mistook His Wife for a Hat and Other Clinical Tales* (New York: Summit Books, 1985).

78. Michael J. Habestrom and Stephen Lescher, *A Coronary Event* (Philadelphia: J. B. Lippincott, 1976).

79. See H. Brody, *Stories of Sickness* (New Haven: Yale University Press, 1987); J. M. Hull, *Touching the Rock: An Experience of Blindness* (New York: Pantheon, 1990); A. Kleinmann, *The Illness Narratives: Suffering, Healing and the*

Human Condition (New York: Basic Books, 1988);*When Doctors Get Sick*, ed. H. Mandell and H. Spiro (New York: Plenum, 1989); E. Rosenbaum, *A Taste of My Own Medicine: When the Doctor is the Patient* (New York: Random House, 1988).

80. L. Churchill and S. Churchill, "Storytelling in Medical Arenas: The Art of Self-Determination," *Journal of the American Medical Association* 262 (1989): 1127.

81. Eric J. Cassell, *Clinical Technique*, vol. 2 of *Talking With Patients* (Cambridge, Massachusetts: MIT Press, 1985).

82. Oliver Sacks, "Clinical Tales," *Literature and Medicine*, 5 (1986): 14.

83. Rita Kielstein and Hans-Martin Sass, "Using Stories to Assess Value and Establish Medical Directives," *Kennedy Institute of Ethics Journal* 3, no. 3 (September 1993): 303–25.

84. E. G. Mishler, T*he Discourse of Medicine: Dialectics of Medical Interviews* (Somerville, N.J.: Able, 1984), 70–90.

85. Sacks, 14.

86. For a comparative analysis of the views of Royce and Husserl, see Jacquelyn Ann Kegley, "Royce and Husserl: Some Parallels and Food for Thought," *Transactions of the Charles S. Peirce Society*, 14, no. 3 (1978): 184–99.

87. Spiro, *Doctors, Patients and Placebos*, 196.

88. Josiah Royce, "Introduction to H. Poincare," in *The Foundations of Science*, tr. G. B. Halsted (New York: Science Press, 1913), reprinted in *Royce's Logical Essays*, ed., D. S. Robinson (Dubuque, Iowa: William. C. Brown, 1951), 279–80. Quote is from reprint.

89. Josiah Royce, "A Critical Study of Reality" (1897), unpublished papers, folio 81.34 Harvard Archives.

90. This view is well presented in Frank M. Oppenheim, *Royce's Mature Ethics* (Notre Dame, Ind.: University of Notre Dame Press, 1993).

91. Ibid., 110–11. See Josiah Royce, "Mind," 1916 in *Encyclopedia of Religion and Ethics*, ed. James Hastings (New York: Charles Scribner's Sons), 8: 649–57, reprinted in *Royce's Logical Essays* (Dubuque, Iowa: William C. Brown, 1951), 146–78. References to this essay will be to the Robinson volume.

92. Ibid., 174.

93. Ibid., 174–75.

94. David Owen, "Medicine, Morality and the Market," *Lancet* 2 (1984): 30–31.

95. Albert Gebhard, Gerlinde Sponholz, and Helmut Baitsch, "Chronic Disease and the Meaning of Old Age," *Hastings Center Report* 24, no. 5 (September/October 1994): 12.

96. Josiah Royce, *The World and the Individual* (New York: Dover Publications, 1959) 2: 219–44.

97. See Gena Corea, *The Mother Machine* (New York: Harper & Row, 1985); *Made to Order*, ed. Patricia Spallone and Deborah Lynn Steinberg (New York: Pergamon, 1987); Mary O'Brien, *Reproducing the World* (San Francisco: Westview, 1989); Gena Corea et al., *Man-Made Woman* (Bloomington: Indiana University Press, 1987).

98. Evelyn Fox Keller, *Reflections on Gender and Science* (New Haven: Yale University Press, 1985); and *A Feeling for the Organism: The Life and Work of Barbara McClintock* (New York: W. H. Freeman, 1983).

99. Josiah Royce, *The Problem of Christianity* (Chicago: Henry Regnery Company, 1968), 2: 42.

100. Charles Sanders Peirce, "Consequences of Four Incapacities" (1868) in *Collected Papers of Charles Sanders Peirce*, vol. 5, *Pragmatism and Pragmaticism*, ed. Charles Hartshorne and Paul Weiss (Cambridge, Mass.: Belknap Press of Harvard University, 1960), 5:314, p. 189.

101. Kay Toombs, "The Temporality of Illness: Four Levels of Experience," *Theoretical Medicine* 11 (1990): 227–41.

102. Edmund Husserl, *The Phenomenology of Internal Time-Consciousness* (Bloomington: Indiana University Press, 1964), 48.

103. Alfred Schutz, "Making Music Together," in *Alfred Schutz: Collected Papers*, vol 2, ed. Arvid Brodersen (The Hague: Martinus Hijhoff, 1976), 171.

104. Josiah Royce, "Kant's Relation to Modern Philosophic Progress," *The Journal of Speculative Philosophy* 15 (1881): 375.

105. Husserl, 51–59

106. Toombs, 237.

107. Jean Paul Sartre, *Being and Nothingness* (New York: Washington Square, 1956), 436–45, 463–70.

108. Toombs, 230.

109. Sartre, 436–38.

110. Ibid., 442.

111. Ibid.

112. Ibid., 466.

113. Ibid.

114. Elaine Scarry, *The Body in Pain: The*

Making and Unmaking of the World (New York: Oxford University Press, 1985), 4.

115. Josiah Royce, *The Conception of God* (New York: Macmillan, 1898), 253.

116. Royce, *World and the Individual*, 2: 276. Italics are Royce's.

117. Sigmund Freud, *Civilization and Its Discontent*, trans. J. Strachey (New York: Morton, 1961), 24.

118. Mary G. Rawlinson, "The Sense of Suffering," *The Journal of Medicine and Philosophy* 11 (1986): 39–62.

119. Ibid., 41.

120. Rawlinson, 42.

121. Ibid.

122. See Josiah Royce, *War and Insurance* (New York: Macmillan, 1914).

123. For the initial discussion of this "will to harmony" see Josiah Royce, *The Religious Aspect of Philosophy* (1885; reprinted, New York: Harper & Row, 1958) 168–70.

124. My discussion of mediation benefits greatly from the explication of this Roycean notion by Frank Oppenheim in his *Royce's Mature Ethics*, 164–69.

125. Talcott Parsons, *The Social System* (Glencoe, Ill.: Free Press, 1951).

126. See Edmund D. Pellegrino, "The Most Humane Science: Some Notes on Liberal Education in Medicine and the University." *Bulletin of the Medical College of Virginia* 2, no.4 (1970): 11–39; reprinted as "The Most Humane of the Sciences; The Most Scientific of the Humanities," in *Humanism and the Physician*, ed. Edmund D. Pellegrino (Knoxville, Tenn.: University of Tennessee Press, 1979), 117–29; "Balancing Head, Heart and Hand in the Physician's Education: A Special Task for Family Practice," *Journal of the American Board of Family Practice* 1, no. 1 (1988): 4–14; and Eric J. Cassell, "The Place of the Humanities in Medicine," in *Applying the Humanities*, ed. Daniel Callahan, Arthur L. Caplan, and Bruce Jennings (New York: Plenum Press, 1990), 167–89.

127. Pellegrino, "Most Humane Science," 17.

128. Cassell, "Place of the Humanities," 171.

129. Ibid., 172–74.

130. Ibid., 175.

131. Ibid., 176–77.

132. Ibid., 179.

133. Ibid., 182–83.

134. Susan Sherwin, *No Longer Patient: Feminist Ethics and Health Care* (Philadelphia: Temple University Press, 1992); Mary Briody Mahowald, *Women and Children in Health Care* (New York: Oxford University Press, 1993); Helen Baquaert Holmes and Laura M. Purdy, *Feminist Perspectives in Medical Ethics* (Bloomington: Indiana University Press, 1992).

135. This is a project funded by the Fund for Improvement of Postsecondary Education (FIPSE). For information on the program contact Sandra P. Levison, Women's Health Education Program, Medical College of Pennsylvania and Hahnemann University School of Medicine, 3300 Henry Avenue, Philadelphia, Pennsylvania 19129.

136. See *Health Care Issues in Black America: Policies, Problem and Prospects*, ed. Woodrow Jones, Jr., and Mitchell F. Rice (New York: Greenwood, 1987); *Health Care for the Other Americans*, ed. V. Bullugh and B. Bullugh (New York: Appleton-Century Crofts, 1982); and J. H. Jones, *Bad Blood: The Tuskegee Syphilis Experiment: A Tragedy of Race and Medicine* (New York: Free Press, 1981).

137. Annette Dula and Sara Goering, *"It Just Ain't Fair:" The Ethics of Health Care for Black Americans* (Westport, Conn.: Praeger, 1994).

138. This is a project funded by the Fund for Improvement of Postsecondary Education (FIPSE). For information contact David J. Hufford, Department of Humanities, Pennsylvania State University College of Medicine, Milton S. Hershey Medical Center, Hershey, PA.

139. Nancy Ann Jeffrey, "HMOs Say 'Hola' to Potential Customers," *Wall Street Journal*, 30November 1995, B1.

140. Ibid., B2.

141. Ibid.

142. Edmund Pellegrino, "The Humanities in Medical Education," *Mobius* 2 (1982): 140.

143. James F Childress and Mark Siegler, "Metaphors and Models of Doctor-Patient Relationships: Their Implications for Autonomy," *Theoretical Medicine* 5 (1984): 17–30.

144. Ibid., 18.

145. See Thomas M. Garrett, Harold Ballilie, and Rosellen M. Garrett, *Health Care Ethics* (Englewood Cliffs, N.J.: Prentice-Hall, 1993) for a discussion of "paternalism" as morally defective, 43–46.

146. For another discussion of the various models of the physician-patient relationship, see Garrett, Ballilie, and Garrett, 18–23.

147. Eric Cassell, "Autonomy and Ethics in Action," *New England Journal of Medicine* 297 (1989): 333–34.

148. Thomas S. Szasz and Marc H. Hollander, "A Contribution to the Philosophy of Medicine: The Basic Models of the Doctor-Patient Relationship," *Archives of Internal Medicine* 97 (1956): 586–87.

149. Ibid., 587.

150. Robert Veatch, "Models for Ethical Medicine in a Revolutionary Age," *Hastings Center Report* 2 (June 1972): 7.

151. Childress and Siegler, 19.

152. "Informed Consent" was enunciated in Salgo v. Leland, Stanford Univ. Board of Trustees, 317 P. 2d 170 (Cal. Dist. Court of Appeals), 1957.

153. A series of celebrated cases gave patients the legal right to refuse treatment, even if this refusal resulted in their death. See Curzan v. Director, Missouri Dept. of Health, 497 U.S. 261 (1990); Superintendent of Belchertown State Sch. v. Saikewicz, 370 N.E. 2d 417 (Mass. 1977); *In re* Karen Quinlan, 355 A.2d 647 (N.J.), *cert. denied,* 429 U.S. 922 (1976).

154. See the discussion of Advocacy in *Rethinking Medical Morality: The Ethical Implications of Changes in Health Care Organization, Delivery, and Financing,* Report of a Research Project, Center of Biomedical Ethics (University of Minnesota, 1989), 21–23.

155. See W. G. Menke, "Professional Values in Medical Practice," *New England Journal of Medicine* 280, no. 17 (1969): 930–36.

156. James E. Sabin, M.D., "A Credo for Ethical Managed Care in Mental Health Practice," *Hospital and Community Psychiatry* 45, no. 9 (1994): 859.

157. Ibid.

158. These three aspects of "Quality Health Care" were set forth in a now classic article by Avedis Donabedian, who initiated outcome assessment of heart surgery at Massachusetts General Hospital. See Avedis Donabedian, "Evaluating the Quality of Medical Care," *Milbank Memorial Fund Quarterly* 44 (1966): 166–206.

159. Wendy K. Mariner, "Outcome Assessment in Health Care Reform: Promise and Limitations" *American Journal of Law and Medicine* 20, nos. 1 & 2 (1994): 42.

160. Ibid., 39.

161. Marc A. Rodwin, "Patient Accountability and Quality of Care: Lessons from Medical Consumerism and Patients' Rights, Women's Health and Disability Rights Movements," *American Journal of Law and Medicine* 20, nos. 1 & 2 (1994): 147.

162. Ibid., 159–61.

163. Ibid., 163–66.

164. Ibid., 153–57.

165. See Albert O. Hirschman, *Exit, Voice and Loyalty: Responses to Decline in Firms, Organizations and States* (Cambridge: Harvard University Press, 1970).

166. Spiro, *Doctors, Patients and Placebos,* 233. Italics are mine.

167. Lawrence B. McCullough, Ph.D., and Frank A. Chervenak, M.D., *Ethics in Obstetrics and Gynecology* (New York: Oxford University Press, 1994), 25.

168. Spiro, *Doctors, Patients and Placebos,* 237.

169. Karen Lebacz, "The Virtuous Patient," in *Virtue and Medicine,* ed. Earl E. Shelp (Dordrecht: D. Reidel, 1985), 275–88.

170. Ibid., 276.

171. Oppenheim, 169.

172. Lebacz, 277.

173. Ibid., 280.

174. Ibid., 281.

175. Ibid., 279.

176. Ibid., 284.

177. Ibid., 282.

178. Edmund D. Pellegrino, "The Virtuous Physician," in *Virtue and Medicine,* ed. Earl E. Shelp (Dordrecht: D. Reidel, 1985), 244.

179. Ibid., 250.

180. Edmund D. Pellegrino and D. C. Thomasma, *For the Patient's Good* (New York: Oxford University Press, 1988).

181. Edmund D. Pellegrino, "Autonomy and Coercion in Disease Prevention and Health Promotion," *Theoretical Medicine* 5 (1984): 83–91.

182. Quoted in Oppenheim, 170.

183. Josiah Royce Lecture, "The Art of Loyalty" (Harvard Archives, Royce Papers, 82, no. 2), 50–51. Quoted in Oppenheim, 137.

184. So aptly stated by Oppenheim, 140.

CHAPTER 8

1. William M. Sullivan, *Reconstructing a Public Philosophy* (Berkeley: University of California Press, 1982).

2. Ibid., 9.

3. Ibid., 11.

4. See Natalie S. Glance and Bernardo A. Hoberman, "The Dynamics of Social Dilemmas," *Scientific American* 270, no. 3 (1994): 76–82.

5. See Jacquelyn Ann Kegley, "Josiah Royce: A Source of New Religious Insights Today," *Religious Studies* 18–19 (1983): 211–24.

6. See Jacquelyn Ann Kegley, "Josiah Royce on Self and Community," *Rice University Studies* 66, no. 4 (Fall 1980): 33–53.

7. Immanuel Kant, *The Doctrine of Virtue,* trans. Mary J. Gregor (New York: Harper & Row, 1964), 99.

8. Immanual Kant, 1785 and 1964. *Groundwork for the Metaphysics of Morals* (1785), trans. H. J. Paton (New York: Harper & Row, 1964), 61.

9. Willard Gayland, "Knowing Good and Doing Good," *Hastings Center Report* 24, no. 3 (May–June 1994): 40.

10. Ibid., 39.

11. Ibid.

12. John Stuart Mill, *On Liberty* (1859), in *The Collected Works of J. S. Mill*, ed. J. M. Robson (Toronto: Toronto University Press, 1977), 18: 226.

13. Gerald Dworkin, "Paternalism," in *Morality and the Law*, ed. Richard A. Wasserstom (Belmont, Calif.: Wadsworth, 1971), 118.

14. Ibid., 116.

15. Mill, 226.

16. Ibid., 281

17. Thomas H. Murray, "Individualism and Community: The Contested Terrain of Autonomy," . *Hastings Center Report* 24, no. 3 (1991): 32.

18. Scott Peck, M.D., *The Different Drum* (New York: Simon and Schuster, 1987).

19. See chapter 3.

BIBLIOGRAPHY

BOOKS

Acuna, Rudolf. *Occupied America: A History of Chicanos.* New York: Harper & Row, 1988.

Alexander, Lamar. *The Nation's Report Card.* Cambridge, Mass.: National Academy of Education, 1987.

Alexander, Lamar, Bill Clinton, and Thomas H. Rean. *Time for Results.* Washington, D.C.: National Governors' Association Center for Policy Research, 1986.

Angelo, Thomas A., ed. *Classroom Research: Early Lessons From Success.* San Francisco: Jossey-Bass, 1991.

Arcana, Judith. *Our Mothers' Daughters.* Berkeley: Shameless Hussy Press, 1979.

Arnold, Richard J., Robert F. Rich, and William D. White, eds. *Competitive Approaches to Health Care Reform.* Washington, D.C.: Urban Institute Press, 1993.

Aronson, E. *The Jigsaw Classroom.* Newbury Park: Sage Publications, 1978.

Astin, Andrew W. *Minorities in Higher Education: Recent Trends, Current Prospects, and Recommendations.* San Francisco: Jossey-Bass,1982.

———. *What Matters in College? Four Critical Years.* San Francisco: Jossey-Bass, 1992.

Astuto, Terry A. *Roots of Reform: Challenging the Assumptions That Control Educational Reform.* Bloomington, Indiana: Phi Delta Kappa Educational Foundation,1994.

Balenky, M. B., B. M. Clinchy, N. R. Goldberg, and J. M. Tarule. *Women's Ways of Knowing.* New York: Basic Books, 1986.

Bane, Mary Jo. *Here To Stay: American Families in the Twentieth Century.* New York: Basic Books, 1976.

Banks, J. A. *Multiethnic Educational Theory and Practice.* Boston: Allyn & Bacon, 1981.

Barber, Benjamin R. *An Aristocracy for Everyone: The Politics of Education and the Future of America.* New York: Ballantine, 1992.

Barber, G. G. *Planning and Organization for A Multicultural Education.* Reading, Mass.: Addison-Wesley, 1983.

Bellah, Robert M. et al. *The Good Society.* New York: Vintage Books, Random House, 1992.

———. *Habits of the Heart: Individualism and Commitment in American Life.* New York: Harper & Row Publishers, 1985.

Bellah, Robert M. et al., eds. *Individualism and Commitment in American Life: Readings on the Theories of Habits of the Heart.* New York: Harper & Row, 1987.

Benjamin, Jessica. *Bonds of Love: Psychoanalysis, Feminism and the Problem of Domination.* New York: Pantheon, 1988.

Berger, Peter, and Richard John Neuhaus, eds. *To Empower People: The Role of Mediating Structures in Public Policy.* Washington, D.C.: American Enterpise Institute for Public Policy Research, 1977.

Bishirijan, Richard. *A Public Philosophy Reader.* New Rochelle, New York: Arlington House Publishers, 1978.

Bogger, R. J., ed. *Our Selves/Our Past: Psychological Approaches to American History.* Baltimore: John Hopkins University Press, 1981.

Bossard, J. H. S. *Ritualism in Family Living.* Philadelphia: University of Pennsylvania Press, 1950.

Brody, H. *Stories of Sickness.* New Haven: Yale University Press, 1987.

Brownell, K., and J. Foreyt, eds. *Handbook of Eating Disorders.* New York: Basic Books, 1986.

Buchanan, J. H. *Patient Encounters: The Experience of Disease.* Charlottsville, Virginia: University of Virginia Press, 1989.

Bullugh, V., and B. Bullugh, eds. *Health Care for the Other Americans.* New York: Appleton-Century Crofts. 1982.

Caplan, Arthur L., and Bruce Jennings, eds. *Applying the Humanities.* New York: Plenum Press, 1990.

Caplan, A. L.; H. T. Englehardt, Jr., and J. J. McCarthy, eds. *Concepts of Health and Disease: Interdisciplinary Perspectives.* Reading, Mass: Addison-Wesley, 1977.

Cassell, Eric J. *Clinical Technique:* Vol. 2 of *Talking With Patients.* Cambridge, Mass: MIT Press, 1985.

Chernin., K. *The Hungry Self: Women, Eating and Identity.* New York: Harper & Row Publishers, 1985.

Clendenning, John. *The Life and Thought of Josiah Royce.* Madison: University of Wisconsin Press, 1985.

Colangelo, W., C. H. Foxley, and C. H. Dustin, eds. *Multiculturual Nonsexist Education: A Human Relations Approach.* Dubuque: Kendall Hunt, 1979.

Coleman, Daniel. *Emotional Intelligence.* New York: Bantam Books, 1995.

Colligan, Douglas. *The Healer Within: The New Medicine of Mind and Body.* New York: E. P. Hutton, 1986.

Condon, J. C., and F. Yousel. *An Introduction to Intercultural Communications.* New York: Macmillan Company, 1988.

Cooper, David. *The Death of the Family.* New York: Vintage Press, 1970.

Corea, Gena. *The Mother Machine.* New York: Harper & Row, 1985.

Corea, Gena, et al. *Man-Made Woman.* Bloomington, Indiana: Indiana University Press, 1987.

Cousins, Norman. *Anatomy of an Illness as Perceived by the Patient.* New York: Bantam Books, 1981.

Cousins, Norman. *The Healing Heart.* New York: Norton, 1983.

Cremin, Lawrence A., ed. *The Republic and the School: The Education of Free Men.* New York: Teachers College, Columbia University Press, 1957.

Degler, Carl. *At Odds: Women and the Family in American History.* New York: Oxford University Press ,1980.

Dewey, John. *Democracy and Education.* New York: Macillan Company, 1916.

Dewey, John. *Freedom and Culture.* New York: G. P. Putnam & Sons, 1939.

Dewey, John. *Liberalism and Social Action.* New York: Columbia University Press, 1935.

Dewey, John, and James H. Tufts. *Ethics.* New York: Henry Holt & Company, 1908.

Dickstein, Morris. *Double Agent: The Critic and Society.* New York: Oxford University Press, 1992.

Diggins, John Patrick. *The Soul of Politics : Virtue, Self-Interest and the Foundations of Liberalism.* New York: Basic Books, 1984.

Dinnerstein, Dorothy. *The Mermaid and the Minotaur.* New York: Harper & Row Publishers, 1976.

Donagan, Alan. *The Theory of Morality.* Chicago: The University of Chicago Press, 1977.

Dula, Annette, and Sara Goering. *"It Just Ain't Fair:" The Ethics of Health Care For Black Americans.* Westport, Connecticut: Praeger Press, 1994.

Edwards, Betty. *Drawing on the Right Side of the Brain.* Los Angeles: Jeremy R. Tarcher, Inc., 1989.

Edwards, Rem B., ed. *Psychiatry and Ethics.* Buffalo, New York: Prometheus Boos, 1982.

Elder, A., and G. Samuel, eds. *"While I'm Here Doctor." A Study of Change in the Doctor-Patient Relationship.* New York: Tavistock Publications, 1987.

Erdich, Louise. *Love Medicine.* New York: Holt, Rinehart & Winston, 1984.

Erikson, Erik. *Insight and Responsibility.* New York: W. W. Norton & Company, 1964.

Etzioni, Amitai. *The Spirit of Community: Rights, Responsibilities and the Communitarian Agenda.* New York: Crown Publishers, Inc., 1993.

Finn, Chester E., ed. *Educational Reform in the 90's.* New York: Maxwell Macmillan International, 1992.

Firestone, Shulamith. *The Dialectic of Sex.* New York: Morrow Press, 1970.

Fletcher, George P. *Loyalty: An Essay on the Morality of Relationships.* New York: Oxford University Press, 1993.

Fogle, B. *Interrelations between People and Pets.* Springfield, Illinois: Charles Thomas, 1981.

Fox, B. H., and B. H. Newberry. (eds.) *Impact of Psychoendrocine Systems in Cancer and Immunity.* New York: Hogrefe, 1984.

Fraiberg, Selma. *Every Child's Birthright: In Defense of Mothering.* New York: Basic Books, 1977.

Freud, Sigmund. *Civilization and Its Discontent.* Translated by J. Strachey. New York: Norton, 1961.

Friday, Nancy. *My Mother/My Self.* New York: Dalacorte Press, 1977.

Garfinkel, Paul E., and David M. Garner. *Anorexia Nervosa: A Multidimensional Perspective.* New York: Warner, 1982.

Garrett, Thomas; M. Harold Ballilie, and Rosellen M. Garrett. *Health Care Ethics.* Englewood Cliffs, New Jersey: Prentice-Hall, 1993.

Gilligan, Carol. *In A Different Voice: Psychological Theory and Women's Development.* Cambridge, Mass.: Harvard University Press, 1982.

Goldfrab, Jeffrey C. *The Cynical Society: The Culture of Politics and the Politics of Culture in American Life.* Chicago: The University of Chicago Press, 1991.

Gollnik, D. M., and P. Chinn. *Multicultural Education.* 2nd Edition. Columbus, Ohio: Charles E. Merrill, 1986.

Goman, Carol Kinsey. *The Loyalty Factor: Building Trust in Today's Workplace.* New York: Master Media Limited, 1990.

Gordon, Linda. *The American Family in the Age of Uncertainty.* New York: Basic Books, 1991.

———. *Heroes of Their Own: The Politics and History of Family Violence.* New York: Vintage Press, 1988.

Gutman, Herbert. *The Black Family in Slavery and Freedom. 1950–1925.* New York: Random House, 1976.

Habestrom, Michael J., and Stephen Lascher. *A Coronary Event .* Phildalephia: J. B. Lippincott, 1976.

Heller, Thomas C., and David Welby, eds. *Reconstructing Individualism.* Stanford: Stanford University Press, 1984.

Halpern, Diane, ed. *Changing College Classrooms: New Teaching and Learning Strategies For An Increasingly Complex World.* San Francisco: Jossey-Bass, 1984.

Henry, Jules. *Culture against Man.* New York : Alfred A. Knopf, 1963.

Hine, Robert V. *Josiah Royce: From Grass Valley to Harvard.* Norman, Oklahoma: University of Oklahoma Press, 1992.

Hirschman, Albert O. *Exit, Voice and Loyalty: Responses to Decline in Firms, Organizations and States.* Cambridge, Mass: Harvard University Press, 1971.

Hocking, William Ernest. *The Coming World Civilization.* London: Geroge Allen Unwin, 1958.

Holmes, Helen Bequaert, and Laura Purdy. *Feminist Perspectives in Medical Ethics.* Bloomington, Indiana : Indiana University Press, 1992.

Hull, J. M. *Touching the Rock: An Experience of Blindness.* New York: Pantheon Books, 1990.

Hutchins, Pat. *Using Cases To Improve College Teaching: A Guide To More Reflective Practice.* American Association of Higher Education, 1993.

Hutchins, Robert Maynard. *Education for Freedom.* Baton Rouge, Louisiana: Louisiana State University Press, 1943.

Jacobs, Jonathan A. *Virtue and Self Knowledge.* Englewood Cliffs, New Jersey: Prentice-Hall, 1989.

Jacoby, Russell. *The last Intellectuals: American Culture in the Age of Academe.* New York: Basic Books, 1987.

Jaffee, Dennis T. *Healing From Within.* New York: Alfred Knopf, 1980.

Jagggar, A., and S. Bordo, eds. *Gender Body/Knowledge: Feminist Reconstructions of Being and Knowing.* New Brunswick, New Jersey: Rutgers University Press, 1989.

James, William. *The Will to Believe.* New York: Dover Publications, 1956.

———. *The Writings of William James.* Edited by John J. McDermott. New York: The Modern Library, 1968.

Jennings, Bruce, James Lindemann, and Erik Parens. *Values on Campus: Ethics and Value Programs in the Undergraduate Program.* Briarcliff Manor, New York: Hastings Center, 1994.

Jennings, Eugene Emerson. *Routes to the Executive Suite.* New York: McGraw Hill, 1971.

Johnson, Coleen Leafy. *Ex-Families: Grandparents, Parents and Children Adjust to Divorce.* New Brunswick, New Jersey: Rutgers University Press, 1988.

Jones, A., and M. F. Rice, eds. *Health Care Issues in Black America: Policies, Problems and Prospects.* New York: Greenwood, 1987.

Jones, J. H. *Bad Blood: The Tuskegee Syphillis Experiment: A Tragedy of Race and Medicine.* New York: Free Press, 1981.

Kant, Immanuel. *The Doctrine of Virtue.* translated by Mary J. Gregor. New York: Harper Torchbooks, 1964.

Kegan, Jerome. *The Nature of the Child.* New York: Basic Books, 1989.

Kegan, Jerome, and Sharon Lamb, eds. *The Emergence of Morality in Young Children.* Chicago: University of Chicago Press, 1987.

Kegley, Jacquelyn Ann K., ed. *The Doctrine of Interpretation: Building Community Out of Conflict.* Hayward, California: California State University, Hayward Press, 1978.

Keller, Evelyn Fox. *A Feeling for the Organism: The Life and Work of Barbara McClintock.* New York: W. H. Freeman, 1983.

———. *Reflections on Gender and Science.* New Haven: Yale University Press, 1985.

Kestenbaum, V., ed. *The Humanity of the Ill .* Knoxville, Tennessee: University of Tennessee Press, 1982.

Kleinmann, A. *The Illness Narrative: Suffering, Healing and the Human Condition.* New York: Basic Books, 1988.

Knors-Cetina, K. D. *The Manufacture of Knowledge.* Elmsford, New York: Pergammon Press, 1981.

Kohlberg, Lawrence. *Essays in Moral Development.* 2 vols. New York: Harper & Row, 1981 and 1984.

Komarovsky, Mirra. *Women in the Modern World.* New York: Basic Books, 1953.

Kouwenhoven, John A. *The Beer Can by the Highway.* New York: Doubelday, 1961.

Kuhn, Thomas. *The Structure of Scientific Revolutions.* 1st and 2nd Editions. Chicago: University of Chicago Press, 1961 and 1970.

Kuklick, Bruce. *The Rise of American Philosophy: Cambridge, Massachusetts 1800–1930.* New Haven: Yale University Press, 1977.

LaFrances Rodgers, Rose. *The Black Woman.* Beverly Hills: Sage Publications, 1980.

Lasch, Christopher. *The Culture of Narcissism.* New York: W. W. Norton, 1979.

———. *Haven in a Heartless World: The Family Beseiged.* New York: Basic Books, 1977.

Larmore, Charles. *Patterns of Moral Complexity.* Cambridge: Cambridge University Press, 1987.

Lazarre, Jean. *The Mother Knot.* New York: Dell, 1976.

Leder, Drew. *The Body in Medical Thought and Practice.* Dordrecht: Kluwer Academic Publishers, 1992.

Lippman, Walter. *The Phantom Public.* New York: Harcourt & Brace Company, 1925.

Lomasky, Loren E. *Persons, Rights, and the Moral Community.* New York: Oxford University Press, 1987.

McCullough, Lawrence B., and Frank A. Chervenak. *Ethics in Obstretics and Gynecology.* New York: Oxford University Press, 1994.

MacIntyre, Alasdair. *After Virtue.* Notre Dame: Notre Dame University Press, 1981.

———. *Is Patriotism A Virtue?* Lawrence, Kansas: University of Kansas Press, 1984.

———. *Whose Justice? Which Rationality?* Notre Dame: Notre Dame University Press, 1988.

MacPherson, C. B. *The Political Theory of Positive Individualism.* London: Oxford University Press, 1962.

Mahler, Margaret, et al. *The Psychological Birth of the Human Infant.* New York: Basic Books, 1988.

Mahowald, Mary Brody. *Women and Children in Health Care.* New York: Oxford University Press, 1993.

Mandell, H., and H. Spiro, eds. *When Doctors Get Sick.* New York: Plenum Publishing, 1989.

Marcel, Gabriel. *Royce's Metaphysics.* Westport, Conn.: Greenwood Press, 1956.

Marshall, Paule. *Brown Girl Brownstones.* New York: Sage Publishing, 1984.

Merleau-Ponty, Maurice. *Phenomenology of Perception.* Translated by C. Smith. London: Routledge & Kegan Paul, 1962.

Mill, John Stuart. *On Liberty.* in *The Collected Papers of J. S. Mill,* ed. J. M. Robson. Toronto: Toronto University Press, 1977.

Millett, Kate. *The Basement: Meditations on a Human Sacrifice.* New York: Simon & Shuster, 1979.

Mishler, E. G. *The Discourse of Medicine: Dialectics of Medical Interviews.* New Jersey: Able Publishing, 1984.

Maccoby, Michael. *The Gamesman: The New Corporate Leaders.* New York: Simon & Shuster, 1976.

Moffat, Michael. *Coming of Age in New Jersey: College and American Culture.* New Brunswick, New Jersey: Rutgers University Press, 1981.

Mueller, Keith J. *Health Care Policy in the United States.* Lincoln: University of Nebraska Press, 1993.

Murdoch, Iris. *The Sovereignty of the Good.* London: Routledge & Paul, 1971.

Murphy, Robert F. *The Body Silent.* New York: Henry Holt, 1987.

Nash, Gary. *Red, White and Black: The Peoples of Colonial America.* Englewood Cliffs, New Jersey: Prentice Hall, 1982.

National Commission on Excellence in Education. *A Nation at Risk: The Imperative for Educational Reform.* Washington, D.C. National Commission on Excellence in Education, 1983.

Navarro, Vincent, ed. *Why the United States Does Not Have a National Health Program.* Amityville, New York: Baywood Publishing, 1993.

Neal, Ed, and Laurie Richlin, eds. *To Improve the Academy.* Stillwater, Oklahoma: New Forums, Inc. Publishers, 1995.

Nearing, Scott. *The New Education.* New York: Arno Press, 1969.

Nisbett, Robert. *Twilight of Authority.* Oxford, England: Oxford University Press, 1975.

Novak, Michael, ed. *Democracy and Mediating Structures: A Theological Inquiry.* Washington, D.C.: American Enterprize Institute for Public Policy Research, 1980.

———. *The Joy of Sports; End Zones, Bases, Baskets, Balls, and the Consecration of the American Spirit.* New York: Basic Books, 1976.

Nozick, Robert. *Anarchy, State and Utopia.* New York: Basic Books, 1968.

O'Brien, Mary. *Reproducing the World.* San Francisco: Westview Press, 1989.

Oppenheim, Frank M. *Roiyce's Mature Ethics.* Notre Dame: University of Notre Dame Press, 1993.

Ornstein, Robert, and Richard F. Thompson. *The Amazing Brain.* Boston: Houghton Mufflin Company, 1984.

Parsons, Talcott. *The Social System.* Glencoe, Illinois: The Free Press, 1951.

Peck, M. Scott. *The Different Drum.* New York: Simon & Shuster, 1987.

Peirce, Charles Sanders. *Collected Papers of Charles Sanders Peirce.* Edited by Charles Hartshorne and Paul Weiss. Cammbridge, Mass: The Belknap Press of Harvard University Press, 1960.

Pellegrino, E., and D. C. Thomasma. *A Philosophical Basis for Medical Practice: Toward A Philosophy and Ethics of Healing Professions.* Oxford: Oxford University Press, 1981.

Phillips, G. M., and E. C. Erickson. *Interpersonal Dynamics in the Small Group.* New York: Random House, 1970.

Pilsnik, M., and S. H. Parks. *The Healing Web: Social Networks and Human Survival.* University Press of New England, 1986.

Ravitch, Diane. *The Schools We Deserve.* New York: Basic Books, 1985.

Rawls, John. *The Theory of Justice.* Cambridge: Harvard University Press, 1968.

Reynolds, Charles H., and Ray W, Norman, eds. *The Longing for Community.* Berkeley: University of California Press, 1988.

Restak, Richard M., M.D. *The Mind.* Tornoto: Bantam Books, 1988.

Rieff, Philip. *The Triumph of the Therapeutic.* Chicago: University of Chicago Press, 1968.

Robinson, Daniel S. *Royce's Logical Essays.* Dubque, Iowa: William C. Brown Company, 1951.

Rorty, Richard. *Philosophy and the Mirror of Nature.* Princeton: Princeton University Press, 1979.

Rosenbaum, E. *A Taste of My Own Medicine: When the Doctor Is the Patient.* New York: random House, 1988.

Rossiter, Clinton, and James Lane, eds. *The Essential Lippman: A Political Philosophy for Liberal Democracy.* New York: Random House, 1963.

Royce, Josiah. *California From the Conquest in 1846 to the Second Vigilance Committee in San Francisco, 1856: A Study of American Character.* Boston: Houghton Mifflin,1886.

———. *The Conception of God.* New York: The Macmillan Company, 1898.

———. *The Feud of Oakfield Creek: A Novel of California Life.* Boston: Houghton Mifflin Company, 1887.

———. *The Hope of the Great Community.* New York: The Macmillan Company, 1916.

———. *Outlines of Psychology: An Elemental Treatise with Some Practical Applications.* New York: The Macmillan Company, 1911.

———. *The Philosophy of Loyalty.* New York: The Macmillan Company, 1908.

———. *The Philosophy of Loyalty.* New York: The Macmillan Company, 1908. Nashville: Vanderbilt University Press, 1995.

———. *The Problem of Christianity.* New York: The Macmillan Company, 1913. Chicago: Henry Regnery Company, 1968.

———. *Race Questions, Provincialism and Other American Problems.* New York: The Macmillan Company, 1908.

———. *The Religious Aspect of Philosophy.* Boston and New York: Houghton Mifflin & Company, 1885.

———. *The Sources of Religious Insight.* The Bross Lectures. Lake Forest College. 1911. New York: Charles Scribner's Sons. 1912.

———. *The Spirit of Modern Philosophy.* Boston and New York: Houghton Mifflin Company, 1892.

———. *War and Insurance.* New York: The Macmillan Company, 1914.

———. *The World and the Individual.* Gifford Lectures. 2 vols. New York: The Macmillan Company. Republished in a Dover Edition, 1959.

Sacks, O. *Awakenings.* New York: E. P. Dutton, 1983.

Sacks, O. *A Leg To Stand On.* New York: Basic Books, 1984.

Sacks, O. *The Man Who Mistook His Wife For a Hat and Other Clinical Tales.* New York: Summit Books, 1985.

Sandel, Michael. *Liberalism and the Limits of Justice.* Cambridge: Cambridge University Press, 1982.

Santayana, George. *Character and Opinion in the United States.* New York: Norton Library, 1967.

Sartre, Jean Paul. *Being and Nothingness.* New York: Washington Square Press, 1956.

Scarry, Elaine. *The Body in Pain.* New York: Oxford University Press, 1985.

Schutz, Theodore William. *The Economic Value of Education.* New York: Columbia University Press, 1963.

Scott, Stanley J. *Frontiers of Consciousness.* New York: Fordham University Press, 1991.

Sen, Amartya, and Barnard Williams. *Utilitarianism and Beyond.* Cambridge: Cambridge: Cambridge University Press, 1982.

Sennett, Richard. *The Fall of Public Man.* New York: W. W. Norton, 1974 and 1976.

Sheikh, Anees A., and Kathrina A. Sheikh. *Eastern and Western Approaches to Healing.* New York: John Wiley & Sons, 1989.

Shelp, Earl E., ed. *Virtue and Medicine.* Dordrecht: D. Reidel Publishing Co., 1985.

Sherwin, Susan. *No Longer Patient: Feminist Ethics and Health Care.* Philadelphia: Temple University Press, 1992.

Schutz, Alfred. *Collected Papers.* Vol. 2. Edited by Arvid Brodersen. The Hague: Martinus Nijhoff, 1976.

Silberman, Robert. *Crisis in American Medicine.* New York: Pantheon Books, 1994.

Sinclair, Upton. *The Goose Step: A Study of American Education.* Los Angeles: The West Branch, 1923.

Skolnick, Arlene. *Embattled Paradise,* New York: Basic Books, 1991.

Smart, J. J. C., and B. Williams, eds. *Utilitarianism: For Or Against.* Cambridge: Cambridge University Press, 1973.

Spallone, Patricia, and Deborah Lynn Steinberg, eds. *Made To Order.* New York: Pergamon Press, 1987.

Spiro, Howard M., M.D. *Doctors, Patients and Placebos.* New Haven: Yale University Press, 1986.

Sprey, Jetse, ed. *Fashioning Family Therapy.* New York , London and New Delhi: Sage, 1990.

Stacey, Judith. *Brave New Families.* New York: Basic Books, 1990.

Stennett, Nick, et al. *Family Strengths: Positive Models for Family Life.* Lincoln and London: University of Nebraska Press, 1980.

Steon, D. *The Interpersonal World of the Infant.* New York: Basic Books, 1985.

Sullivan, William M. *Reconstructing Public Philosophy.* Berkeley: University of California Press, 1982.

Sykes, Charles. *Prof. Scam.* Washington, D.C. Regnery Gateway, 1988.

Szekey, E. *Never Too Thin.* Toronto: Women's Press, 1988.

Takaki, Ron. *Strangers From a Distant Shore.* Boston: Little Brown, 1989.

Thorne, Barrie, and Marilyn Yaloom, eds. *Rethinking the Family: Some Feminist Questions.* Boston: Northwest University Press, 1992.

Tillich, Paul. *The Courage To Be.* New Haven: Yale University Press, 1952.

de Toqueville, Alexis. *Democracy in America.* Translated by Henry Reeve. New York: Abelaid & Saunders, 1838.

Tolstoy, Leo. *Writings on Civil Disobedience and Non-Violence.* New York: New American Library, 1968.

Trebilcot, Joyce. *Mothering: Essays in Feminist Theory.* Towata, New Jersey: Rowman & Allenhe, 1983.

Turner, Bryan S., ed. *Citizenship and Social Theory.* London: Sage, 1993.

Walzer, Michael. *Spheres of Justice. A Defense of Pluralism and Equality.* New York: Basic Books, 1983.

Wassterstrom, Richard, ed. *Morality and the Law.* Belmont, California: Wadsworth Publishing Company Inc., 1971.

Weiss, L. *Between Two Worlds: Black Students and An Urban Community College.* Boston: Routledge & Kegan Paul, 1985.

Weston, Kath. *Families We Choose: Lesbians, Gays, Kinship.* New York: Columbia University Press, 1991.

Williams, Bernard. *Ethics and the Limits of Philosophy.* Cambridge: Cambridge University Press, 1985.

Winnicott, D. *Playing and Reslity.* New York: Basic Books, 1971.

Wingspread Group on Higher Education. *An American Imperative: Higher Expectations for Higher Education.* Racine, Wisconsin: The Johnson Foundation, 1993.

Wilson, Jackson. *In Quest for Community: Social Philosophy in the United States 1860–1920.* New York: John Wiley & Sons. Inc., 1968.

Zaner, R. M. *The Problems of Embodiment: Some Contributions to a Phenomenology of the Body.* The Hague: Martinus-Nijhoff, 1964.

JOURNALS

Agich, George J., "Disease and Value: A Rejection of the Value Neutrality Theory." *Theoretical Medicine* 4 (1983): 27–41.

Apple, Dorian. "How Laymen Define Illness." *Journal of Health and Human Behavior* 1 (1960): 219–25.

Blum, Lawrence. "Gilligan and Kolhberg: Implications for Moral Theory." *Ethics* 98 (April 1988): 472–91.

Blum, Lawrence. "Iris Murdoch and the Domain of *Morality*" *Philosophical Studies* 50 (1986): 343–67.

Boorse, Christopher. "Health as a Theoretical Concept." *Philosophy of Science* 44 (1977): 542–73.

Cassell, Eric J. "The Nature of Suffering and the Goals of Medicine." *The New England Journal Of Medicine* 306 (1982): 640–52.

Childress, James F., and Mark Siegler. "Metaphors and Models of Doctor-Patient Relationships: Their Implications for Autonomy." *Theoretical Medicine* 5 (1984): 17–30.

Cottingham, John. "Partiality, Favourtism and Morality." *The Philosophical Quarterly* 36, no. 44 (1987): 357–73.

Dewey, John. "Challenge to Liberal Thought." *Fortune* 30 (August 1944): 155–57.

Donabedian, Avedis. "Evaluating the Quality of Medical Care," *Milbank Memorial Fund Quarterly* 44 (1966): 166–206.

Gewirth, Alan. "The Justification of Morality." *Philosophical Studies* 53 (1988): 245–62.

Gutman, Amy. "Communitarian Critics of Liberalism." *Philosophy and Public Affairs* 14 (1985): 308–22.

Herman, Barbara. "Integrity and Impartiality." *The Monist* 66, no. 2 (April 1983): 233–50.

Kegley, Jacquelyn Ann K. "Josiah Royce: A Source of New Insight for Religion Today." *Religious Studies* 18 (1979): 221–24.

———. "Josiah Royce on Self and Community." *Rice University Studies* 66 (Fall 1980): 33–53.

———. "Royce and Husserl: Some Parallels and Food for Thought." *Transactions of the Charles S. Peirce Society* 7 (Summer 1978): 184–99.

Mariner, Wendy. "Outcome Assessment in Health Care Reform: Promise and Limitations." *American Journal of Law and Medicine* 20, nos. 1 & 2 (1994): 37–58.

Kielstein, Rita, and Hans-Martin Sass. "Using Stories to Assess Value and Establish Medical Directives." *Kennedy Institute of Ethics Journal* 3, no. 3 (September 1993): 303–25.

Nagy, Paul. "The Beloved Community of Jonathan Edwards." *Transactions of the Charles S. Peirce Society* 7 (Spring 1971): 93–104.

Oldenquist, Andrew. "Loyalties." *The Journal of Philosophy* 54, no. 14 (April 1982): 173–93.

Oppenheim, Frank M. "A Roycean Road to Community." *International Philosophical Quarterly* 10 (September 1970): 341–77.

Pellegrino, Edmund. "The Humanities in Medical Education." *Mobius* 2 (1982): 138–48.

Rawls, John. "Dewey Lectures: Kantian Constructivism in Moral Theory." *The Journal of Philosophy* 77, no. 9 (September 1980): 515–72.

———. "Justice as Fairness: Political and Not Metaphysical." *Philosophy and Public Affairs* 14 (Summer, 1985): 223–51.

Rodwin, Marc A. "Patient Accountability and Quality of Care: Lessons from Medical Consumerism and Patients' Rights, Women's Health and Disability Rights Movements. *American Journal of Law and Medicine* 20, nos. 1 & 2 (1994): 147–68.

Royce, Josiah. "The External World and Consciousness." *Philosophical Review* 3 (1894): 513–45.

———. "Is There a Science of Education?" *Educational Reform* 1 (1891): 15–25, 121–32.

———. "The Life Harmony." *Overland Monthly* 15 (1875): 157–64.

———. "The Modern Novel as a Mode of Conveying Instruction and Accomplishing Reform." *Berkeleyan* 1 (April 1874): 1; 10–11.

———. "On Certain Psychological Aspects of Moral Training." *International Journal of Education* 3 (1893): 413–36.

———. "Present Ideals of American University Life." *Scribner's Magazine* 10 (1891): 376–88.

———. "The Problem of Class Feeling." *Berkeleyan* 1 (February 1874): 5.

———. "The Psychology of Invention.." *Psychological Review* 5 (1898): 113–44.

———. "Recent Discussions of Class Feeling." *Berkeleyan* 1 (January 1874): 7.

———. "Review of Recent Literature on Mental Development." *Psychological Review* 3 (1896): 201–11.

———. "The Social Basis of Conscience." *Addresses and Proceedings of the National Educational Association* (1989): 196–204.

———. "Truth in Art." *Berkeleyan* 2 (April 1875): 3–4.

Slote, Michael. "Morality and Self-Other Assymetry." *The Journal of Philosophy* 31, no. 4 (April 1984): 179–92.

———. "The Schizophrenia of Modern Ethical Theory." *The Journal of Philosophy* 73, no. 4 (August 1971): 453–62.

Shulman, Lee S. "Teaching as Community Property: Putting an End to Pedagogical Solitude." *Change* 25, no. 6 (1993): 6–10.

Szasz, Thomas, and Marc H. Hollander. "A Contribution to the Philosophy of Medicine: The Basic Models of the Doctor-Patient Relationship." *Archives of Internal Medicine* 97 (1956): 586–87.

Toombs, Kay. "The Temporality of Illness: Four Levels of Experience." *Theoretical Medicine* 11 (1990): 227–41.

INDEX